C000196544

LEWIS IN HISTORY AND LEGEND

THE WEST COAST

For Chris

LEWIS IN HISTORY AND LEGEND

THE WEST COAST

BILL LAWSON

BIRLINN

First published in 2008 by
Birlinn Limited
West Newington House
10 Newington Road
Edinburgh
EH9 1QS

www.birlinn.co.uk

Copyright © Bill Lawson 2008

The moral right of Bill Lawson to be identified as the author
of this work has been asserted by him in accordance with
the Copyright, Designs and Patents Act 1988

All rights reserved. No part of this publication may be
reproduced, stored or transmitted in any form without the
express written permission of the publisher.

ISBN13: 978 1 84158 368 6
ISBN10: 1 84158 368 5

British Library Cataloguing-in-Publication Data
A catalogue record for this book is available from the British Library

Typeset by Brinnoven, Livingston
Printed and bound by MPG Books Limited, Cornwall

CONTENTS

PROLOGUE

The Dun at Carlabhagh sits brooding on his hill-top, looking out to the sea loch of Loch Rog and across it to the island of Bearnaraigh, and thinking of past days, when his building was entire – not the partial ruin it is now.

Dun is the Gaelic word for a fort, but Dun Charlabhaigh was more than just a fort. In his youth, over two thousand years ago, he was a mansion house to his Iron Age builders and occupants. In a land short of timber, it was little wonder that builders had specialised in stone-work, and the roundhouses they had built at first had gradually evolved into round forts. As the local chieftains had begun to vie in importance and wealth, so they had begun to build more impressive duns – indeed there had grown up a profession of 'dun architects' willing to construct for any chieftain with sufficient resources and sufficient manpower to do the physical work of gathering stones and dragging them to the site.

The wealthier the chieftain, the larger the dun, and if the local chieftain in Carlabhagh was not necessarily the richest in the whole of Lewis, he certainly wanted the Dun to look as if he was – the Iron Age equivalent of some of the houses in Rathad Shanndabhaig, Steornabhagh, today!

The Dun was not the oldest building in the area, and it could be argued that he was not even the most important. Two thousand years and more before his day, the great stone circle of Calanais and its many subsidiary circles had been built around the area. There had been a powerful chieftain then too, to be able to organise the labour which brought the stone from the quarry beyond Breascleit, and a wise one also, to have been able to plot the layout of the avenues and circle. They said that some of the stones were even aligned on particular stars in their seasons, but that lore had been lost, and with so many stones, there were only too many possible permutations.

There had been plenty of good land then – plenty for all the people who were in the area – but then the weather had begun to

1. Dun Charlabhaigh

change. The prevailing wind changed from east to west, bringing
more rain, and as the ground got wetter, the peat began to spread in
the valleys until much of the good land was lost and people began
to fight about the land that was left. That was when they began
to build the forts to protect their arable land and give warning
of dangers, which would usually have been arriving from the sea.
Strong chiefs had arisen who could organise the protection of their
land, and now times were more settled once again, and the Dun,
which had once been a guardhouse against danger, had now become
a showpiece.

Then the missionaries had come, followers of the early Christian
saints – probably not followers of Columba himself, as they had
concentrated more on the mainland, but followers of Maelrubha of
Applecross and Moluag of Lismore. Nothing was left of the buildings
of this era – the Vikings had seen to that – but the ground they
consecrated remained in use as graveyards, and the later churches
were usually rebuilt on the old sites.

The hill of Beinn an Duin blocked the view, but the Dun knew
that the old burying ground was still in Cirbhig, to the north-
east. There had been a church there, dedicated to St Michael, but

that was a later dedication. The old site was just referred to as the Teampall – a reminder that the early church had used the Latin language, so their Templum and Ecclesia had become Teampall and Eaglais in Gaelic.

The Dun could remember the churchmen, and he could also remember the first time he had seen a Viking boat coming into the entrance to Loch Charlabhaigh – a long timber ship, with a square, coloured sail. He had had no idea who the crew could be, but the local people soon found out, as the Vikings slew and plundered their way through the area. At first, the Viking raids were short, as the crew returned to their ship laden with booty and headed home again to Norway, but after a while they came not to raid but to settle, and by their sheer ferocity took over the land and enslaved its inhabitants.

He remembered one of them, Karl, a tall, red-haired man with sword and helmet. (Why did they insist today on showing Vikings with horns on their helmets? – he didn't remember them like that – probably one of the many Victorian additives to history!) Karl had grouped around himself a war-band of Vikings, ready to follow his bidding so long as the takings were good. They had based themselves around the sea loch and anchorage over behind the Dun – and it was still called Carlabhagh – Karl's Bay – today.

As they became more settled and less fierce, the Norse settlers began to loosen their links with Norway, and when the King of Scots decided to try to wrest the Islands back from Norse control, the settlers in Lewis had no great support for either – both were a long way away. After the battle of Largs in 1264 and the Treaty of Perth which followed it, the Hebrides became part of Scotland – and probably no one in Lewis noticed the difference!

Many of the Norse settlers had perforce to take local wives, and the people of the Islands had become a hybrid race, part Norse, part Scots – the Gall-Gaedhil – the 'foreign Gaels'. Greatest of the Gall-Gaedhil was Somerled, the first Lord of the Isles. His successors in the Lordship ran it as a semi-autonomous kingdom to the west of Scotland, and for a time the Scots kings had enough to do, consolidating their power on the mainland, and paid only nominal attention to the Lordship.

But in 1462 the then Lord of the Isles entered into the Treaty of

2. Diagram of possible interior layout of Dun Charlabhaigh

Ardtornish, agreeing with Edward IV of England to assist his later invasion in return for recognition of the Lordship as a separate kingdom, with himself as king. This was too much for the Scottish king, and in 1494 John, the last Lord of the Isles, was forced to submit to James IV of Scotland.

Defeating the Lord of the Isles and enforcing Scottish rule in the Lordship were two very different things, and in 1506 the earl of Huntly was sent to subdue MacLeod of Lewis, who had been backing his nephew Donald Dubh, who was trying to reclaim the Lordship for himself. The Dun could remember the heavy tread of Huntly's armed men, coming along from Allt an Torcan at Acha Mor, where they had defeated the MacLeods, some heading north to join their allies the Morrisons, and others heading west to deal with the MacAulay rebels in Uig.

A sort of nominal peace followed, but the MacAulays and MacLeods never forgave the Morrisons for joining Huntly. The tread of cattle was what the Dun remembered now, cattle from Nis being driven south by the MacAulays, and cattle from Uig being driven north by the Morrisons – and very often they met in the debatable lands around Carlabhagh, and many a clan battle had been fought in that area.

The MacLeods of Lewis – Clann Torcaill – had been the heirs of the Lordship in Lewis, but they had been a quarrelsome lot. Rev. James Fraser of Wardlaw, outside Inverness, had put it succinctly in 1699 in his *Polychronicon*:[1]

> The clan Torkil in Leis were the stoutest and prettiest men, but a wicked bloody crew whom neither law nor reason could guide or model, destroying one another, till in the end they were expelled that country, and the McKenzies now possess it.

The poet gave them this satyr:

> She mi varrell er Chland Leod
> Gir cossvil ead re Poir I Duse
> The shin mis is mo
> Ichis I te Oighe tuse

(in modern Gaelic)

> 'S e mo bharail air Clann Leoid
> gur cosmhuil iad ri poir an t-uisge
> An te is sine, mas i mo
> ithis i an te is oige duibhs

> It is my opinion of Clan Leod / that they are like pikes in the water. / The oldest of them, if the biggest, / eats the youngest of them.

Roderick, the last MacLeod chief of Lewis, had at least nine sons, four from his three marriages, and at least five others. Their infighting, some for their father and some against, and some solely for themselves, gave the MacKenzies the opportunity to wait until they had exhausted each other, and then take the spoils of Lewis for themselves.

It is in the period of the MacKenzies, later the Seaforths, that we have the first detailed estate rentals, showing the better lands occupied as farms by the MacKenzies and their allies, and the poorer

3. Dun Charlabhaigh

land divided among joint tenants. The Dun could remember when the whole area between Tolastadh a' Chaolais and Dal Beag had been occupied as five tacks – farms under written lease – and two of the tacksmen had been MacKenzies and the other three MacIvers!

But times changed, and Seaforth, like so many other landlords, came to think less of family and past support, and more of money. Tacksmen, who had held their land as a social upper class, found that they were expected to bid against mainland farmers for what they reckoned as their own family land, and many emigrated, mostly to the Carolinas, setting a trend for emigration which has never halted since then.

Some of their tacks were divided among joint tenants, and the Dun remembered the lands between his site and his loch of Loch an Duin being made into the separate township called Dun Charlabhaigh after him, and the people coming in and dividing the land amongst themselves, though Sandaig at the shore end of the township had remained for a time as a tack, along with Cirbhig.

About the same time a new industry – kelp – came to the Islands. Kelp was made by the controlled burning of seaweed in kilns, and was a valuable source of minerals, especially when Britain was at war in the late 1700s and early 1800s. Kelp gathering and burning was a labour-intensive process, so, to get as many people as possible on to the land, the old joint tenancies were changed to long, narrow crofts. Most of them ran from the hill to the shore, and along the shores were the kelp kilns – the Dun could remember the acrid smoke drifting from them, across the township and on to his hill. Some of the crofters were able to gather some capital from their pay as kelp-workers – though, of course, the landlord got most of it – and many of these had used their capital to pay their passage across the Atlantic and to buy new land in Cape Breton.

Then, after the French Wars were won, there was no more demand for kelp, and the crofters had no employment to help them pay the rents, which had been set high in the days of the kelp. At the same time, medical care came to the Islands and the childhood killer diseases, which used to be the great fear of parents, were largely eliminated. The population grew apace, at the same time as the average income dropped, and poverty began to grow. The crofts were subdivided among the families – it was against the estate rules; but who could refuse a potato plot to a brother? – but the smaller the crofts became, the less possible it was to make a living from them. Carlabhagh had been lucky – it had a good harbour and good fishing banks were within a reasonable distance – but other places were not so lucky. The potato had become the main article of food, as no other crop could produce so much from so little land; and when potato blight arrived in the 1840s, and the crop failed year after year, destitution threatened.

Outright famine was avoided, largely by aid organised by the Free Church on the mainland, and also by the new proprietor James Matheson, but it soon became clear that the problem was too great for these essentially temporary measures. Either employment or a source of income had to be found for those threatened with starvation, or else large-scale emigration was necessary. Matheson had introduced some new industries and had created new croftlands, but the scale of the problem was too great for these measures.

Emigration seemed the only answer, and it was taken up by a great many families, especially of landless cottars, whether willingly, or solely from lack of alternative. Arrangements were made for their transport to Canada, and for land to be available when they arrived there, but emigration, however well arranged, is still a wrench, and the Dun remembered the weeping families on the hill behind him, watching their relatives being taken out to the ships riding at anchor at the mouth of the loch, ready to start the journey across the Atlantic to a new home in the New World.

With some of the pressure of over-population taken away, and recovery from the potato blight, matters improved in Lewis, but life was still dangerously near to subsistence level for many, and one bad year could spell utter ruin. Eventually the government was forced to pay attention to the distress of the crofters, and a Royal Commission of Inquiry into the Conditions of the Crofters and Cottars in the Highlands and Islands of Scotland, better known as the Napier Commission, was set up to look into its causes and suggest reasons for its cure. The Commission was in Lewis in 1883, and the evidence given before it is a valuable record of the history of Lewis. Of course, not all the evidence was wholly accurate – much of it was about happenings more than a generation ago, and memory can get the details wrong – but the sheer mass of evidence of oppression over the previous century is compelling. The Commission recommended a limited degree of security of tenure for crofters, and after the passing of the Crofters Act in 1885, much of the harassment of crofters by factors ceased.

In 1918 Lord Leverhulme appeared on the scene, and though his story belongs mainly to the areas nearer to Steornabhagh, it had repercussions on the rest of Lewis also. The Dun chuckled when he thought of the Carlabhagh underpass – Leverhulme's plan to build a railway to the fishing port came to naught, but the bridge across the railway had been built and might as well be used!

The Dun had been adopted in his old age by Historic Scotland, and he had thought that his story would be told properly then, but for many years there was only a sign telling visitors how much they would be fined if they damaged him! A few years ago, however, not only did he get a proper sign, but a visitor centre was built with details of how he was built, and even a craft shop selling local souvenirs, many of them to do with his lifetime – and if some of them might appear to him a little bit tawdry, that was what some of the visitors wanted!

The Dun settled himself more comfortably on his rock, thinking back over the varied history that had unrolled around him – Vikings, clansmen, farmer and crofters. One thing he did not like about the crofters – they had taken away parts of his walls to use the stones for building their houses. Much of the west side had gone, but that meant that he now had a clear view out to the sea. The missing wall also meant that it was a bit draughty too, and he had worried for a time that the gales might blow down his remaining walls, but his builders had known what they were doing, and he remained as firm as the day he was built. They could not build like that today – and he noticed that the new visitor centre had been built largely underground – that way it could hardly blow down!

Now he had plenty of visitors, but he thought that he probably liked the archaeologists best – they were always arguing about how he was built and why he was built. Theory was replaced by theory, and they were forever making guesses about his story. The Dun chuckled – he did not need to guess – he knew!

4. Dun Charlabhaigh township from the Dun

PART 1 – SGIRE NIS (NESS)

Sgire Nis, at the northernmost point of Lewis, comes as a surprise to the first-time visitor – side-by-side housing along the length of the road. The croftland itself is flat, above low sea-cliffs and merging into flat peat-moor, stretching into the far distance to the hill of Beinn Dhail, noticeable in this flat land, though only 164 m in height.

The people are different too – physically so – with a far greater proportion of slim, tall, fair- or red-haired people, evidence still of the Norse ancestry of the Nisich. The first Viking raids on the Hebrides were in the 800s, and Nis would have been the obvious place to settle as a base for raids further south. In most of the Islands, the Norsemen appear to have been a ruling elite, but Nis was Viking country, settled in far more depth than most of the rest of the Islands, and you find Norse placenames, not only in the main settlements along the shores but even in little spots out in the moor where there were summer grazings. The suffixes are still recognisable – -bhat for a loch, -nis for a headland, -dal for a valley, -bost for a town – though sometimes the meaning of the suffix has been forgotten, and duplicated in Gaelic, so that we find Loch Langabhat – Loch Long Loch.

5. Tabost, Nis

The Nisich consider themselves – not without reason – to be the best seamen in Lewis, and no doubt this also is an inheritance from their Viking past, along with many Norse-derived words in their Gaelic, especially in relation to the sea and fishing. Their typical boat – the sgoth – was of a style unique to Nis, and you can still see one – the *Sulaire* built a few years ago by John Murdo MacLeod, of the boatbuilder family from am Port.

John MacCulloch, the geologist, writing in 1819[2] notes:

> The people themselves are also strikingly dissimilar to the general population of the islands, preserving their unmixed Danish blood in as great purity at least as the inhabitants of Shetland; and probably with much of the manners and appearance of the times when this country was an integrant part of the Norwegian kingdom. They constitute even now an independent colony among their neighbours, who still consider them a distinct people, and almost view them in the light of foreigners. They possess almost universally the blue eye and sanguine complexion of their original ancestors, and with their long matted hair never profaned by comb or scissors, can not be distinguished from the present race as we still meet them manning the northern ships. Notwithstanding their rude aspect and uncouth dress, they are mild in manners, and are esteemed acute and intelligent.

The prime targets of the Viking raids were the early Christian churches, and there are a surprising number of old church sites in Nis – none of them dating back so far as the pre-Norse times, but usually on the site of an older foundation.

As the Islands became more Scots and less Norse, power there was assumed by the Lordship of the Isles, which in its heyday had its own judicial system, with a series of local judges or brieves in their own areas. Hugh MacDonald of Sleat tells,[3] in about 1680, that 'there was a judge in every isle for the discussion of all controversies, who had lands from MacDonald for their trouble and likewise the eleventh part of every action decided, but there might still be an appeal to the Council of the Isles.' The brieves in Lewis were Morrisons, based in Nis, and also they seem to have had a supervisory role among the other judges, as there is a reference in a charter of Angus, Lord of the Isles, in 1485 to 'Hullialmus Archijudex' – William, the High Judge.[4] It may seem odd that the chief judges were situated at the far north end of the Lordship, but there is a gathering amount of evidence to suggest that there was another group of Brieve families in Kintyre, at the far south end of the Lordship, with strong links with the Morrisons, if not sharing their name.

The origin of the Morrisons is obscure; a website for the 'clan' claims that they are descended from a son of Leod the Viking who was shipwrecked and washed ashore in Nis. This is probably based on the early-nineteenth-century writings of Canon MacLeod of Dunvegan, who claimed that the Morrisons were descended from a bastard son of Leod, the progenitor of the MacLeods, who married the heiress of Clan Gow of Pabaigh in Harris. The canon was anxious to establish the superiority of the MacLeods, and he was not above rewriting history to prove his claim!

Canon MacLeod's connection of the Morrisons with Pabaigh seems to be an attempt to explain the presence of the name Morrison in Harris. There are certainly two main groups of Morrisons in the Islands, those of Nis and of Harris, but there are also many other Morrisons in Scotland, especially in Aberdeenshire and Ayrshire, who have no connection with either of these groups. Morrison is a translation of the Gaelic MacGille-Mhoire – son of a follower or devotee of St Mary – so the name can occur anywhere there is a church dedicated to Mary. I myself am not convinced that there need be any connection between the Morrisons of Nis and Harris, other than the translation of their name into English, and it would be interesting to see if DNA trials would prove or disprove a link.

A description of Lewis by John Morrison of Bragar in about 1680[5] claimed that the Morrisons' descent was from 'Mores the son of Kennanus whom the Irish historiance call Mackurich, whom they make to be a naturall sone to one of the kings of Norway' The reference to Norway is too vague to be given much credence, especially as it was the fashion at the time to claim a Norse ancestry for all the major clans, but of more interest is the name Kennanus, which appears in more recent days in the forename Cian or Cain, found only among the Morrisons and their descendants. Rev. William Matheson points out that this appears to be the same as the Irish name Cano, so that the Morrisons, far from being of Norse extraction, might in fact belong to their Irish-Celtic enemies – a descent which could also account for the continuing bad relations between the Morrisons of Lewis and their avowed Norse neighbours.

On the other hand, Captain Thomas, in his *Traditions of the Morrisons*,[6] claims that the Morrisons of Nis at least are really MacDonalds!

> The current tradition throughout the island is that the heiress of the Morrisons, having determined that she would only marry with a Morrison, Cain, who was a MacDonald from Ardnamurchan, passed himself off for a Morrison, became the husband of the lady, and consequently brieve also. The Harris Morrisons claim to have been of the original stock.

The problem with that tale is that the name Cain is certainly still found among the Morrisons – but only in descendants of the Harris Morrisons! I think that we just have to admit that no one knows for sure!

So long as the authority of the Lordship of the Isles existed, the Morrisons were safe in their lands in Nis, but when that authority was removed, they were forced to fight for survival, and it is interesting to note that in every attempt to restore the authority of the Lordship, the Morrisons were on the opposite side from their MacLeod and MacAulay neighbours.

It is claimed that there were twelve successive Morrison Brieves, the last being Iain mac Uisdein, who was killed in 1600. Even allowing for succession by brothers on occasions, rather than father to son, this suggests that the Morrison Brieves date from the earliest time of the Lordship of the Isles.

The descendants of the Brieves, as befitted their social position, were the tacksmen – farmers under written lease for a number of years – of the best farms in Nis, and also supplied the Church with a large number of ministers. They also provided seamen, as shown in the list of 'Those with Murdo McLeod in his galley in January 1600 at the capture of Balcomie'[7] – one of the ill-fated Fife Adventurers who tried to settle in Lewis – but more of that when we reach Steornabhagh – which includes John Dow McBrief and Angus McKeane (for MacIain) McBrief.

The citation of the present 'Chief of the Clan Morrison' claims that, since the line of the Brieves of Lewis can no longer be traced, the line of the Morrisons of Ruchdi in North Uist is the most senior line. Both parts of the claim are nonsense – there are plenty of known descendants of the Brieves still in Nis, and there is no evidence to suggest that the Morrisons of Ruchdi are in any way a senior branch of the Morrisons of Harris, never mind of Lewis. Rev. William Matheson was of the opinion that the best claim to be of the senior branch of the Morrisons currently in Lewis lay between the late Paidean – Peter Morrison – of 12 Dail bho Thuath – and the late Donald Morrison – mac Dholaidh Lisa – of an Rathad Ur – and I see no reason to dispute his judgement. I am afraid that the chiefship of Morrisons, like so many other chiefships, partakes more of fiction than of historical fact!

There are arguments at times about the seniority, and even the legitimacy, of those who spell the name Morison with one 'r', and those who use Morrison, with two 'r's. The earlier records do tend to use Morison, but then a new registrar comes along who starts to use Morrison. We have to remember that it was rarely the person so-named who was writing it down, so the name and the spellings as they appear are the choice of the clerk, not the person himself – I remember showing a friend of mine in Steornabhagh, who insisted on Morison, that his father's death certificate may have been Morison, but his birth certificate was Morrison – to my friend's great consternation!

And on the subject of spellings, I should point out that I have purposely used the accepted Gaelic names for most places in my own text – why on earth should we spell them in a foreign language? – but I have left all the original spellings in passages quoted from other writers – which will also show that even English-spellers could never agree about them! The purist may argue that originally Norse names in a Gaelic version are less than wholly authentic, but to then translate them into English makes them far worse.

Most of the older croftlands of Nis lie on the shore side of the main road, and many of the townships were originally on the machair land closer to the shore. Machair is a land-form unique to the Atlantic coasts, where centuries of shell-sand blown ashore from the beaches have sweetened the basically acid soil to create a fertile arable land. From pre-historic times, this has been the area of settlement, and the advancing seas, eating into the shoreline have exposed many interesting sites of early habitation.

Those of the old townships which were not tacks would have been joint tenancies, with the tenants holding land in common and sharing it out year by year as required. In the later 1700s, Seaforth, the landowner, realised that the tacksmen were subletting much of the land at a profit, and that, if he let the land directly to tenants, he would be able to acquire this profit himself, so many of the old tacks were broken up.

In the early 1800s, the kelp or seaweed trade became important to the economy of the Islands. The kelp trade was very labour-intensive, and the joint tenancies were converted to crofts, with each tenant holding his own particular piece of land, and liable each for his own rent, as a means of getting the maximum number of people on to the land as a potential workforce. The change was unpopular with many tenants, especially the women, who were being separated from their neighbours, and many families left Lewis at this time.

New crofts were also made from the moorland on the east side of the main road, but whereas the old machair crofts were usually long narrow strips of arable land running from the main road to the shore, the new crofts tended to be rectangular blocks of poorer land reclaimed from the moor.

Commercial fishing also became important in Nis, and new fishing townships, like Port Nis and Sgiogarstaidh, were created on land which had formerly been grazings for the machair townships but had facilities for the construction of piers and harbours.

In 1819 the whole of Nis was reckoned to have a population of 1,132 persons over the age of six. By 1851 every township in Nis was held in crofts, apart from small farms in parts of Suaineabost and Cealagmhol.

Filiscleitir

Filiscleitir may appear a strange place to start a survey of Nis, but, as well as being geographically at the edge, it is also a prime example of how short-term and ephemeral history can be. There are the ruins of an Iron Age dun or fort on the headland, but the main ruins are those of a house and church – and why would anyone build a church

6. Ruins of Dun Fhiliscleitir

in such a desolate place? Yet if one could go back even one hundred years, Filiscleitir would be very different.

The whole agricultural basis of Nis was based on the airidh or shieling – where the cattle were taken out onto the moor in the summer to enjoy the fresh grazing there and, more importantly, to relieve the pressure on the in-bye croftlands of the townships. With the cattle went many of the women and children, and a whole community lived out on the moors for a period in the summer, living in little bothags, some of turf, some of stone.

Each township had its own area for airidhean – Port Nis had the area around Allt an t-Sulair, an Cnoc Ard had Cuisiadar, and Lional had Filiscleitir itself. I remember myself what could be called the descendants of the airidhean – little timber cabins and even caravans along the river at Cuisiadar, though by that time the cattle had gone, to be replaced with sheep, and the airidhean were used more as summer holiday cottages than for any agricultural purpose. Some people lived out there most of the summer, and I remember gratefully Angus MacLean – Aonghas Dhomhnaill Tinceir – from Steornabhagh, who spent the summers there with his daughter; gratefully, as they were a very welcome source of tea and a rest for a hiker trekking across the moors!

John Nicolson – Iain Fiosach – was originally from Lional but had spent many years in the United States, and came back to Nis with his American wife, Nora Cushing. He built the house – Dune Tower – on the edge of the cliff, and in the summer it would have been at the centre of a busy bustling community, though in the winter, as now, it would have been incredibly lonely, especially for Nora, who latterly was blind.

Alasdair Alpin MacGregor in his *Haunted Isles*[8] describes some of the problems of building on such a site:

> For the building of it nine tons of sand from Vatisga Bay were carried up the face of the cliffs in sacks to an altitude of considerably over two hundred feet, each sack containing about a pailful. It was found impossible to carry more at a time, as the journey between Vatisga Bay and Dune Tower is precipitous and perilous. The sand-carriers slung the sacks over their shoulders; and, while one hand was engaged in holding the sack, the other was used in manoeuvring the cliffs where foothold was inadequate. The sand was mixed with four tons of cement, every ounce of which was carried on the backs of human beings from the Port of Ness, over six miles of broken moorland.

Iain Fiosach had become a Baptist in America – I do not think that he was ever a minister, but he was certainly a lay preacher, and

7. Church at Filiscleitir

he built a Baptist church beside his house for the people of the airidhean. I remember an old lady in Port Nis saying that she never heard a sound to match the sound of the psalm-singing, coming across the moor at Filiscleitir.

John Wilson Dougal, the geologist, knew this area well and refers to it in his *Island Memories*:[9]

> The crag on which Dune Tower is built is surrounded by a stout fence abutting the precipitous cliffs, and within this enclosure two young goats were privileged to nibble the rich grass. Near the gateway a lone burial-place holds the bones of an unknown man, whose corpse was found on the shore. About one hundred yards away stands a tiny place of worship where the shieling folk gather at sunset. Situated on the cliff edge it overlooks the bay, into which Leum Langa river leaps as a waterfall beneath the shadow of the wild rocks of Cellar Head.

On one of his geological expeditions Dougal, who was the discoverer of what he termed flinty-crush beds of rock in the Islands, lived alone in Dune Tower for a week or so, but seems to have been unaffected by the loneliness of the site:

> There was an eerie feeling in the house at times with wind noises, creaks of doors and windows, contraction in the beams when the house cooled at night, sea noises in the cave underneath the house. Alarms would arise from movements in the steep rock slices and crush rocks which are prominent near the Dune Crag – especially in cold weather and hard frosts. One night only was there an odd experience. About midnight I shifted the window screen to view the lighthouse flashes, and watch the lights of two trawlers fishing the near banks. A galaxy of stars and the full moon gleamed on the dark waters. Many white-crested waves careered shorewards, and one remembered the stories of the Blue Men of the Shiant Islands, who are supposed to ride the waves of the Minch.
> While gazing outward, the presence of four living eyes, yellow in colour, in two sombre bearded faces shone out of the darkness into the window. The period of sight and recognition was short, before knowing that the two goats were sheltering under the window eaves.[10]

The summer airidh was the great place for making and meeting friends – and for courting! Though Nis and Tolastadh are a good

8. Taigh Iain Fhiosaich, Filiscleitir

distance apart by road, their airidhean on the moor north of Muirneag were very close, and many a match was arranged at the airidh, which explains the many marriages between couples from Nis and Tolastadh.

From Filiscleitir a track leads towards Tolastadh, along the side of the stream where Coinneach Beag mac Choinnich a' Ghearrlaich – little Kenneth son of Kenneth of the Gairloch people – made a well which it is still possible to find – and to use – before he left for America, but perhaps he only repaired the well, for Dougal refers to it as the Well of the Stone of Angus's son – Tobar Clach mhic Aonghais. Then you follow the track above the strange valley of the Maoim, down towards Diobadal – and out of the range of this book and into the next volume.

9. Taigh Effer, Cuisiadar

I have not been at Filiscleitir for a few years, and I am told that it has changed again. The Nisich no longer put sheep onto the moor – at least not in quantity – and in much of it the grass has become rank. The paths are overgrown, and if it was always difficult to find a footing among the peat hags, it will be more so when they are disguised with a matting of old grass.

Cuisiadar

There was at one time a little village here, occupied by a family of MacFarlanes, but it was remote, even by that time's standards. The people left in 1877 and the area was added to the common grazings. I still remember one thatched house, Taigh Effer, kept up for use as an airidh.

In the heyday of the job creation schemes of the 1970s, many unsurfaced roads were made or improved as access roads to the peat banks, and one was made out to Cuisiadar and a bit of the way towards Filiscleitir. There was talk of making a road right through to Tolastadh in Lord Leverhulme's day. Both ends of the road were begun, but the project was abandoned; it still crops up now and again. It would certainly open up another part of the island, but it is mainly through bleak moorland – and one doubts in any case whether the conservation bodies, which have so strong a grip on any development here, would allow it. 'Nothing must ever be allowed to change' appears to be their motto, and yet, as we saw at Filiscleitir, change is happening all the time. At least, the track has been maintained and I am told that it is good for mountain bikes – though whether mountain bikes are good for it is a different matter!

From Cuisiadar there is a track along the side of the stream to Airidh a' Bhealaich, then over the hill of the Campar with its radio masts to the back of Tabost, or we can follow the peat road to Sgiogarstaidh past the headland of Caithaisiadar, which is easily confused with Cuisiadar. There was never a village at Caithaisiadar. Its sole claims to fame are the white cairn erected near the shore to commemorate John Wilson Dougal, the geologist, and the offshore Brag Rock, where there have been a few shipwrecks over the years.

Sgiogarstaidh (Skigersta)

Sgiogarstaidh was one of the fishing villages set up to capitalise on the new commercial fishery in 1824. Its early years were unlucky – so many of its men were drowned that the township became known as Baile nam Banndrach – the town of widows. Five were lost in the drowning of 1836 and another six in 1851. There was a Sgiogarstaidh crew lost in the great drowning of 1862 also. Then in 1885 the *Dun Alasdair*, heading from Dundee to America, was wrecked off Sgiogarstaidh in a fog – but no one was lost that time.

It was not only out at sea that there was danger – Kate Murray was down cutting feumainn – seaweed – on the shore when she was carried away by a wave – and it was at Stromness in Orkney that her body came ashore.

There were happier times at the shore too, as Donald MacKenzie[11] remembers in his 'Amhran Cladach Sgiogarstaidh':

O nach truagh nach robh mi fhathast
Na mo bhalaich air an traigh
O 's e laithean doigheal m' oig
A dh' fhagas sona mi gu brath.

Ann an Stiogha Tuath is mi 'nam sheasamh
'S mi ri 'g amharc mach am bagh
Toirt 'nam chuimhne 'n uair bha mi og
Sgiogarstaidh, sud ait' mo ghraidh.

Isn't it sad that I am no longer / a boy on the beach / it is those carefree days of youth / that leave me forever happy. / Standing at North Stiogha, / looking out across the bay, / brings back memories of when I was young / Sgiogarstaidh, the place I love.

I must repeat here what I said in the very first book in this series, that I am well aware that translations of poetry, unless by another poet, tend to be merely doggerel, but nonetheless I feel constrained to put in some translation, to give our monoglot English friends at least an idea of the meaning, if not of the poetry, of the verse.

Sgiogarstaidh has a good harbour, and it is from there that I have gone to the offshore islands of Ronaidh and Sulaisgeir, forty-odd miles to the north.

Ronaidh

The journey by fishing boat to Ronaidh is a long one – about six or seven hours – and to me, a landsman, the most interesting time on the journey was when we hit Abhainn Ocaisgeir. This is a tidal race in the sea, coming round from the Butt of Lewis, and I remember being as aware of the current as if we had met a real river flowing through the sea, pushing the boat eastwards. Somehow I had never thought of the sea having its own currents as well as tides – which shows how bad a seaman I would have been!

Ronaidh itself is a beautiful island; the south end is a low hill, with good grazing, and it is to sheep-shearing fanks that I have gone there, with balaich Glen from Suaineabost, who had the lease of the island then, though they were thinking of giving it up because of the depredations of sheep-rustlers from east-coast fishing boats. Though the grazing was good, it was reckoned that a sheep could only be left there for a short number of years, or else her flesh would become too rank, and that a sheep taken from Ronaidh could be kept on the mainland for a week or two to lose excess fat, but after that she would have to be slaughtered as she would never prosper

on mainland grazings after being used to the lush, salty grazings
on Ronaidh.

At the north end of Ronaidh is the peninsula of Fianuis, tide-
lashed by storms, especially in the winter-time. I think that the
most impressive evidence I have ever seen of the force of the tide
is along the west side of Fianuis, where a cliff of some 100 feet in
height is topped by a storm beach of boulders, thrown up by the
violence of the sea.

Our first detailed account of Ronaidh is from Martin Martin's
Description of the Western Islands of Scotland[12] in 1703:

> The Island Rona is reckon'd about 20 Leagues from the North-east
> point of Ness in Lewis, and counted but a Mile in length, and about
> half a Mile in breadth; it hath a Hill in the West part, and is only
> visible from the Lewis in a fair Summers-day.

Martin did not visit Ronaidh himself, but had a description of its
people from Rev. Daniel Morrison, minister of Barvas:

> They have Cows, Sheep, Barley and Oats and live a harmless Life,
> being perfectly ignorant of most of those Vices that abound in the
> World. They know nothing of Money or Gold, having no occasion
> for either; They neither sell nor buy, but only barter for such little
> things as they want; they covet no Wealth, being fully content and
> satisfy'd with Food and Raiment.[13]

10. Fianuis on Ronaidh

I think that this has to be taken as an example of distance lending attraction to the view; Martin cannot always be acquitted of the charge of playing to the gallery, as when he tells that 'There are only five Families in this small Island . . . They take their Sir-name from the colour of the Sky, Rain-bow and Clouds'[14] – which sounds rather exotic, but presumably only means that they used by-names such as Ruadh, Gorm, Ban and Dubh, as did every other community in the Gaidhealtachd. Martin also tells us how the community there had been wiped out:

> About 14 years ago a Swarm of Rats, but none knows how, came into Rona, and in a short time eat up all the Corn in the Island. In a few months after, some Seamen Landed there, who Robbed the poor People of their Bull. These misfortunes, and the want of supply from Lewis for the space of a Year, occasion'd the Death of all that ancient Race of People. Some Years after, the Minister (to whom the Island belongeth) sent a new Colony to this Island, with suitable Supplies. The following Year a Boat was sent to them with some more supplies, and Orders to receive the Rents; but the Boat being lost, as it is supposed, I can give no further account of this late Plantation.[15]

MacCulloch the geologist, in his *Description of the Western Islands of Scotland*,[16] published in 1819, tells of another extinction of population:

> Some years have now past since this island was inhabited by several families, who contrived to subsist by uniting fishing to the produce of the soil. In attempting to land on a stormy day, all the men were lost by the upsetting of their boat, since which time it has been in the possession of a principal tenant in Lewis. It is now inhabited by one family only, consisting of six individuals, of which the female patriach has been forty years on the island. Twice in the year, that part of the crop which is not consumed on the farm, together with the produce of the sheep and the feathers obtained from the sea-fowl, which he is bound to procure, are taken away by the boat from Lewis, and thus his communication with the external world is maintained.

The shepherd at the time of MacCulloch's visit was a Kenneth MacCagie, who later came ashore with his family to am Port where he used the surname MacRitchie, whereas Finlay MacCagie, his

11. Teampall Ronaidh

predecessor on Ronaidh, came ashore with the name MacKay. To be more accurate, these are the surnames given to the MacCagies by the keepers of the Old Parochial Register of Baptisms and Marriages, and it is likely that neither Kenneth nor Finlay ever saw the names which were written down for them, nor could have read them if they had! All through the registers and census returns in the Islands, we see clerks changing names which they may have found difficult to spell into better-known names, which may have had only the slightest similarity to the originals.

The last record of shepherds on Ronaidh is in the census of 1841, when there were three, apparently unrelated, shepherds there on census night. Thereafter the island had only visits from working parties with the sheep until 1884, when a rather bizarre occurrence led to a small resident population for some months. A dispute had arisen in the church, and two of the men involved, Malcolm MacDonald and Murdo MacKay, decided to go to Ronaidh as shepherds. They were left there on 20 June, and visitors in August found them well. Projected visits later that year had to be cancelled due to bad weather, and the next boat to succeed in visiting Ronaidh was not until April 1885, when both men were found dead. What made the deaths even more strange was that the minister concerned in the

12. Tobha Ronaidh

dispute, Rev. Duncan MacBeath, was said to have predicted that neither MacDonald nor MacKay nor another party, MacPherson, would die a natural death – and MacPherson went missing and was never found.

Several books have been written about Ronaidh, in much more detail than is appropriate here, of which *Rona, the Distant Island*[17] by Michael Robson gives a particularly detailed account of the island and the sources for its history.

It is some years since I was last on Ronaidh, and my fondest memory is of a beautiful summer's day visit on the *Calina*, taking some sheep to the island and bringing others back, when the sea at Geodha Sto was so calm that they could sit the boat alongside the rock and drive the sheep directly off the deck and onto the island – not a very common occurrence!

Frank Fraser Darling, in his *A Naturalist on Rona*,[18] gives a very different picture:

> Fianuis becomes an inferno when a big northerly or westerly gale is blowing. It is certainly not safe for a human being to go looking at the wonderful spectacle of wild sea . . . Immense seas break over the cliffs as far as the storm-beach and spray rises twice or thrice the height of the cliffs. The spray breaks the full three hundred feet

13. Heading for Ronaidh

of height of the western cliffs of Rona in a winter gale and is driven
right over the island.

A wild place, but a beautiful one, which I hope to visit again.

Sulaisgeir

In contrast to Ronaidh, Sulaisgeir is an island which I am happy to
remember, but have no wish to revisit!

If Ronaidh to me is lush grass and seals, Sulaisgeir is jagged rock
and lice! It lies some ten miles west of Ronaidh and at about the
same distance – forty miles – from Nis. I have been there on a few
occasions, either landing the Niseach boys for their annual guga cull,
or taking them off again with their booty. Theirs is a dangerous and
dirty task, and I have the utmost admiration for them, and for their
determination to keep the tradition going, despite the attempts of
some of the wilder conservation bodies to stop them.

For those who do not know, a guga is a young gannet, and the
Niseach boys catch and kill them on the rock ledges of Sulaisgeir,
then split and salt them in piles like a small peat stack. The boys
stay there for about two weeks, living in little rock-shelters with
absolutely no mod cons. Everything for that period has to be taken

14. Sulaisgeir

with them, even water, for there is none on the rock and rainwater cannot be collected for use as it would be fouled by the birds, and then at the end it has all to be taken away again, along with the gugas. Among the luggage is a dismantleable chute, down which the gugas are slid from the top of the cliff to the ledge where the boat can come alongside. A novice like myself is given the job of catching the birds from the chute to pass them to the boat, and no one thinks to point out that, as the chute gets greased by the oil of the gugas, their speed on the chute increases till you inevitably are hit by a barrage of ill-smelling, oily carcases!

You can tell from that description that I am not a Niseach, for to a Niseach the smell of a guga is the most beautiful perfume, and the taste a great delicacy – neither of which sentiments I can share!

At one time the guga was a very necessary part of the diet of the Nisich, and the tradition continues. The cull does not seem to affect the number of gannets breeding on the rock, and indeed the only noticeable drop in bird numbers took place during the last war, when the cull could not take place. Perhaps it is because only a certain proportion of the birds are ready for taking – too young and they are not worth having – too old and they are able to fly away. Anyway,

15. Arriving at Sulaisgeir

the Nisich have a special dispensation from the Protection of Birds Act of 1954, allowing them to take two thousand birds a year. Every so often, there are calls for the cull to be prohibited, but since the bird numbers do not appear to be adversely affected, is it necessary to destroy a few hundred years or more of tradition, and to deprive local people of a delicacy? I remember when I was project team leader for the IDP (Integrated Development Programme for the Western Isles) – a partly European-funded programme to develop crofting and fish-farming – Peigi, my secretary, had a call from the Department of Agriculture and Fisheries in Edinburgh enquiring whether I had any views on the guga cull. Peigi was able to reply that, although I was away from the office, she could say without any doubt that I was in favour of it – for that is where I was!

That the guga-hunt has been going on for many centuries can be seen from the descriptive text accompanying the *Blaeu Atlas* of 1654:[19]

> It only rises into black cliffs, which black moss covers, and the white wave of the sea opens up. Here sea-birds lay their various eggs every-where, and hatch their chicks and fatten them with prey. But

16. Bothy on Sulaisgeir

before they cut through the air on sprouting wings, a large crowd
from the neighbouring shores sails out to prey on them, and gives
up eight days to collecting them and drying them in the air and the
blast of Phoebus, until they fill their small boats with the feathers
and stiff flesh.

A fascinating and detailed account of a guga-hunt on Sulaisgeir can
be found in John Beatty's *Sula – the Seabird Hunters of Lewis*.[20]
I have said that I do not enjoy the taste of guga, but I have to
admit that our local hotel at Roghadal in Harris had 'Guga Stovies'
on the menu on one occasion and I very much enjoyed them, as
the mixture of potato meant that we got all the flavour of the meat
without the oiliness – but any true Niseach will already have put
this book aside as sacrilege!

A truer Niseach view of the guga appears in a poem by Angus
Campbell,[21] better known as am Bocsair, to distinguish him from
his brother am Puilean – also named Angus Campbell:

An guga Niseach liath-ghlas
Is milis e fogh'n fhiacail
Thar gach uile biadh tha e cail-mhor,
Roghainn na fir-mhora

17. Preparing to leave Sulaisgeir

'O Sgigearsta gu Rodul
'Nuair gheibh iad air a bhord le buntat' e.

'N guga glas is lith air
Mac an athair rioghail
Sulaisgeir thug ire cho trath air.
'S cha b'e fear gun chli ann
A bheiridh dhachaidh mir as
Ach maraichean nach diobradh sa' ghabhadh.

The dark-grey Nis guga is sweet to the tooth / beyond any other
meat it is tasty / The choice of the great men / from Sgiogarstaidh
to Roghadal / when they get it on the table with potatoes. / The
grey, greasy guga, / son of a royal father, / Sulaisgeir is the place of
its youth / It won't be a feeble man that will take that food home /
but seamen who never shirk dangers.

I am afraid that Sulaisgeir to me is a smell – and not a pleasant one! The only time I can remember being seasick was lying off the shore to the east of Sulaisgeir, waiting for the swell to go down enough to allow us to land. With the difficulty of getting there, and the danger and the conditions on the island, the boys going for the gugas have my admiration – I am very glad that I have been there – but do not trouble to ask me to go back again!

Eorodail and Adabroc

These are two small crofting townships created in the space between Sgiogarstaidh and Port Nis. To me, the only thing special about them is the road which divides them in such a way that at first Eorodail is on the east side and Adabroc on the west, then Eorodail on the east and Lional on the west and finally Port Nis on the east and still Lional on the west! That is unfair – Eorodail also has an interesting Iron Age fort or dun on the shore, while Adabroc was the site where the Adabroc Hoard of Later Bronze Age material was found in a peat bank in 1909 by Donald Murray – was he the Donald Murray whose sister Kate was drowned at Sgiogarstaidh?

Ian Armit, the archaeologist, describes the hoard as 'a collection of bronzes, including a range of tools such as gouges, a hammer, socketed axe, chisel and whetstones, and weaponry including a spearhead, along with beads of amber, gold and glass.' He also points out that, quite apart from their intrinsic value, showing a relatively affluent society, 'some items show Irish and continental affiliations, while the use of amber suggests north European contacts.'[22]

Joseph Anderson, who wrote a paper on the hoard soon after its deposit in the Museum of Antiquities in Edinburgh, adds a more personal touch:

> One feature which distinguishes the Adabrock hoard from the general character of these deposits is the presence of the amber and glass beads and the bead of gold. These personal ornaments may have belonged to the wife or daughter of the owner of the rest of the hoard, which consists of industrial tools.[23]

I like the mental picture of the lady of three thousand years ago sweeping the floor, hunting for the beads she had dropped! The

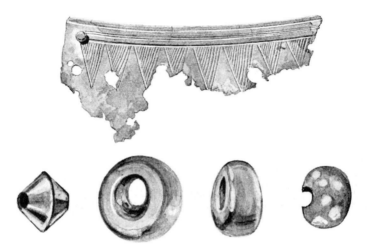

18. Items from Adabroc Hoard

prehistoric population of the Islands was not nearly so primitive as earlier text-books would have us believe!

The hoard also contained the rim of a decorated vessel, which may have originally been the container of the rest of the hoard.

Port Nis or Cealagmhol (Port of Ness)

Am Port today is a very trim little village, giving no great sign of its heyday as a centre of the fishing industry. A list of persons liable for militia duty in 1827 notes 'Port Cealaquol is a new colony of fishermen, and can hardly be said to be occupied, and the people presently reside in the neighbouring villages.' There were two groups of houses to begin with, one at Tobhta Gormaig, near the present-day Cealagmhol Farm and the other at Garbost, at the Buaile Muigh on the cliff-top above the sand beach, though they were later combined into one crofting township under the name of Cealagmhol, or Port Nis, or just am Port.

There had, of course, been fishing from Nis before this time, but MacCulloch mentions[24] that it was not commercially developed:

They are reputed industrious fishermen, but they only fish for their own consumption; appearing to abound in food, as they are all fat

19. Port Nis

and ruddy. Numerous fishing boats are generally to be seen about the Butt, manned each by nine men rowing eight oars in double banks, a practice nowhere else to be observed.

This style of seamanship must have been discontinued soon after MacCulloch's time, for in the stories of drownings, of which there are many in Nis, the normal boat's crew appears to have been six.

It was with the collapse of the kelp trade in the early 1800s that the fishing industry was introduced on a more commercial basis. Laying out new fishing villages was a part of the development, but much needed on the wild open coasts of the north and west of Lewis were safe harbours. Surveys were made in 1828, but not until 1835 was a pier built at Cealagmhol at a cost of £1,645, of which the Herring Fishery Board provided just over £1,000 and Seaforth the balance.

James Wilson, in his *Voyage round the Coasts of Scotland*,[25] was quite impressed by the new harbour in 1842:

The harbour was found to be well constructed, and had about a dozen boats lying within its shelter. There is also a nice slip, on which in stormy weather boats can be drawn quite up upon the quay. The chief thing that is wanted is the cutting away a little more rock at the mouth, which is too narrow, and where lives have been lost in consequence. Raising the storm wall a few feet would be likewise an advantage. There is a road of approach to the harbour, and a considerable extent of curing-houses, some of which were occupied by those engaged in curing ling.

Wilson was less impressed by the village:

> Farther on was a kraal of the most miserable huts ever seen, resembling those of Barra in external form, but infinitely worse. The St Kilda huts in comparison to these were palaces. The first object which met the eye (and nose and feet) within the threshold was a dunghill, from which the visitor has the option of descending either by the right hand into the cow's apartment, or by the left into that tenanted by human beings. Yet many of these people were making handsomely by fishing.

W. Anderson Smith in his *Lewsiana*[26] describes the harbour at am Port in 1873:

> It consists of an opening in the rock a few yards wide, up from which a pavement has been laid by the laird to enable the fishermen to draw up their boats. This is all their harbour. Out of it no boat can be launched, even on the calmest day, without the men pushing them out up to their waists in water; remaining in this wet condition during the whole time at sea, which is often prolonged for two days. On returning, they are again obliged to leap into the water, to remove mast, oars and ballast, and then, after a hard day at sea, pull their boats high and dry up the paved beach. The severity of this labour is very great, and the men are said to age rapidly under it. When at sea these men often spread raw cod-livers on their bannocks, and at all times consume a great quantity of livers. This doubtless assists them to endure long exposure in wet clothes; the oil alike supplying heat to the system and lubricating the lungs to as to secure them against cold.
>
> Even with all disadvantages the Nessmen generally show a good average fishing per boat – say three thousand ling. Besides the money value of these to be obtained from the merchant, they are allowed to take so many cod home to their families; while the heads, the skate, dogfish and fish-roes contribute to the sustenance of the household. A good fishing will give each man from £15 to £23, besides otherwise benefiting the household.

Many attempts were made to improve the harbour at am Port, but none were wholly successful. The lack of wholly reliable harbours was in part the cause of many drowning accidents – a boat from Sgiogarstaidh was lost in 1836, one from Lional in 1844, one from na Coig Peighinnean in 1847 and one from Gabhsann in 1849 – though there was some doubt about how the Gabhsann boat was lost, as we shall tell when we come to that township. In 1862 was the Bathadh Mor – the great drowning, when five boats and their crews were lost, and another two driven across the Minch and wrecked on the shore at Scourie. A boat from Dail was lost in 1882 and two from Eoropaidh in 1885, then in 1889 two boats, one from Dail and the other from Lional, were wrecked coming into the harbour, though another four boats managed to make Steornabhagh in safety. Am Port itself lost a boat in 1900 on Latha na Droibh – the day of the cattle sales.

Donald MacDonald in his *Lewis – a History of the Island* reports an eyewitness account from the *Lewisman* of the drowning of 1889:

> The scene in the bay was something terrible to the anxious friends and relatives who crowded the outlying points and approaches to the harbour, knowing full well the danger in which the boats were placed owing to the heavy seas and the cross seas caused by the violence of the gale and the action of the strong tideways which run along the coastline. Hour after hour the little fleet dodged under low sail, but as the tide made, the sea became heavier. About 5pm the first boat ran the harbour entrance safely, but the *Look Sharp* with Donald Smith, North Dell, as skipper, was struck and capsized by a heavy sea, all aboard being drowned in full view of the relatives and friends.[27]

The other boat lost on this day was from Lional, skippered by Donald Morrison, known as an Sasunnach because he wore a jacket, instead of the peitean – lapelled waistcoat – worn by most other men at the time.

Sometimes it is the small details in a story which are the most poignant, and I was always struck by the story of John MacLeod from Eoropaidh who was lost in the 1885 drowning. The boat was too far out to sea for the watchers on the cliff-top to identify who was still on board, but as one man was swept overboard, his wife saw a flash of light from his peitean, and knew that it was her husband, as she had left a needle in the lapel when she was mending it earlier that morning.

It was a major complaint at the time of the Napier Commission in 1883 that the bigger boats coming in for the herring fishery were spoiling the local fishing. According to John MacDonald of an Cnoc Ard:

> I remember myself the boat of which I formed one of the crew landing 6400 ling in a season, and a neighbouring boat 8000, and now they can make scarcely 1000 in a season. The ling fishermen stay out for two or three days . . . they are bound to stay out and watch their lines, otherwise these may be destroyed by the herring boats.[28]

Murdo Morrison of Lional agreed, when asked if the people might do more by way of fishing:

> They risk their lives as it is, and since the herring fishing commenced off the shore here they cannot well leave out their lines – the herring nets break them. Almost all their success at the fishing now is in the winter and early spring, before the herring fishermen come. The cod and ling fishing is carried out by leaving lines out at night, and these lines must have buoys upon them, and if you leave a line out, it may be that before morning it will be in Stornoway.[29]

Another of the complaints of the Nisich was that they could only use small boats, as they had to be hauled up on to the shore every night. Various extensions were made to the pier at Cealagmhol and John MacLeod, the boat-builder there, was critical of the work, in 1883, as he thought the chance should have been taken to make a proper deep-water harbour:

> It is just a piece they are running on the front out to the sea, and there is not a back to it. If there was another one at the back of it, and a hearting and a parapet the same as the rest of it, it would be sufficient to stand the waves; for the out-sweep of the sea here is stronger than at any place the Stevensons (the contractors) saw in their life, and I am afraid it will take the corner of the outer pier out.[30]

Much work had been done, and much money spent, on the harbour since then – but still it silts up!

There were two main gathering places at am Port: the tobar – the well – for the women and the barometer for the men. The barometer was first put up in 1836 on one of the salting houses, but it was moved up later to the post office. The men used to gather there

20. Port Nis

to look at the glass and decided what was to be done that day, and the bodaich – the older men – would stay there to chat and reminisce. Almost across the road was the tobar, and between the tobar and the glass there wasn't much that happened in am Port that wasn't discussed!

Am Port is much changed today. It is a very trim village, almost too much so – almost suburban – and the only fishing out of am Port today is for pleasure. Donald MacLeod put it well in his poem 'An t-Iasgach bha 'm Port Nis':[31]

Tha Calaigmhol air caochladh
Is faodar sin a radh,
Chan fhaicear lang, air sgaoilteach ann
Gan caoineachadh mar bha:
Chan fhaicear bat' le salainn
Tighinn an t-astar so gu brath,
'Se 's coltach g' eil an t-iasgach
Air criochnachadh san ait'.

Dh'fhalbh na tighean saillidh,
Chaidh iad seachad mar an corr,
Gun cail ann ach na laraichean
Air fas 'nan toman fheoir;

Na h-eathraichean bha 'g iasgach ann
Gun sgail air gin de'n t-seors',
'S than 'n ait' 'na aobhar cianalais
Do dhaoin' tha fhathast beo.

Cealagmhol has changed, / I have to say / you don't see ling / spread
there for drying / you won't see a boat with salt / making its way here
any more / it looks as if fishing / is finished in the place. / The salting
houses have gone / they are past like the rest / with no trace but the
foundations / grown up with clumps of grass / the boats that used to
fish there / there is not a shadow of that kind now / it's a place now
to cause homesickess / to the people who are still living.

On a personal note, am Port has changed greatly for me too – my
home-from-home there was with Dolaidh and Mairead at Cliff
House and Anna Bheag, their daughter. Mairead was almost as
obsessed by sloinntearachd – family history – as I am, and many a
night she and I spent trying to sort out families and their history,
with a slightly bemused Dolaidh in the background phoning around
checking answers for us – and now both Mairead and Anna Bheag
are gone, tragically young, and there is a great hole at the heart of
that most hospitable household.

21. Port Nis

An Cnoc Ard and na Coig Peighinnean (Knockaird and Fivepenny)

These two townships were originally one, and the latter name gives some idea of the length of their history, for the five pennies refers to the value of the land for tax purposes in Norse times. The earliest detailed rental of Lewis is preserved in the Forfeited Estate Papers – the Seaforth of the time had been involved in the 1715 Jacobite Rebellion and his estates were for a time forfeited to the government – and Fivepenny is shown then as shared between twenty-four named tenants. The only problem is that the Gaelic patronymics used at that time were spelled phonetically by government clerks, and can take quite a lot of unravelling. Faced with a name like 'macoilicormett', you have to try pronouncing it until you can imagine what it was the clerk thought he heard, and then you can break it down into mac Dhomhnaill mhic Thormoid – son of Donald son of Norman.

Patronymics were the usual way of reference to a person then, and indeed they still are in day-to-day Gaelic usage, much the same as in Iceland, as with the late Magnus Magnusson. Some families, however, use the equivalent of surnames, though not of the same style as in English. So one of the tenants in Fivepenny in 1715 is Mccoilbuy, where Mccoilbuy stands for mac Dhomhnaill Buidhe – literally the son of yellow-haired Donald – but the meaning of mac can also be extended to mean 'descendant of', and this particular Donald may have been one well known at a much earlier phase in local history, so that Buidhe is not so much a personal description as a family by-name.

In the same way, we find the by-name 'Rivich' in Fivepenny, for the Gaelic Riabhach – pock-marked or freckled – and that is still the by-name for a family in the area, though officially they are now MacLeans.

An Cnoc Ard was split off from na Coig Peighinnean in 1754, and was originally named Garenin. The village was then down near the shore of Loch Stiapabhat, but was later moved up the hill to its present site and renamed an Cnoc Ard. Loch Stiapabhat was for a time an example of the inconsistencies of conservation, where the crofters of the land surrounding it were under strict restrictions in order to preserve the wildlife on the loch, which is notable for wading birds and ducks, which the shooting parties from the estate would then come in and shoot! I believe that that anomaly was dealt with a few years ago, and the situation would hardly arise now in any case, as the estate has been bought out by the crofters.

Nis is an area famous for its singers and songwriters – almost every village had its own bard to write in its praise – and na Coig Peighinnean was no exception, as Donald Morrison 'Geinidh' wrote:

> 'N teid thu leam, mo nighean donn,
> Falbh thu leam gu tir mo ruin
> 'N teid thu thairis leam thar thonn,
> Null gu eilean donn an fhraoich
> Dh'aindheoin ait' 's an robh mi riamh,
> Ged a thriallainn an Roinn Eorp'
> 'S e na Coig Peighinnean mo mhiann,
> 'S far an iarrainn crioch mo lo.[32]

> Come with me, my brown-haired maid / Leave with me for the land of my love / Come with me across the sea / Over to the brown heather isle. / Despite all the places I have seen / Although I have travelled Europe / na Coig Peighinnean is my choice / for where I would want to end my days.

The coast behind an Cnoc Ard is one of low cliffs with some isolated stacs, among them Dun Eisdein. This, as the word Dun tells us, was a fort, a refuge used by the Morrisons of Nis in time of trouble. Although the dun can be reached on foot at a very low tide, it is a steep climb down and up again, and so an easily defended position. It was not the main residence of the Morrisons, which was at Tabost, but a secure defensive site, whose name is used by the Clan Morrison as a slogan, in its original meaning of a rallying cry.

Now the word clan is used in varying senses. To some it is a group of people in an area, owing allegiance to the same leader, and in that sense it is sound history. To others it has come to mean a group of people, all of the same name and all with a common ancestor, and in that sense it is unsound, as the same name has been used in English to represent several names in Gaelic, and many names are in any case territorial rather than family-based. And for those to whom a clan is a group of people all entitled to wear the same tartan, I am full of admiration for the salesman who imposed on their gullibility!

Most tartans today are of recent origin, few going back beyond the Sobieski-Stewart brothers in the 1820s, and their patterns were as spurious as the pedigree they claimed for themselves – grandsons of Bonnie Prince Charlie! Certain regions wore tartans of certain colours, because these were the dyes available locally, but the idea of each clan wearing its own distinguishable tartan arose largely from Sir Walter Scott, and the subsequent 'Balmoralisation' of Scottish history under Queen Victoria. Let us just say that certain tartans are very attractive, and some people enjoy wearing them to demonstrate a loyalty – and why not?

I have no patience whatever with the clan chiefling who parades around ill-informed hosts in America, gathering donations for the maintenance of the ancestral home – often in Essex or elsewhere in the south of England – but on the other hand there are clan societies who do a lot of good work, welcoming visitors to their area and financing the upkeep of local historical buildings, etc. The Clan Morrison have been able to gather finance to build a bridge across to Dun Eisdein, allowing the intrepid visitor to cross to the rock, and envisage himself defending the clan against assault from their enemies.

It is easy to mock the emotional appeal of places like Dun Eisdein to the overseas visitor, whose Morrison ancestry may well have nothing whatever to do with Scotland, never mind Lewis, but we cannot deny that that appeal exists, however ill-founded it may be.

Eoropaidh (Eoropie)

Eoropaidh is the furthest-north township in Lewis. Its name is said to be derived from the Norse *eyrr* – a shore – hence shore town, and it was to its shore that a pair of strangers came in 1608, fleeing from the mainland after being involved in an affray in Dornoch in which Charles Pape, the sheriff clerk of Sutherland, was killed. The affray began in a common enough way. William and Thomas Pape, ministers of Dornoch and Rogart and brothers of Charles, were at an inn in Dornoch:

As they were at breakfast, one John Mackphaill entered the house and asked for some drink for his money, which the mistress of the house refused to give him, thereby to be red of his company, because she knew him to be a brawling fellow. John Mackphaill taking this refusal in evil pairt, reproved the woman, and spok somewhat stubbornlie to the ministers, who began to excuse her; wherevpon Thomas Pape did threattin him, and he agane did thrust into Thomas his arme ane arrow, with a broad forked head, which then he held in this hand. So, being parted and set asunder at that tyme, Mr William and his brother Thomas came the same evening in to the churchyaird, with their swords about them, which John Makphaill perceaveing, and taking it as a provocation, he went with all diligence and acquented his nepheu Houchein Mackphaill and his brother-in-law William Murray, the bowyer . . . And meitting them in the churchyaird, they fell a quarrelling, and from quarrelling to fighting. Charles Pape hade been all that day abroad, and at his returne, vnderstanding what case his brethren were in, he came in a preposterous haste to the fatall place of his end and rwyne. They fought a little while; in end, Charles hurt William Morray in the face, and thervpon William Morray killed him.[33]

The Pape brothers were bad enemies to have made, and the case was raised with the Privy Council, where MacPhail and Murray were declared rebels. Sensibly they had already left Dornoch, and Rev. William Matheson makes a very good case for asserting that they were the strangers who arrived on the shore at Cunndail. MacPhail may have been the instigator of the brawl in Dornoch, but it is his brother-in-law William Murray who is best remembered in Lewis, as he became a famous blacksmith there – the Gobha Gorm. Gorm is generally blue in English, but it also is used for the very glossy raven-black shade found in the hair of some island families. The Gobha may have had this colouring, but there is another tradition that the colour referred to a wound on his face – perhaps that given him by Charles Pape. However that may be, the Gobha Gorm is reckoned as the ancestor of most of the Murrays in Lewis – most, because some others are known to have adopted the name later, for various reasons. The knowledge of smithying was carried down in his family, many of who also were blacksmiths, as is shown in their by-name of Gobha – or Gow, as it appears in many of the older rentals.

John Roy MacPhail apparently made his way down to Bragar,

where we will find him in dispute with Donald Cam MacAulay, and there are still many MacPhail descendants in that area.

Older than the Gobha Gorm is the old church in Eoropaidh – Teampall Mholuidh, dedicated to St Moluag of Lismore. It is thought that the original building may date from the fourteenth century, but is has been largely, and tastefully, modernised.

Martin Martin, in his *Description of the Western Islands of Scotland* in 1703[34] tells us that John Morison of Bragar told him 'that when he was a Boy, and going to the Church of St Mulvay, he observ'd the Natives to kneel and repeat the Pater Noster at four Miles distant from the Church'. He also tells us:

> The Inhabitants of this Island had an ancient Custom to sacrifice to a sea-god call'd Shony, at Hallowtide, in the manner following: the Inhabitants round the Island came to the Church of St. Mulvay, having each Man his Provision along with him; every Family furnish'd a Peck of Malt, and this was brew'd into Ale: one of their number was pickt out to wade into the Sea up to the middle, and carrying a Cup of Ale in his Hand, standing still in that posture, cry'd out with a loud Voice saying 'Shony, I give you this Cup of Ale, hoping that you'll be so kind as to send us plenty of Sea-ware, for inriching our Ground the ensuing Year; and so threw the Cup of Ale into the Sea. This was perform'd in the Night-time; at his return to Land, they all went to Church, where there was a Candle burning upon the Altar; and then standing silent for a little time, one of them gave a Signal, at which the Candle was put out, and immediately all of them went to the Fields, where they fell a-drinking their Ale, and spent the remainder of the Night in Dancing and Singing etc. The next Morning they all return'd home, being well satisfy'd that they had punctually observ'd this Solemn Anniversary, which they believ'd to be a powerful means to procure a plentiful Crop. Mr Daniel and Mr Kenneth Morison, Ministers in Lewis, told me that they spent several Years, before they could perswade the vulgar Natives to abandon this ridiculous piece of Superstition, which is quite abolish'd for these 32 years past.

The map-makers had fun with the name Eoropaidh. William Daniell's *Scotland* refers to it as Oreby[35] – and he was not impressed!

> Their huts are of the simplest construction that could have been devised for attaining the advantages of warmth, shelter, and security.

Those near the point of Oreby have neither doors nor windows; and the entrance is by holes in the roof, near the top of the walls. A stranger might take these structures rather for rustic sepulchres than dwellings, unless he saw, as was the case on the present occasion, some of the inmates looking forth from their battlements, and presenting, with their unshaven chins and matted locks, no faint image of the aboriginal Britons who combated against Agricola.

The Victorians were even worse, and their atlases insist that the correct name is Europa Point – as being the furthest point of Europe!

A narrow road leads north from Eoropaidh village, among an incredible array of fences – when the crofts were first made, in the early 1800s, they were made as long, narrow strips from the hill to the shore, so that all tenants would share some of the different types of land. It is hard to imagine a shape of land-holding less suitable for the use of modern machinery, or more expensive to fence, but the first requirement of any agricultural usage of land is that the stock on it can be controlled, so the plethora of fences is inevitable, without a complete change in the system of land tenure. Having said that, while I see the need to fence stock in, I have less sympathy with some of the more recent croft-tenants in the Islands, who have no intention of ever using the land agriculturally, and whose fences are purely for the purpose of keeping others out!

The road leads to the Butt of Lewis and its lighthouse, perched above horrendous cliffs. Some of the offshore rocks are bent into incredible shapes, while the seas rushing between them make a deafening noise in a storm.

The light is now automatic, but I stayed many times in the Lighthouse Cottages with Angus MacCuish, then principal lightkeeper there, and his wife Ina, who was from Shetland, and whose ability to knit wool into incredibly intricate patterns was matched only by her aptitude as a baker – and her hospitality in feeding her baking to all visitors! The lighthouse is in a beautiful spot, and well worth a visit on a fine day, but it is also incredibly exposed, and I remember one day being bothered by hearing heavy rain falling on the flat roof of the houses but seeing none through the windows, until it dawned on me that the 'rain' was actually the sea breaking on the cliffs behind the house, and rising up over them to fall on the roof!

22. Rocks at the Butt

MacCulloch the geologist found the cliffs impressive also – up to a point!

> At the Butt these cliffs are broken into rugged forms of an aspect peculiarly savage, being at the same time hollowed into innumerable caves into which the western swell beats with almost incessant volume and noise. Arches and pillars detached by the power of the turbulent sea form a series of objects from which a painter might select detached parts with great effect; but the whole is unpleasing to a cultivated eye; there is too much of that which, sparingly used, is conducive to the most powerful effects in painting as in poetry.[36]

Why does the word pompous come to my mind?

Perhaps he would have been happier a few hundred yards to the east of the lighthouse, where the suddenly appearing inlet of Port Stoth has, in the sunlight, a blazingly white beach above a sea blending from azure to ultramarine in the distance.

Behind the lighthouse there are more cliffs, with a marker where a young lad from Liurbost – Angus Martin – was lost playing football at a picnic in 1953, and then, almost at the Butt itself, the offshore stac of Luchruban, like Dun Eisdein accessible at certain low tides but only with difficulty. Dean Munro mentions it in his *Western Isles of Scotland* of 1549:[37]

23. Butt of Lewis lighthouse

At the north point of Leozus thare is ane little Ile called the Pygmeis Ile, with ane little kirk in it of thair awn handie wark. Within this kirk the ancients of thet cuntrie of Leozus sayis that the saids Pygmeis hes bene earthit thair. Mony men of divers cuntries hes delvit up deiply the fluir of the said kirk, and I myself amangis the lave, and hes fundin in it deip under the earth certane banes and round heids of very little quantitie, alledgit to be the banes of the said Pygmeis.

Martin Martin mentions it also in 1703: he calls the Island 'the Isle of Little Men', and calls the pigmies 'Lusbirdan'. The island was certainly well known; *The Blaeu Atlas of Scotland* of 1654 shows it as Ylen Dunibeg – for Eilean nan Daoine Bige.

W.C. MacKenzie wrote a paper on Luchruban for the Society of Antiquaries in Scotland in 1905, with the results of a dig carried out there by his brother, who found some pieces of pottery, some bones and some peat ash. Fourteen pieces of bone were sent to the Natural History Museum, where they were identified as belonging to oxen, young lambs, a dog, rock pigeons and gulls. MacKenzie heard a local tradition that the pigmies were 'Spaniards, but big yellow men came from Argyll and drove the little men from Cunndail (a cove near Luchruban) to the latter island; but when the pigmies got numerous, they emigrated to Europie and Knockaird in the same vicinity. They lived on buffaloes, which they killed by throwing sharp-pointed knives at them.'[38] Is this a folk memory of the taller Iron Age Celts arriving and replacing the smaller, darker Iberians? Or should Luchruban be treated as a version of Leprechaun?

I can tell from my own experience that there are traces of a building on the summit of the stac, most likely those of an early anchorite cell – a place for meditation by monks of the early Celtic Church, of which there are many in similar situations around the coast. MacKenzie's article included a site plan of the buildings, which look, as he says, very like the buildings on a similar site in the Flannan Isles.

MacKenzie has a fascinating side-note:

> The local tradition at the present day connects a saint named Frangus with the pigmies of Luchruban. St Frangus is said to have been an outlaw who lived on the sands at Lionel at Ness. According to the tradition, which was recently taken down from the lips of an old inhabitant of Ness, Frangus was unkind to the pigmies, who hanged him on a hill, which is called Bruach Frangus to this day.[39]

Further west still, to the very point of Rubha Robhanais, there is a natural arch, leaving a hole like an eyelet through the face of the cliff. At one time Lewis lay much further to the south, and all the islands, right down to Barra Head, formed a continuous block of land. This was in the days of the Vikings, and they were rather worried by the distance they had to sail from Norway to reach Lewis, so they gathered a fleet of ships, attached strong hawsers through the Eye of the Butt, and started to pull the Hebrides closer to Norway. Matters went well for a while, but then Barra got stuck on an undersea rock. They pulled harder and harder, and their hawsers were so strong that eventually it was the islands which tore apart – and that it why the Outer Hebrides are now a string of detached islands – or so they say!

Lional

The road between Eoropaidh and Lional leads through the machair, the sandy plain between the sandy beaches and the moor. It is good arable land and a riot of flowers in the summer-time. Normally, I would place the machairs of Harris and the Uists above those of

Lewis, but Lional machair in the late summer, covered in drifts of brilliantly red clover, is a sight to see and to smell!

Lional itself runs along the main road to am Port with a branch to Adabroc. On the slope below the junction was Tobar Lionail, not just a well but a fancy metal standpipe and pump. It was beautiful water and many a time I went to Tobar Lionail for flagons of water that was far better-tasting than the mains supply. Now the tobar is closed, due to pollution from the surrounding land and roads, and though the mains water supply to Nis is now better than it used to be, it does not have the distinctive taste of the water from Tobar Lionail!

Alexander Nicolson, brother of John Nicolson of Filiscleitir, wrote in praise of Lional:

Fhuair mi m'arach am baile Lional
A laigheas sgiamhach an Eilean Leodhais
'S a dh'aindheoin boidhchead gach aite thriall mi
'S an ann a dh'iarainn gu siorruidh comhnuidh

Tha Muirneag ainmeil is Beanntan Bharbhais
'Nuair ni thu falbh as chi thu mar cheo iad
Tha iad na 's airde os cionn gach aite,
Tigh soluis la iad do'n bhat' tha seoladh[40]

I was born in the township of Lional / the bonniest place in the Isle of Lewis / though I have travelled many a bonny place / it is there that I would ever wish to live. / Muirneag is famous and the hills of Barabhas / when you are leaving you see them like mist / they are so high above each place / they are a day-time lighthouse to the boats that sail.

It is very true that the Barabhas hills and Muirneag, though they have no great height, are dominant landmarks for many miles out in the Minch, and even from the west coast of the mainland.

Nis not only had good land, but also had the fishing to rely on, and even in times of scarcity was better off than other parts of the island. John Munro MacKenzie, who was factor of Lewis in 1851, kept a diary of his work at a time when most of Lewis was reeling from the effects of the potato blight of the previous years. MacKenzie travelled around the island explaining that the landlord, Sir James Matheson, would no longer support the poor of the island,

and that they would be expected to pay their rents or emigrate. In Nis he notes[41]

> the greater number of the people of these places are fishermen, and can pay their rents if inclined. I fixed on depriving 79 fishermen of their lands if they do not pay up their arrears of rent, or get the fishcurers to become bound for the payment of their rents. Many of the Ness men are supposed to have money in the bank, tho' in arrear of rent, but they must pay up now, or want land.

A great drawback in using MacKenzie's diary as a historical source is that we hear of the actions he threatened in that one year, but not whether they were carried out. When we look at the rentals of Nis before and after 1851, we find very few changes in tenancies – apparently his threats were successful in inducing payment of rents, so avoiding any large-scale evictions. It would be interesting to find out if the fishermen did indeed have bank accounts in Steornabhagh!

Tabost (Habost)

Tabost in its day was the most important township in Nis, and the largest in terms of population. It was also the seat of the Morrison Brieves, who as well as lawmen, were also famous warriors. We told in our *Harris in History and Legend*[42] how Hugh Morrison, son of the brieve of the day, led a raid of Morrisons into Harris and over to the Isle of Tarasaigh, where they were defeated and Hugh barely escaped with his life, swimming the two miles from Tarasaigh to Torgabost on the Harris machair with arrows sticking in his back! Rev. William Matheson, in an article in the *Stornoway Gazette*[43] tells the sequel to the story.

> A good number of years after the raid on Harris, John MacLeod – Iain mac Dhomhnaill mhic Aonghais – of Bearnaraigh, so the story has it, went to Lewis to buy horses. His quest took him as far as Ness. There he entered into conversation with a man who was kind enough to offer him hospitality for the night. The house to which he was brought turned out to be the House of Tabost, and his host none other than the Brieve of Lewis. We are not told whether the Harrisman tried to conceal his identity, or whether he realised that the other was the same who had swum the Sound of Taransay so

many years before. Whether he did or not, he enjoyed the best of entertainment, and the two worthies sat up conversing amicably until a late hour. Before going to bed the man of the house stood up with his back to the fire and lifted his nether garment to warm the backs of his legs. The terrible marks of former lacerations so startled the visitor from Harris that he exclaimed 'It was not at the fireside that you got those marks, my friend'; to be met with the reply 'Bu dhian do dha laimh 'gan cur ann' – 'Your two hands were busy putting them there'. However this was followed by the assurance that what was past was past. 'If you had not served me so, I would have done the same for you.' So they retired for the night, and when parting in the morning, the Brieve presented his guest with two of the best horses from his stable as a token of goodwill.

Tabost was also the site of one of the earliest schools in Nis, with its teacher James Thomson, who is said to have come there from the east coast of Scotland in 1738. All the Thomsons in Lewis are descended from him, and where the name James occurs in Nis, it can usually be traced to the schoolmaster.

Tabost also had its bards, and it is strange that two of the most famous singers from Lewis should have become so much associated with two such well-known songs, of such different styles, from two bards from the same township,

The late Calum Kennedy sang Murdo Morrison's song 'An Cia-ora', about the trip out from the Clyde on a ship of that name:

O 'se thusa, fhaoileag bhoidheach
Tha ri seoladh os mo chionn,
Ma thadhalas tu duthaich m'eolais,
'S e sin Steornabhagh an Leodhas,

Innis dhaibh gu bheil an Cia-ora
Seoladh aotrom bharr nan tonn
'S i ri deanamh cursa direach
Air na tirean fada thall[44]

You bonny seagull / flying over my head / if you call on my homeland / that is Steornabhagh in Lewis / tell them that the Cia-ora / is sailing lightly on the tops of the waves / setting a straight course / for the faraway lands.

– while Ishbel MacAskill can ensure instant silence from her audience with Malcolm MacLean's heartbreaking 'Deireadh Leave, 1940' – 'Returning from Leave, 1940':[45]

O Leodhais mo ghraidh, dean innse dhomh 'n drasd
An am dhomh bhith fagail do ghlinn
'N teid mi thairis air sal 'n duil tilleadh gu brath
No an slan le mo Thabost a chaoidh?

Am faic mise tuilleadh a' ghrian ri dol sios
'N Taobh Siar de dh'Eilean mo ghraidh?
No'n cluinn mi na buillean bhios tonnan a' chuain
A' bualadh bith-bhuan air a thraigh?

O Lewis my love, tell me now / now that I am leaving your glens / when I cross the sea will I ever return / or is this farewell forever to my dear Tabost? / Will I ever again see the sun going down / on the west side of my dear island / Will I hear again the noise of the waves of the ocean / breaking eternally on the beach?

Taigh Dhonnchaidh in Tabost was the family home of Duncan Morison, pianist and music teacher in Steornabhagh. Duncan was very much a society pianist in his youth, and accompanist to singers like Father Sydney MacEwan – his style of playing was unmistakable, and my wife, Chris, was listening to a radio programme one day when a recording of Paul Robeson was played, singing the 'Eriskay Love Lilt' – and the piano accompaniment could have been played by none other than Duncan! It seemed a most unlikely combination, but Chris checked, and Duncan had indeed made such a recording.

Chris had Duncan – Major, as he was better known locally – as a music teacher in school, and she tells me that, memorable as his piano performances might be, nothing that he did could ever be as important as the love of music he was able to instil into that generation of schoolchildren. Taigh Dhonnchaidh is now used for the study of Gaelic music and for concerts.

The Comann Eachdraidh, across the road, have a fascinating collection of historical material, as well as photographs and artefacts. It is very easy to lose all track of time browsing through their collection, which varies from substantive items like St Ronan's Stone from the Isle of Ronaidh, a worn cruciform stone pierced by three holes and carrying on its surface the shadowy outline of

24. Smithy at Tabost

a person – perhaps the Crucifixion, but perhaps some even older icon – to some of the domestic crockery of years not too far past today but destined to become history in the future. They have also a most welcome tea-room in the summer months!

Suaineabost (Swainibost)

Near the river on Suaineabost machair are the remains of Teampall Pheadair, clearly a major church in its day, and with many interesting stones in its graveyard – it is said that the Gobha Gorm himself is buried there, but there is, of course, no visible sign today.

Suaineabost was a farm until well into the 1800s, when part of it was made into crofts. More crofts were made in 1840 to accommodate tenants removed from the Eadar dha Fhadhail area of Uig – so much so that Suaineabost was known for a time as Baile na h-Uigich – but still a small area was left as a farm, and it is still such today. The Uigich cannot have been too happy in their new home, as many of them left Suaineabost in the 1850s and 1860s to settle in the Eastern Townships of Quebec. We shall look at the Eastern Townships in more detail when we come to Uig, from where many of the first emigrants left, but we should mention here the story of one emigrant from Suaineabost – Malcolm MacAulay,

25. Teampall Pheadair, Suaineabost

born in Suaineabost in 1846, a son of Malcolm MacAulay and Kirsty MacRitchie, originally from Baile Niceal in Uig. Malcolm's family settled in Winslow Township in Quebec in 1851, and Malcolm's later history appears in a short biography in Channell's *History of Compton County*.[46]

> He left Winslow in 1864, enlisted in the Army of the North, was ordered south, and remained there until the close of the war. Came back to Boston, Mass., in August 1865. After living there two years, he returned to Winslow in February 1868, and has lived in the county since that date. His business has been principally contracting and farming. He had several contracts on the old International and Q.C. Railways. He also put in the Cookshire water works and sewerage system. While in the Union Army he served under General Thomas, and was in the battles at Nashua, and Springfield, Tennessee. He held the office of mayor of Whitton and also of Lake Megantic, each for four years, and many other public offices. He is a justice of the peace for the St. Francis District. He joined the 58th Battalion in 1869, as Lieutenant, having graduated from the Montreal military school that year. He has secured gradual promotion until he now holds the honourable position of Lieutenant-Colonel of the Battalion.

26. Lt Col MacAulay's house in Quebec

A grand example of 'local lad made good', yet if he is known at all in Lewis today, it is as the villain in the story of the Megantic Outlaw, which will be told when we come to Cnip in Uig – obviously there are two sides to every story, not least in folk tales!

The farm of Suaineabost was for many years in the hands of the Murrays, descendants of the Gobha Gorm, who is said to have set up his smithy there, after coming ashore at Eoropaidh. Neil Murray, believed to have been his great-grandson, appears as tacksman of Suaineabost in rentals of 1718 and 1728, in the latter case as Neil Gow – for Gobha, or blacksmith. Neil's great-grandson, Alexander Murray, was the last of the family to have the tack of Suaineabost, from which he moved to Dail bho Thuath, but he was buried at Teampall Pheadair, in 1857, in what is claimed to have been the same spot as his ancestor the Gobha Gorm. There are many families in Lewis with the name Murray, not all of them connected with the Gobha Gorm, and the sign of those who are so descended is that they are still given the name Gobha in Gaelic.

Many of the other Murray families in Nis are descended, not from the Gobha Gorm, but from his companion in adversity, John Roy MacPhail. There is a tradition that he had a sister married in

Carlabhagh area, and the family members who went to that area
have retained the name MacPhail, whereas in Nis, those in an Cnoc
Ard and that area became Morrisons, and those in Dail became
Murrays! This could be an attempt by a minor family to obtain the
protection of a more important one, but it could also be the result
of the unwillingness of many church and estate clerks to accept an
unusual name, which they would replace with one better known to
them – and easier to spell!

Cros

Cros in the old days was another tack tenanted by a Morrison family.
In 1754 a judicial rental was held, to establish what each tacksman
was claiming in rent from his subtenants. Cros was held then by
Donald Morison:

> Compeared Finlay Beaton, tenant in Cross, a married man aged
> seventy one years . . . depones that the tack of Cross consists of four
> pence lands, that two pennies thereof is possest by four tenants, and
> the oyr. two by the said tacksman; depones that each halfpenny pays
> one pound nine shillings ten pence sterling money rent yearly . . . a
> weekly days services, a cock and hen, a peck of meal, a coil of heather
> rope, and as much butter as each tenants cows yields in a week.[47]

The part-payment of the rent in butter is quite unusual, and
suggests that Cros was more of a dairy farm than its neighbours.
Oddly enough, cattle crop up also in a later story about Cros. In the
early 1820s, the tacksman there was William Morrison – mac Iain
mhic Ailein – and his family included a daughter Sibla. William
and Sibla were in Steornabhagh on Latha na Droibh – the day
of the cattle sales – and so was Angus Morrison – Aonghas mac
Fhionnlaidh – from Tarasaigh, with cattle to sell for his father.
Angus fell for Sibla, and he used his father's cattle for the usual
dowry; Angus went to Cros, where there are descendants still – and
neither the cattle nor their price went back to Tarasaigh!

Nis is officially part of the parish of Barvas, but was separated
quoad sacra – for religious purposes only – into the parish of Cros.
In the *Statistical Account* of 1797, before the separation, Donald
MacDonald, minister of Barvas, notes that the church 'in the district
of Ness, an old Popish Church, called St Peter's, was enlarged and

27. Traigh Chrois

rebuilt last year; it is thatched with heath.'[48] In the *New Statistical Account* of 1836, Rev. William MacRae of Barvas notes that the parish 'originally embraced a district called Ness, at the eastern extremity, where there is a Government Church, and which has been erected into a separate parish called Cross.'[49] A parliamentary church was built in Cros in 1828, to a design by Thomas Telford.

The minister at Cros at the time of the Disruption of the Church of Scotland in 1843 was Mr John Finlayson, who led his congregation into the new Free Church, though he left them after a few months to take up a charge in Bracadale in Skye. His former congregation was left without a church until 1846, when a Free Church was built in Dail bho Dheas, replaced in 1891 with a church in Cros.

The politics of Church unions and disunions are not a subject into which I care to enter too deeply, but the church history of the time can be summed up in a phrase from my late mother-in-law – 'Until the Union, we had two churches, but after the Union there were four.'

At Cros a road branches off the main road to lead to Sgiogarstaidh – Cross-Skigersta Road in English – an Rathad Ur – the new road, locally. Along the Rathad Ur are fishermen's holdings, made in the early 1900s. The Board of Agriculture, in its wisdom, numbered the holdings along one side of the road, following up and down each side-road, then back down the other side of the road, then filled in the gaps. So No. 36 is opposite No. 45 in one direction and opposite No. 148 in the other, and No. 67 is next to No. 126! A stranger does not need a guide-map to find his way around the Rathad Ur, he needs an astrologer!

Dail bho Thuath (North Dell)

Dail bho Thuath was a tack as far back as we can trace in the Seaforth Papers, occupied by a family of Morrisons. Allan Morrison, the tacksman in 1797, complained to Seaforth that the wife of one of his subtenants, Iain Ruadh, had threatened to set his house on fire, and asked permission to evict him. As is always the case with information from such records, we have to remember that we are hearing only one side of a story, and it is quite possible that this pretext was used to hide quite a different disagreement – probably Morrison wanted John Roy's land for himself.

The township of Dail bho Thuath was at that time nearer the shore, near Airnistean, and the old track can still be seen leading from there through the other machair villages to the old church at Suaineabost – Rathad Beag an t-Searmoin – the wee road of the sermon. The farm was on the slopes of the river – Abhainn Dhail – with the farmhouse at Baile Glom, about halfway between Airnistean and the present road. The tacksman also had a mill on the river, and as in most areas of Lewis, the tenants in the neighbouring townships were 'thirled' to that mill, that is they were bound to take their meal there for milling, paying a percentage, usually about a twelfth share, of the meal to the miller. This payment was known as a 'multure' and even if a tenant did not take his meal to that mill he still had to pay 'dry multures'. Originally, this would have been a reasonable payment towards the cost of upkeep of the mill, but later became merely another element in the rent that could be charged, and was much resented by the tenants, who preferred to use their own querns, or one of the so-called Norse mills whose ruins can still be seen on many rivers.

New mills were built by Seaforth for some of his tacksmen in the 1820s, and the mill for the whole of Nis was based at Dail bho

Thuath. Originally it was run by the tacksman, Alexander Murray, late of Suaineabost, but it passed into separate hands – first a Donald Munro from the mill at Griais, but originally from Halkirk in Caithness, and then to Alexander MacFarquhar, of a Steornabhagh family from Redcastle in the Black Isle. MacFarquhar's son Murdo eventually obtained both the mill and the farm.

It is not long since the last tenants, Morrisons from Lional, had the mill running, and I believe that it is still in working order, though no milling is done now.

In the 1830s part of the mill land was made into crofts for tenants evicted from Griais on the east side of Lewis – the Baile Ghriais. One of the families changed not only their home but their name also – they were MacMillans leaving Griais, but Campbells when they reached Dail! When Murdo MacFarquhar got both farm and mill, he exchanged the Baile Ghriais for the land around the farmhouse at Baile Glom.

Another Campbell family there claims to have been MacIvers, according to Norman Campbell:[50]

> The branch of the great clan of which my father, Malcolm Campbell, came was not a direct offshoot from Argyll, but from Glenorchy, the Marquis of Breadalbane's district. The family came to Port Ness from Cape Wrath about the year 1663. They were the descendants of Kenneth Buey MacIver and his brother Farquhar, who left Argyllshire about 1560 with a large number of clansmen, and marched northwards to Caithness, scouring the country as they went. The details of their history are lost in the haze of tradition.

Dan Ferguson – mac Eoghainn Dhomhnaill – mentions some of these places in his song in praise of Dail bho Thuath:[51]

> Tha 'm baile sgiamhach seo 'na mhais na laighe 'n eilean Leodhais
> Tha iomadh ait' ann 's leam bu mhiann bhi deanamh orra sgeoil
> Bho Airnistean gu ruig Gleann Dail 's mach a' Mullach Mor
> 'S tha Baile Glom cur tuilleadh mais air Dail fo Thuath an
>   Leodhas

> This bonny village in all its glory lies in the Isle of Lewis / there are many places in it that I would tell you about / From Airnistean till you reach Gleann Dail and out to Mullach Mor / and the Baile Glom adding to the beauty of Dail bho Thuath in Lewis

Actually in Dail bho Thuath is the misleadingly named Cros School, with its former schoolhouse, which was the home of the earliest stage of Comann Eachdraidh Nis – Ness Historical Society – working under the Van Leer project, with workers employed through the job creation scheme of the time. I had helped with the layout and early stages of gathering information, and there were two ladies in particular who worked with us, gathering updated information and generally trying to find answers to the questions we were posing. I have already mentioned the late Mrs Margaret Morrison – Mairead a' Ghiomanaich – from am Port, to whom the Comann Eachdraidh owes a great debt for her work and support, but I must also mention here Miss Murdina Smith – Murdag Scotaidh – of Dail bho Dheas. Murdag began on the scheme with little or no interest in genealogy, but it was not long before she was complaining that 'This is worse than the drink, if it gets a hold of you!' Get a hold of her it did, and Murdag has been busy ever since, gathering information from registers, tombstones and obituaries, which will be of tremendous importance in the coming years.

The aim of the Van Leer project was to strengthen the local community, and one way of doing this was to involve the local children in interviewing the older people in the area, making both groups feel involved in the gathering of information to supplement

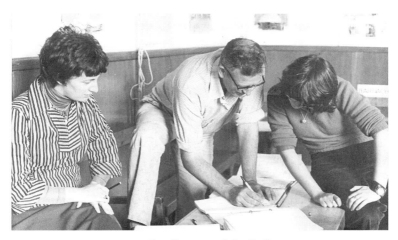

28. Family research in Dail

the data I had gathered from more formal sources on the history of the families and crofts of the area.

The prime mover in the Comann Eachraidh then, as in so many projects in Nis, was Anna Mhurchaidh Mhurdaig – Mrs Annie MacSween – Annie MacDonald at that time – and she still tells of her embarrassment the first time I stayed at her parents' house in Dail bho Thuath. Annie had a pet hen, which had made its way into the house and into the bedroom her mother had prepared for me – and had it been an egg it had laid, it would not have been so bad!

Dail bho Dheas (South Dell)

The oldest building in Dail bho Dheas is the old Free Church manse, now unfortunately in a poor state of repair. An old grey stone building, of course, with its roof turned bright orange by generations of lichen, it has a character of its own – it exudes history! – and I hope that it will not be allowed to deteriorate until demolition is the only viable option. But it is the usual problem – there is little point in preserving a building unless it can be used for something, and can generate sufficient income to prevent it sliding into disrepair once more.

Rev. Roderick MacRae from Kintail was the first minister to live there, to be followed by Rev. Duncan MacBeath from Applecross, who is unfortunately most remembered for another dispute within the Church when he fell out with three elders in his congregation. He is supposed to have prophesied – to call it a curse would surely be un-Christian – that none of the three would die in their beds, and sure enough two of them, Malcolm MacDonald and Murdo MacKay, went, as we saw, to the Isle of Ronaidh and died there, while the third, Kenneth MacPherson of Cros, walked out of his house and was never seen again.

At the far west end of Dail bho Dheas, in the area known as Aird Dhail, was Tobht' an t-Saighdeir – the ruins of the soldier's house. The saighdear was Donald MacLeod – Domhnall Thormoid Bhain – sergeant of the 78th Regiment, and he was in the Waterloo campaign, perhaps at that battle itself. He was in the same company as a Sergeant Harry Gunn from Thurso in Caithness, and they had made a compact that if either of them was killed the other would make a point of going back to tell his family. Harry Gunn was killed, and Donald not only went back to tell the widow, whose name was Binnie Campbell, but married her himself and brought her and her daughter back to Dail. Binnie became Peenidh in Niseach Gaelic, and she is still remembered as Peenidh na Teadha, as she is said to have introduced tea-drinking to that part of the island. It is said that, some time previously, a ship-load of tea had come ashore, and the locals had no idea what it was for, and eventually spread it on the fields as manure – but much the same story is told of many other places also.

Saighdear na h-Airde was not the only old soldier in Dail bho Dheas. Donald Gunn was there also, who according to tradition was taken by the pressgang and sent to the war in India in the early 1800s. He was a married man with family at the time, and it is said that his eldest son, Angus, was sent to Ronaidh so that he at least would escape the pressgang. The story cannot be quite accurate as it stands, as the pressgang had been disbanded by this time and, in any case, it was 'recruiting' for the navy, not the army, but there is no doubt that many men were 'persuaded' to join the armed services by fair means and foul, and the danger was perceived as a definite threat at the time. This is quoted at times as a reason for some of the changes of surname in Lewis, as men took the surname of the main landholder in the area, as a means of invoking his protection against the recruiters.

Dail was among the townships from which emigrants left to go to the Eastern Townships of Quebec. The first Gaelic settlers there had gone in 1838, but several more families went out in the 1840s. In Sir James Matheson's scheme of assisted emigration in 1851 (which we will refer to more fully when we reach the townships of Siadar) several families from Dail joined them, till there was a village called Dell in Quebec! One of the emigrants well remembered in Nis was Angus Smith – Aonghas mac Ailein Dhomhnaill Bhain. He was sixty-three years of age when he left with most of his family; a lament for their parting was written by his brother Donald in an Cnoc Ard, and is well known today from the singing of the incomparable traditional singer Mairi Seocaidh – Mary Smith – Donald's great-granddaughter.

Tri fichead bliadhna 's a tri b'e sin an aois mun a robh thu
Cha mhor tuilleadh de shaoghal tha cuid a dhaoine ri faighinn
Dhol a dh'fhagail do dhilsean b'fhaoin an ni dha do leithid
Dhol a ghearradh nan craobhan, och, gus an seann duine
    chaitheamh.

Chan e do bhoidhchead no t'ailleachd tha mi'n drasda ri achainn
Ach nach fhaic mi gu brath thu latha Sabaid no seachdainn
Sinn cho fada bho cheile 's tha 'n cruinne-ce 's e cho farsaing
Sinn gun sgriobhadh gun leughadh, och, gu sgeula thoirt
    eadrainn.[52]

Sixty-three years was your age / there aren't many who get more
years in the world / going to leave your kin, a foolish thing for your
like / going to cut the trees, wearing out an old man. / It is not your
beauty or your handsomeness that I am missing now / but that I will
never see you, Sabbath or weekday / We are as far from each other
as the world is wide / for us, without reading or writing, a divide
has come between us.

The best compliment I can pay to Mairi Seocaidh's singing is
that she sings as though she was making up the words as she goes
along – her singing is so immediate and so personal.

Another emigrant from Dail to the Eastern Townships was John
Campbell, of whom all that I ever heard was that his son Angus
traded his first wife for a horse! – but there must surely be more to
the story than that!

Asmigearraidh (Asmigarry)

Asmigearraidh was a little shepherd's house between Dail bho Dheas
and Gabhsann, near the headland of Tobha Ghabhsainn. It is a
beautiful little spot of green among the browns of the moor between
the road and the sea, nestling under a little hill to shelter it from the
south-west wind. What it would be like in a winter north-easter is
a different matter!

The first shepherd I can trace there was a Roderick Morrison,
who was there from 1812 to 1816, then moved into Dail bho Dheas,
from where he emigrated to Quebec in 1851. The next shepherd was
a John MacIver – Iain Dhomhnaill Bhain – whose first wife was a
lady from Pabail whose name is remembered locally as Beinti. This

is a very rare name in Lewis, though it does occur also in South Lochs, and the register clerk at the time entered her in the marriage register as Sophia. Beinti died young, and a mythology has grown up about her: that she was Greek, and had been washed ashore from a shipwreck with only a woollen gown with her name embroidered on it. It is not impossible – it is a brave man who would claim that for a family story! – but I cannot help wondering whether the whole story has built up from the English translation Sophia, which may have been decided on by the clerk, who could not think of anything else to replace Beinti.

In the 1840s and 1850s the shepherd there was an Alexander Nicolson, originally from Mealabost Bhuirgh. He belonged to a family of Nicolsons known as the Fiosaich – seers – presumably because of some ancestor who had, or claimed, that facility. After he died in 1854, his widow went to Quebec with all the family except one son, also Alexander, who remained and settled in Lional, where he was the father of Iain Fiosach of Filiscleitir and Alexander, better known locally as Billy an Fhiosaich, the poet and songwriter.

Gabhsann (Galson)

In the days of the Seaforth rentals there were two townships in Gabhsann – Gabhsann bho Thuath, which was crofted, and Gabhsann bho Dheas, which was a farm. In 1819, the farmer was a William MacGregor, originally from Gairloch, who moved to Strathconon in Easter Ross in 1848, and his main claim to fame today is that his son Roderick emigrated to the Philippines, where he set up what became the Del Monte pineapple plantations. So, to paraphrase the television advertisement, the man from Del Monte, he says 'Tha'.

MacGregor had subtenants on the farm, but his successor Hugh MacPherson had them removed to the new township of am Baile Ur – New Gabhsann – opposite Gabhsann bho Thuath, on the moor side of the road, where they were joined by landless cottars from Gabhsann bho Thuath. In MacPherson's time also, the townships of Borgh Mheadhanach and Mealabost Bhuirgh were cleared of their tenants and added to the farm. In 1863 Gabhsann bho Thuath and am Baile Ur were also added to the farm, which retained its new

B'ann air an là seo

12mh Fhaoilleach 2007

a ghabh muinntir Oighreachd Ghabhsainn

sealbh air an fhearann aca fhèin

29. Commemorative stone for Gabhsann Estate buy-out. 'On this 12th day of January 2007 the people of Gabhsann Estate took over the ownership of their own land.'

boundaries until 1924, when it was broken down into the crofting townships of Gabhsann bho Dheas, Gabhsann bho Thuath and Mealabost Bhuirgh.

In 2007, a community trust was able to buy out the ownership of virtually all the land from Barabhas Uarach to Eoropaidh and Sgiogarstaidh from its previous private owners, and what more appropriate name could the trust take than Urras Oighreachd Ghabhsainn – Galson Estate Trust. Most of Lewis had been in private hands since it was sold off in the collapse of Lord Leverhulme's schemes in the 1920s, other than the parish of Steornabhagh, which was given to the Stornoway Trust to manage. This idea of community-led trust ownership is now being spread to several areas of the Highlands, and although it will not be a panacea for all the many problems of the area, it does at least give local people a say in the running and development of the land they occupy.

Gabhsann bho Thuath was cleared of all its people in 1863, and how this happened is still a contentious point. We can tell the story as it appears in a section of the *Croft History* we produced for Urras Oighreachd Ghabhsainn,[53] to celebrate the day of the buy-out:

William MacKay, the Chamberlain of Lewis, gave evidence to the Napier Commission in 1883:

> The Crofters of this township petitioned to be sent to America in 1863, as they could not maintain themselves on the lands they held. There were forty-three crofters; twenty-four emigrated, and nineteen were provided with vacant crofts in other townships. The rental of the township was £154; and at the time of their removal they were £289.11.11 in arrears of rent, which was wiped off, and they got valuation for such of their stock as they could not otherwise dispose of.
>
> There were no crofters evicted forcibly, and no legal proceedings taken except the notice of removal, and even this same was not given in the case of the Galson crofters. The people were allowed to remain in their holdings till they had fixed on another place – some one, two and three years; and assistance in most cases was given to build new houses.[54]

The amount quoted for arrears is actually fairly low, less than two years' rent, but it includes many tenants who were up to date with their rentals and others badly in arrears. Writing off these arrears would have been no great loss to the estate, as they would probably have been irrecoverable anyway, but Sir James Matheson, the proprietor, paid the costs of travel to Ontario, amounting to between £20 and £30 for each emigrant family.

A very different version of events was given to the Napier Commission by John MacDonald of Dail bho Dheas, who was himself born in Gabhsann. The questions asked of him and his answers can be combined as follows:

> The last clearance was twenty years ago, in Sir James Matheson's time, and without his knowledge, and the land given to the tacksman. I could not ask to be better off than we were at North Galston, and almost all of the other crofters were so at first, but at a later period the tenants of South Galston were added on to them, and then they were not so well off. Of upwards of 100 families about 40 of them went to America and the rest was scattered all over the country. It was against our will that we were put out of Galston, but we went away without being summoned. I don't know one who benefited by it except one family, Angus Graham, now in Shader, he got better land where he went to than the land he was put out of. There was reason for giving a favour too; he built a slated house in that place.

30. Tin-type photograph of Norman Morrison and Christina MacLeod
who emigrated from Gabhsann to Ripley, Ontario

> I would like to go back to North Galston – I would have some of
> my furniture there before I slept if I got it.[55]

The two accounts, as so often with evidence, appear completely
contradictory. No doubt MacKay was truthful in saying that
the crofters petitioned to be removed, but why did they do so?
Gabhsann does not appear to have been any worse in arrears than
other townships, so why was it specially selected, unless because it
was so handy for an extension to Gabhsann Farm? There had been
a few bad seasons of crops, and no doubt those tenants not in arrears
would be finding difficulty in raising the money for the rent.

Did the estate make the offer of relatively generous terms of
emigration or other crofts, with the alternative of eviction without
any compensation? If so, it would be little wonder if the hard-
pressed tenants opted for giving up their crofts and making the
best of matters.

The *Inverness Courier* of July 1863 gives details of their embarkation:

Emigration from the Lews

The late adverse seasons and the severity of our weather during the past spring led many of the crofters to consider the propriety of emigrating with a view to bettering their condition, and nearly 500 souls have had their wishes gratified by the kindness of Sir James Matheson, who largely assisted them with means to provide passages to Canada, whither they have been forwarded. The largest batch left Carloway on the 29th ult, by a steamer for Londonderry, where they were transhipped to the *Elizabeth*, a sailing vessel which sailed for Quebec in the 3rd inst. The emigrants seemed to be in excellent spirits, and were met by Mr Munro, the Chamberlain, and Mr Murray, emigration agent, Glasgow, who superintended their embarkation. The latter gentleman accompanied them to Derry, and saw every attention paid to their comfort for the voyage across the Atlantic.

Would it be churlish to suggest that Munro, the chamberlain, was making sure they left?

From Canadian sources we know that the *Elizabeth* arrived in Quebec on 1st August, when her passengers dispersed, some to Goderich in Ontario, and others to join relatives in the Eastern Townships of Quebec.

We will approach the questions of emigration and clearance in more detail when we reach the Carlabhagh section of this book, as that was the main port of embarkation in later emigrations, but it is worth making the point here that, after decades of ignoring the Highland Clearances, popular history has now swung to the opposite extreme and tends to blame everything on the Clearances. Unfortunately, history is never as simple as that, and as we see in the Gabhsann story, widely differing interpretations can all be true – up to a point – and all equally false – up to a point!

A writer in 1901 states:

He (Sir James) assisted many poor people, utterly unable to help themselves, to emigrate to Canada. Many of these it has been my privilege to visit after many years in their new homes amid vastly improved circumstances.

31. Donald MacLeod and Janet Graham, who married in Ripley, Ontario, in 1885

– and this was no stranger to the Islands but Roderick Campbell from Dail bho Thuath, in his autobiography *The Father of St Kilda*.[56]
Though Gabhsann has such an interesting modern history, we must not forget its ancient history. The sea, eating into the shores below the township has, over the years, exposed a series of middens and graves, which, if not wholly unique in the Western Isles, are accessible and so better researched and documented than some remoter sites. Ian Armit in his *The Archaeology of Skye and the Western Isles*[57] notes that:

> excavations have revealed a long cist cemetery dating to around the fourth century AD . . . In 1984 and 1985 erosion of the beach front brought to light a series of four cists, of which two were examined

albeit not in ideal conditions . . . The two excavated skeletons had both been buried with their heads to the west. One was a robust young woman, perhaps in her mid-twenties, who had apparently suffered illnesses in childhood; she had suffered back problems in life resulting from heavy work and pelvic damage resulting from child-birth trauma. The other was a muscular adult male, perhaps around 35/40 years old. He too would have suffered back pain resulting from heavy work. This evidence supports that adduced from five burials excavated on the site in the 1950s which again stressed the heavy workloads endured by each of the individuals examined.

It is fascinating to think that science today can tell so much of the life and lifestyle of persons who died so long ago.

At a later date, there was Teampall an Cro Naomh – the Church of the Holy Cross – surrounded by its graveyard, on the shore below Gabhsann farmhouse. According to T.S. Muir in 1885:[58]

the walls nearly entire, but wanting the gables. The windows are flat-headed, and placed, one in the east end and one towards the east end of each of the side walls; the west end blank; the doorway, broken, is south-west.

By 1928 the earth outside the church had reached almost to the wall-heads, and now little can be seen of the site. However, we can obtain a good idea of what it did look like in 1819, for William Daniell made it the subject of one of the drawings he made during a visit to Lewis in that year.

In the vicinity is an architectural ruin, pretty nearly in the same state with that of the Chapel at Ness. There are numerous tombstones in the cemetery, but none of them bear traces of inscriptions; if any ever existed, they have probably been obliterated by time and the effect of the sea breezes from the westward. This ruin, like the former, has its legendary mystery, which still retains some hold on the superstitious feelings of the people. It was visited till within these few years by many of the peasantry, who would assemble here at stated periods to feast and dance for two or three successive nights. At one of these merry meetings it was ascertained that a man had taken an indecorous liberty with a female; the hallowed purity of the temple was in consequence destroyed, and it has not since been resorted to. As a proof of the high offence taken at this indignity by the genius

32. Teampall Ghabhsainn

of the place, it is asserted, and firmly believed by the islanders, that a taper lighted within the walls is instantly extinguished.[59]

To return to the crofting township of Gabhsann bho Thuath – in 1849 a boat-load of fishermen set out from Gabhsann; no trace was ever seen of them again. As the years passed, they were given up for lost, though it was strange that nothing at all of the boat, or its gear, or its crew, ever appeared on the shore, and the story grew up that perhaps they must have been taken by pirates. At least one of the widows remarried – an economic necessity in these days for a woman with a young family and no breadwinner. One day, many years later, a stranger came to the village, and asked about this woman, naming her by the name of her dead first husband. 'Oh, they said, you mean bean so-and-so', naming her by her second husband. They pointed out the house, but the stranger just thanked them and went away again. Later that night, someone noticed the stranger again, standing outside the house, gazing in through the little window at the family gathered inside, then he turned and went away, and was never seen again in Gabhsann. Was this her first husband, having made his way home to claim his wife and children, but deciding that, in the circumstances, he would be better to remain dead?

PART TWO – SGIRE A' CHLADAICH (SHORELANDS)

A few miles south of Gabhsann, a wide ditch has been dug across the moorland. It can hardly be a drainage ditch, as it runs in places against the fall of the land; traditionally it marks the boundary between Nis and Cladach. Cladach – the shore – is the old name for the area from here to Siabost, and we have used it, rather than the modern name of Sgire Bharabhais – Barvas parish – to avoid confusion between the parish and the township.

Though the Norse influence in still strong in Sgire a' Chladaich, it is less so than in Sgire Nis. Although the main placenames are Norse, the smaller areas in the moors tend to have Gaelic names, suggesting that the extent of the Norse domination here was less comprehensive. There are no real natural harbours on this stretch of the coast, so fishing was to a smaller scale than further north.

There is a small dun, or Iron Age fort, south of the boundary ditch, known as Dun Bhuirgh, though *Dun* in Gaelic and *Borg* in

33. Ruins of Dun Bhuirgh

Norse both mean fort. Rev. Donald MacDonald of Barabhas, in the *Statistical Account*[60] of his parish notes that:

> Betwixt Borve and Galson, upon an eminence at a small distance from the sea, may be seen the ruins of a pretty large dun or Danish fort, of a circular form, with passages and small apartments in the walls; the only entry was from the top. Tradition says that there was subterraneous communication to it from the sea, of which no vestige can now be traced.

Duns are, of course, far older than Viking times, and they are of two main types – the residential duns, as in Carlabhagh, and the chain of lookout duns on the shores, each within signalling distance of the next. Little remains of Dun Bhuirgh now – a round foundation and one small section of wall, but even so, it is a noticeable landmark in such a flat terrain.

Where Nis was Morrison country and Uig belonged to the MacAulays, Sgire a' Chladaich had no one dominant family – since both Morrisons and MacAulays had to pass through on their way to battle each other, Sgire a' Chladaich became a bit of a buffer zone between them.

One surname, which does not appear anywhere in Lewis today, but is said to have been common in Sgire a' Chladaich at one time is MacGill'Eadharain. Donald Morrison, a Harris man living latterly in Steornabhagh in the 1840s, and better known as an Sgoilear Ban tells a story about them, published in the *Morrison Manuscripts – Traditions of the Western Isles*:[61]

> At this time there was in Lewis a race of men called the MacLarens, all living on the west side, whom MacDonald got pledged to stand by his standard, promising them free lands in Lewis or Skye, should he be successful. When the battle began on the west side, MacDonald called out 'Separate, separate yourselves, MacLarens, do today as you promised me yesterday'. Immediately 140 of the MacLarens, wearing blue bonnets, joined the MacDonald corps.
> The battle began and lasted a whole day. In the end, the MacDonalds and MacLarens were beaten and a great slaughter took place. MacDonald himself narrowly escaped, leaving behind him most of his men. The few MacLarens who survived the battle betook themselves to Skye, in the terms of MacDonald's promise to give them land there, should he fail to conquer Lewis. But MacDonald

only gave each of them a cow and a boll of meal and told them to go about their business, as he said 'I have no confidence in you since you have betrayed your own countrymen and proprietor by joining me in fighting against him.' Thus the MacLarens never had any footing in the Highlands since this memorable battle.

But, as with many of the Sgoilear Ban's tales, there is a problem. There were never MacLarens in Lewis, but this is the Sgoilear Ban's attempt at MacGill'Eadharain. The problem is that there are many MacDonald families on the west side of Lewis who are known to have been MacGill'Eadharain at one time – Donald Cam, the folk hero of the MacAulays of Uig, was married to a daughter of Finlay MacGill' Eadharain, tacksman of Gabhsann bho Thuath. But if the few who survived the battle went to Skye, how were there so many MacGill'Eadharains left behind in Lewis? On the other hand, if there were, one can see why they would have changed their name!

The north end of the parish comprises the townships of na Buirgh – the Borves – Mealabost Bhuirgh, Borgh Mheadhanach and am Baile Ard to the north of the river and Borgh na Coig Peighinnean to the south.

Mealabost Bhuirgh (Melbost Borve)

Although this is the name of the township today, its first appearance in the Seaforth Papers under that name is not until 1810; prior to then it appears as Ulbost. In 1718 the tacksman of Ulbost is an Angus Morrison, but this changes in 1726 to William Ross, whose family retained the tack until 1787. Ross is not a local name in Lewis, and the only occurrence of the name in the 1718 rental is William Ross, tacksman of Lional, no doubt the same man as later moved to Ulbost. Since Ross is a name from Easter Ross, it is tempting to see the Rosses as a family who came from there with the MacKenzies when they took over Lewis from the old MacLeod chiefs, but that was in the early 1600s, so one would expect more than one tacksman of that family by 1718 – of course, the Rosses could have been like the later Rosses in Harris, who specialised in daughters, so that their name died out.

After the Rosses, the tack of Mealabost Bhuirgh passed to two former soldiers – Donald Graham, late sergeant in the 78th Regiment and Donald MacKenzie, late of the same regiment – according to a rental of 1787.[62]

This was the old 78th Regiment, raised by Seaforth himself, as we shall tell when we reach Uig, and though they later had a successful campaign in India, the regiment's history begins with a mutiny – as told by Colonel David Stewart in his *Sketches of the Highlanders of Scotland*:[63]

> In the year 1778, the Seaforth Highlanders were marched to Leith, where they were quartered for a short interval, though long enough to produce complaints about the infringements of their engagements, and some pay and bounties which they said were due to them. The regiment refused to embark, and marching out of Leith, with pipes playing and two plaids fixed on poles instead of colours, took a position on Arthur's Seat, of which they kept possession for several days, during which time the inhabitants of Edinburgh amply supplied them with provisions and ammunition. After much negotiation . . . the causes of the soldiers' complaints were investigated and settled to their satisfaction; they then marched down in the hill in the same manner as they had gone up, with pipes playing; and with the Earls of Seaforth and Dunmore and General Skene at their head.

It sounds rather as if it should have been the Duke of York at their head!

The regiment embarked for India on 1 May 1781, but Seaforth died on the voyage:

> Before they reached Madras, on 2nd April 1782, 230 men had died of scurvy, and out of 1,100 who had sailed from Portsmouth, only 390 men, when they landed, were fit to carry arms. In the month of October, the health of the 78th was so much re-established that upwards of 600 men were fit for duty, and ever afterwards they preserved their health and efficiency in a remarkable manner. The colours, which had been laid up, were again unfolded, and in April 1783 the regiment joined the army under Major-General James Stuart for the attack of Cuddalore.[64]

In these early Indian campaigns in the French Revolutionary Wars, it is clear that the French and their ally Tippoo Sahib, were not the main dangers to be feared.

The soldiers did not retain the tack for long, and by 1807 the township had been divided between sixteen tenants, two of whom were Rosses, no doubt descended from the former tacksmen, but the last of that family moved to Siadar Iarach, then went to Quebec along with the emigrants from Gabhsann in 1863.

There was a family of Nicolsons in Mealabost Bhuirgh, related to the Fiosaich we met at Filiscleitir. Donald Nicolson in Mealabost was married to Gormelia Murray, who claimed to have been born on Ronaidh in about 1780 – did she belong to the settlement there from which all the men were drowned, as MacCulloch related?

Their daughter Ann was married to a John MacLeod, and they set up a shop, with the contents, it is said, of a purse she found on the shore – it was probably merely malicious gossip that suggested there had been a body attached to the purse!

Another unusual name in Mealabost, and later in Siadar and Borgh was Saunders, who are said to have been descended from a salmadair – precentor and psalm-teacher – who came originally from Dundee, though he may have been in Caithness for a time. The family names he brought to Lewis included Robert, James, Emily and Merriett, and where any of these names are found in Sgire a' Chladaich there is probably a Saunders in the family background somewhere.

Mealabost Bhuirgh itself was cleared in 1853, to add to the tack of Gabhsann, of which it formed a part until the break-up of the farm in 1924.

Borgh Mheadhanach and am Baile Ard (Mid and High Borve)

Borgh Mheadhanach was a township on the northern slopes of Abhainn Bhuirgh. In 1780 it was a tack leased to one of the Ross family, along with the little farm of Begnigearraidh near Siadar Iarach.

> Donald Ross, Tacksman of Begnigarry, agrees to accept of his present possession and of the Town and Lands of Middle Borve as possessed by the tenants thereof for the space of Seven years for the payment of twenty Pounds Stg. of rent.[65]

Later the township was split, with tenants on the upper slopes and a farm nearer the river, then in 1851 the farm was divided into crofts

34. Am Baile Ard

for tenants evicted from Riof, and given the name of am Baile Ard.
According to John Munro MacKenzie, the factor in 1851:

> The part of Mid Borve farm formerly held by Robert Murray is now
> occupied by 8 families from Reef who own a Wick boat & nets and
> can pay their rents; they seem quite satisfied with the change they
> have made. The other tenants of Mid Borve are the most destitute
> in the Parish and are all old men.[66]

In 1853 the crofters of Borgh Mheadhanach were evicted, mainly
to crofts in Siadar, and their land was added to Gabhsann Farm,
though in 1863 it was taken away from the farm, and added to the
crofts of am Baile Ard.

Borgh na Coig Peighinnean (Fivepenny Borve)

Borgh na Coig Peighinnean is the formal name of this township,
though it is now generally referred to simply as Borgh. The penny
lands were a measure of tax from Norse times, and as well as na
Coig Peighinnean in Nis and here, we have na Seachd Peighinnean
as a generic name for the townships of Siadar, and even na Ceithir
Peighinnean Deug in the Bhaltos area of Uig.

The villages of the Cladach have the reputation in the rest of Lewis of being 'fad air ais' – far behind – and Borgh in my first memory certainly gave that impression. I remember going along the inner road through the township in a bus, and noting the apparently endless row of ruins of thatched houses, so many as to dominate the more modern houses and almost give an impression of a ruined township, had it not been for the haze of peat smoke everywhere. No doubt this was unfair, as I must have hit just on the point of transition from the old housing to the new, but such was my first impression.

Borgh will always appear congested, because of the narrowness of the crofts, which was not helped by the prevalence of further subdivision – the thirty-two crofts set out in 1851 had become forty-seven by 1871, and by 1891 the number of households had grown to sixty-two.

In a rental of 1756[67] Donald Roy paid his rent of £1 8s 6d by five pecks of meal, worth 2s 9d, a cow to the factor, worth £1 2s 2d, and cash of 3s 7d; in the following year he paid with eight pecks of meal, a stot, valued at 19s 4d, and the balance in cash of 3s 5d. Others were paying with the value of cattle supplied to Borline, or to Charles MacSween, cattle-drovers from Skye, with again a small balance in cash.

There is an interesting point here: it is generally accepted that the economy of rural Lewis at that time was a barter economy, yet here we see, as early as the 1750s, part of the rent being paid in cash. Where did the cash come from? It was not through selling cattle to the factor or to his drovers, as these are listed separately. So what were the tenants of that time selling? And, even more intriguing, who was buying it?

A list of stock in Barvas parish in 1824[68] shows Fivepenny Borve as having a total stock of 59 horses, 133 cows and 73 sheep. John Munro MacKenzie had a difficult time in Borgh in 1851, when he went to collect cattle as rental payments in 1851:[69]

> Went to Borve and after having sent three messengers to Five Penny Borve to attend with Cattle or Money to pay their rents and seeing that but few appeared, went to the sea shore where their cattle were pasturing. Collected their cattle and horses and drove them to the road, but before we got them so far the greater number of them were

secured in their houses. Tho' no one could be seen when they were sent for, men, women and children now appeared in all directions, some driving off a cow, some running away with a horse etc. etc. Being overpowered by numbers we succeeded in taking but few of their cattle, and the greater number of those we did get we had to let go as we could not ascertain the owners names . . . The people of this township have a good stock of Sheep and Cattle and have always had good crops, there is no doubt that the greater number of them could pay if they pleased.

Borgh was one of the townships from which several men went off to work for the Hudson's Bay Company in the 1820s. Many of them married there, and some brought wives and families back to Lewis – it is surprising just how much Cree Nation blood there is in Borgh and Siadar.

In January 1953, the shore at Borgh was the scene of a shipwreck – the *Clan MacQuarrie*. James Shaw Grant, at that time a reporter though later the publisher of the *Stornoway Gazette*, tells the story in his book *The Hub of my Universe* [70]

When I went to get the car out there were occasional flurries of snow and a wind such as I have never experienced before or since. It was a struggle to open the garage door. It was a greater struggle to keep the car on the road across the Barvas moor. When eventually I stopped, I was blown ten yards backwards before I got the hand-brake on. When I got to Borve I could see the lights of a large vessel close inshore, the *Clan MacQuarrie*. She was in ballast, rearing high out of the water. A perfect target for the vicious wind, she had been driven helplessly on to a reef.

The Lifesaving Crew from Stornoway were on the scene by this time. They had to leave their vehicles and manhandle their gear, including an electric generator, for about a mile across a broken moor to get near the wreck. They were pushed here and there by the wind. Flung in to ditches. Battered with hail and flying spray. The wind was now gusting well beyond a hundred miles an hour, and a huge wave drowned the generator, plunging the rescue team into total darkness. There was little they could do but wait for daylight. In the meantime there was the *Clan MacQuarrie*, on a lee shore, with more than sixty men on board, in imminent peril.

I will never forget the sight that met my eyes when I got back to Borve. Crofters and fishermen had gathered from all the villages

35. The *Clan MacQuarrie*

along the coast. Big burly men who had lived with the sea all their lives. The Lifesaving Crew had got a line aboard the *Clan MacQuarrie*, and a hundred willing helpers were holding it taut, as the bosun's chair shuttled back and fore above the breakers. Every man on board was taken safely off, even the ship's cat. And they didn't get their feet wet. It was the biggest rescue by breeches buoy in the history of the sea, up to that time at least, and so far as I know, it has not been surpassed since then.

Living in Ayrshire at the time, I remember that night as the night the Stranraer ferry the *Princess Victoria* was lost. My wife remembers it as the night one of her neighbours had a baby boy – known thereafter as Hurricane Bill!

Siadar a' Chladaich (Shader)

The name Siadar comes from the Norse *setr* – a grazing settlement – and is a common element in Lewis placenames. Siadar a' Chladaich comprises three main units – Siadar Iarach, Begnigearraidh and Siadar Uarach. Together they comprised na Seachd Peighinnean – Seven Pennies – a name which appeared on a Bartholomew atlas as late as 1896, though it has now gone out of use.

It is interesting in the light of recent controversy about road signs that that atlas shows almost all of the village names in the Western Isles in both Gaelic and English – the move to monoglot English names only came in the last century.

In the general relotting of Lewis townships in 1851, the Siadar townships were moved to new sites, not to the liking of many of the crofters, many of whom, as we shall see, decided to emigrate rather than settle on the new lands proposed for them.

Siadar Iarach (Lower Shader)

Originally the crofts of Siadar Iarach were along the hill ridge near the shore – Cuidhbhatotar – with the little farm of Begnigearraidh to the south, but in the 1840s the village was moved to its present site nearer to the main road and Begnigearraidh became a part of the township. An old track still runs from the shore at Mol Eire along the ridge of Cuidhbhatotar, and the remains of the old houses are still clear there. I remember on one occasion taking a party of MacIvers from Penticton and elsewhere in British Columbia to see the village their ancestors had left from; it is hard for us to comprehend the emotional effect that seeing their visible history has on their descendants.

Across the main road from the present village is Loch an Duin, with, as the name implies, a fort on an island, accessible only by a causeway, now largely below water level. On the slope above it is Steinacleit, the remnants of a chambered cairn, and to the north, the five-foot-high standing stone of Clach Stei Lin.

Siadar Iarach must in its day have been an important religious centre, as there is a grouping of early Christian sites there, listed by Finlay MacLeod in his *The Chapels of the Western Isles*.[71]

The chapel of Teampall Pheadair is situated on a green sward above Mol Eire in Shader. A grassy knoll can still be seen on the site with a small amount of wall still showing. It was over 33 feet long and apparently it comprised two rooms; these were the nave and the chancel. Beside the chapel is Creag Gille Phadraig. Clach an t-Sagairt (the priest's stone) could at one time be seen by the shore until it was eroded by the force of the sea some years back. St Andrew's Well, mentioned by Martin Martin, can be found east of the chapel, and Tobar Mhoire (Mary's Well) is slightly to the south of it. Rubha na h-Annaid lies 100 yards east of the chapel and the large stones which are called Clachan na h-Annaid are about 100 yards south of Rubha na h-Annaid near St Andrew's Well.

Annaid is an ancient name for a church location.

Martin Martin's reference is to the diagnostic powers of the well:[72]

> St Andrew's Well in the village Shadar is by the vulgar Natives made a Test to know if a sick Person will die of the Distemper he labours under. They send one with a wooden Dish to bring some of the water to the Patient, and if the Dish which is then laid softly upon the Surface of the Water turn round Sun-ways, they conclude that the Patient will recover of that Distemper; but if otherwise, that he will die.

Several families from Siadar Iarach were among the emigrants to the Eastern Townships of Quebec in the 1850s, and there was an area there known as the Baile Shiadair, as well as the nearby Baile Bharabhais. Baile Shiadair was the only place where I have come face to face with a wild black bear, and I am glad to say that I was in a car at the time, and it was not actually its face it had towards me as it ambled off into the secondary forest-growth.

Among these settlers from Siadar Iarach was a John Smith family. They settled in the area a little to the east of the Baile Shiadair, in an area later known as Giosla, where, as Duncan MacLeod in his *History of Milan, Quebec*[73] tells us, his family had an eventful life:

> Donald 'Cyclone' Smith and two sisters lived on a farm towards the Middle District, off the town-line road. Their home was destroyed by the cyclone in 1917. They were in the house when the cyclone struck and were severely injured but survived. The house was picked up off its foundation and turned topsy-turvy, coming down on the roof, completely destroyed. Willie MacDonald was on his way to visit the family and witnessed the event, he having to take refuge in a ditch to escape being killed.

Other families went to Ontario, mainly to Bruce County, including a James MacIver family, whose son Murdo and family later settled in Kincardine Township.

36. Murdo MacIver family in Kincardine, Ontario

Siadar Uarach and Baile an Truiseil (Upper Shader and Ballantrushal)

Siadar Uarach originally lay at Cleitir, on the moor side of the road, to the south and east of Siadar Iarach, but it also was moved in the resettlement plans of 1851, with two new roads being laid out towards the sea at Mullach an Thoil and Baile an Truiseil. A great number of families left both townships of Siadar at that time, at what is frequently, but in this case inaccurately, referred to as 'the Clearances'. Clearance, as it happened in some other parts of Lewis, involves the removal of the population of a township or area, to be replaced with a farm or other non-local usage, as happened in parts of the parishes of Uig and Lochs, whereas in Siadar area, the townships had even more crofters after the clearance than before!

In a list of households in 1819,[74] Siadar Uarach had twenty crofter households and six cottar widows, a total population of 124 persons above the age of six; by 1841, this had increased to forty-one households with 230 persons. The main food crop of the period was the potato, but when it failed in successive years in the late 1840s, starvation was only avoided, as elsewhere in Lewis, by destitution funding from the Churches, through the Highland Relief Board, and from Sir James Matheson, the then owner of the island. Matheson expected that the cost of his meal would be repaid eventually – though it rarely was – but he did at least provide food at the time when it was most needed.

I considered the sequel in my lecture on *The Clearances in Lewis – Truth or Myth* – the Third Angus Macleod Memorial Lecture in October 2006:[75]

> Things were bad enough for the crofters, but many times worse for the cottars. The policy of discouraging and even preventing emigration, to provide a workforce for the now-defunct kelp trade, had meant that a much greater than usual number of young married couples had settled on small unofficial shares of their relatives' land. Improvement in the availability of health care had lessened the impact of infant mortality, and the population had expanded far beyond the ability of the land under crofting to maintain them. If a croft could no longer maintain a crofter family, still less could it maintain extra cottars.
>
> By 1850 both Matheson and the Highland Relief Board had given up the task as being beyond the extent of the resources available to them – it was no longer a short-term problem but a danger of long-term famine. It was estimated that over 12,000 people were in receipt of help through the Relief Board, out of a total population of just under 20,000. Emigration was thought to be the only answer to the immediate danger – especially emigration of the ever-growing body of cottars. Matheson encouraged emigration with both carrot and stick – the promise of free transport to Canada, to areas where land was available, and the threat of cessation of relief works and funds.

In addition to this inducement and compulsion to emigrate, the people of Siadar were also faced with the prospect of removal to their new townships, and, especially in the case of Siadar Uarach, of breaking in new lands.

John Munro MacKenzie, in his *Diary 1851*,[76] was conscious of dissent in the area:

> The people of Shaders are yearly falling more into arrears of rent; they show no wish to pay & it would seem as if a combination existed amongst them not to pay the landlord as many of them are

in possession of a good Stock of Sheep and Cattle, tho' others have few or none. 10 families from Lower Shader emigrated and 2 from Upper, & many of the rest are preparing to follow & have no desire to pay rents.

My reading of the situation is that MacKenzie was quite right, and there was a 'combination' against the landlord. I think that many of the families decided that, if faced with leaving their old homes and breaking in new ground, they would do so on their own terms and for their own benefit – in Canada! No fewer than thirty-three families left Siadar between 1851 and 1855, twenty-nine of them for a new settlement in Bruce County, Ontario.

Norman Robertson's *History of the County of Bruce*[77] has an account of the arrival of the settlers, provided by Angus Martyn, himself a son of an emigrant from Siadar.

> They came on sailing vessels and landed at Quebec in the 4th August, 1851. They then went by boat to Port St. Francis, where the party of emigrants divided, the majority going to the county of Compton, Lower Canada, and the remainder went on the same boat to Montreal, from there by another boat to Hamilton, touching at Toronto. From August to December they remained in Hamilton, the men working on the Great Western Railway, which was then in the course of construction. In December they scattered, going to Guelph, Stratford, Galt and Goderich. All met in Goderich in the summer of 1852. Some more emigrants from Lewis came to Canada in 1852 and joined the others at Goderich in the fall of that year, when all moved to Huron Township in the County of Bruce. There were one hundred and nine families in all.

It has become fashionable to look on the Lewis emigrants as poor, helpless people, being sent across the Atlantic to a land of which they had no conception, but an article on the above Angus Martyn in *Ripley – Huron's Hub*[78] notes of his father 'Donald Martyn had been a trader with the Hudson's Bay Company and spoke Gaelic, English, French and an Indian language.' Donald himself was originally from Begnigearraidh, but had moved into Siadar Iarach in the 1840s.

Huron Township is a few miles inland from the shores of Lake Huron, and when I was last there was mainly cattle country, with its hub the Pine River Cheese factory. Looking at the flat farmlands

37. Pine River, Ontario

today, it is hard to imagine what it looked like when the first settlers arrived – virgin forest, and scrub along the shores of the Pine River itself.

It must have been hard work clearing the forest, but was it any worse than the drudgery of peats and tilling an unproductive soil at home? And at least in Bruce County the results belonged to you alone, with no share to be given to a factor. Those who remained behind must have thought so, for, of the twenty crofter families settled in Baile an Truiseil in 1850, fifteen emigrated to Canada in the next ten years.

When the railroad came through the area, the town of Ripley became a commercial centre. According to *Families and Farms of Huron:*[79]

> In 1930 there were thirty-one places of business in Ripley. These included two millinery stores, three large grocery stores, two hardware stores, a jewellery store, bakery, ice cream parlour, printing office, harness shop, flax mill, a planning and lumber yard, a bank and two hotels. There were three doctors and a dentist, and three churches.

My first visit to Ripley was to Jack and Mary MacDonald. Jack's great-grandfather Donald MacDonald – called Donald 'Dory' to distinguish him from the eleven other Donald MacDonald heads of household in Huron Township in the census of 1861! – was originally from Siadar Uarach, and was married to Marion MacDonald from Gearraidh Shiadair – and so called Sarah 'Yarrie'.

The first time I was in Ripley the leather and harness-maker's shop was still there. That was where all the older men gathered in the mornings – I think a George MacLean ran it, but I am not quite sure of the name – and I still have in my office patterned leather desk mats I was given there. But like all the small country towns in Ontario, Ripley is now in decline, especially since the railroad closed, and only a few businesses are left today.

Another quote from *Ripley – Huron's Hub*: [80]

> One of the Ripley residents with a very interesting background was Angus 'Indian' MacDonald. Donald MacDonald from Upper Shader, went to western Canada with the Hudson's Bay Co. at York Factory.
>
> He married or had a country wife Jane Robison. She was a Metis with a white father and an Indian mother. Donald and Jane had a son Angus and perhaps a daughter. Donald left his Metis wife and returned to Scotland with young Angus in 1844. In Lewis, Donald MacDonald married Mary MacDonald of Upper Shader. Donald and Mary had a son Isaac Hunter MacDonald, named after Dr Isaac Hunter of the Hudson's Bay Co.
>
> Young Angus grew up around Shader and in 1873 married Kate MacRitchie of Upper Shader. In 1883 they came to Canada to settle in Ripley with other Gaelic-speaking Lewis Island cousins.

The old Pioneer Cemetery was on the shores of the Pine River, but erosion has been a problem, and most of the stones were removed some years ago to a memorial cemetery.

The Huron Township community was too diverse for Gaelic to survive as a community language, unlike the Eastern Townships of Quebec. A schoolmaster there in 1865 reported:

> Fully half of the younger boys and girls who attended the school could not speak a word of English at first, but in less than six months not a word of Gaelic could be heard in the playground, and their parents, instead of raising a national cry over it were only too glad and proud that their children had learned the common language of the country, and in so short a time.[81]

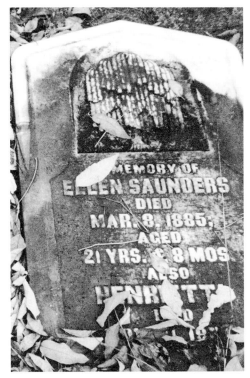

38. Gravestone in Huron Pioneer Cemetery, Ontario

I was privileged to meet the last two Gaelic speakers in the area, Mrs Picot and Mrs Hendry. The latter was a darling lady – absolutely stone deaf, but she loved talking, and so long as she could see you asking questions, it did not worry her whether she heard them, but just answered whatever question was in her own mind at that moment. I think that our best crossed-wires came when I asked her how many brothers her grandfather had, and she told me 'Eighteen Hundred and Fifty Two'.

Many more settlers came to Ontario in the following years; Huron Township was soon fully settled, so the next major group, in 1863, settled closer to Goderich. The Bruce Peninsula, north of Owen Sound, had been declared by treaty to be Indian land, but as pressure grew on the settled land, the treaties were revised and revised until little was left to the First Nations except what is now the Cape Croker Reserve – where incidentally one of the most common surnames is MacLeod! There were settlements of Lewis people around Lion's Head and Wiarton but the main new settlement was at Stokes Bay, in its day a fishing community, now largely deserted except for holiday homes, and with a graveyard full of stones with Lewis names.

Jane Yemen's *Scrapbook* of her life in Bruce County contains many obituaries, such as this:

> Cupar, Saskatchewan, Dec. 28, 1926 – The death of Kenneth McLay, 83, an early settler of the Cupar district, occurred Christmas Day at his home. Deceased was born in the Highlands of Scotland in March 1844, where he lived until seven years of age. He came with his parents to Lower Canada and lived a few years near what is now Sherbrooke, Quebec. He moved when a young man to Upper Canada, to the district later included in Bruce County when the province of Ontario was formed. He came west in 1899 and lived near Fort Qu'Appelle for two years before coming to the farm near Cupar where he resided until the time of his death.[82]

From our own records at *Co Leis Thu?* we can identify Kenneth as a son of Kenneth MacLeay of Siadar Iarach and Mary MacDonald of Dail bho Thuath, who took up one of the new crofts in Baile an Truiseil for a year or so, then left for Canada. Like so many of the early settlers there, their children moved further west to the Prairies as land became available there.

At the time of my first visit to the area, the main real estate company was MacLay's, of Siadar ancestry, with branches in Wiarton, Lion's Head and elsewhere in the Bruce Peninsula.

Another emigrant from Siadar Uarach was Murdo Morrison of Niagara Falls, whose 'Coinnichidh mi an gleann an fhraoich'[83] is still very popular, especially as sung by Kathleen MacDonald, herself from Siadar Uarach:

> Nuair dh'iathas ceo an fheasgair dluth
> Cur smuid air bharr nam beann,
> 'S an crodh bho'n innis cnamh an cir
> Cho sgith a' tighinn do'n ghleann;

'Nuair bhios a' bhanachaig 'm beul na h-oidhch'
Don 'n laoigh toirt deoch le meoir,
Coinnichidh mi an gleann an fhraoich
Mo ghaol, mo ribhinn og.

When the mists come down in the evening / putting a mantle on
the hill-tops / the cattle from the grazing chewing the cud / tired
coming back to the glen / when the milkmaid in the evening /
gives milk to the calves with her fingers / we will meet in the glen
of heather / my love, my young girl.

Of course, Siadar Uarach has its ancient history too, centred
around the massive standing stone of Clach an Truiseil, 5.7 m. in
height. Rev. Donald MacDonald in the *Statistical Account* of 1797[84]
was not impressed:

It is famous for nothing but its size, having no figures upon it, as is
erroneously related. The vulgar tradition concerning it is too absurd
and superstitious to deserve any notice.

So for stories of Clach an Truiseil, both ancient and modern, I
would refer you to that much underrated book *Devil in the Wind*
by Charles Macleod.[85] Superficially it is the story of his attempt
to relocate from Glasgow back to his native 'Sevenpenny' as he
calls it, but the atmosphere of the island seeps in through every
page. There are some excellent vignettes, above all the story of the
wedding in the snow, when a groom from Bru and a bride from
Baile an Truiseil were just going to get married when an exceptional
snowfall blocked all the roads on the island, and there was no way
to get the groom to the bride – or the minister to either. The men
of Bru and Siadar and all the intervening townships turned out with
spades and shovels to clear the road sufficiently to allow a bus, with
the minister on board, to make its way to Siadar – the groom, of
course, was wielding a shovel too! And, in the bus, sat the minister.
And Macleod makes it clear, without saying so in so many words,
that not only would the minister not have considered helping with a
spade, but he would not have been welcome if he had – two worlds,
and never could they meet.

Marvellous little pictures, such as two old men discussing a party
which had turned out better than they had expected: 'I will never

39. Clach an Truiseil

forget what I can remember of it.' But I am not going to quote any
more – you should read it for yourself!

Clach an Truiseil was one of the antiquities pictured by William
Daniell:

Daniell describes the stone: [86]

> On leaving Galston, a small deviation was made from the direct
> route, for the purpose of inspecting another relic of more remote
> antiquity. Its actual site is between Barvas and Shather, in a deep
> moss, its height from the surface being about sixteen feet. Its entire
> length, if we judge from its probable depth in the ground, must be
> much more. There are no stones in the immediate vicinity, and,
> being placed at a considerable distance from the sea, it cannot but
> be a matter of wonder and conjecture from whence so ponderous a
> mass was secured, how it was brought hither, and by what means it
> was fixed in its present position.

Murdo Morrison speaks for the stone in his poem 'Clach an
Truiseil', quoted in Ian Stephen's 'Siud an t-Eilean': [87]

> Dearcaidh mi bho thaobh mo chuil
> Air Muirneag a' chuil duinn
> Is chi mi ceo gach feasgar ciuin
> Ag iadhadh dluth sna glinn;
> Chi mi bhuam an t-arbhar lan
> Air Mullach ard an Toil;

O, b' eolach mi air tuar gach ait
Mus tainig na tha beo.

Behind me I see the rise / Of Muirneag in the brown moor, / And
in the calm of the dips / To the quiet evening mists / Trailing shade
over glens / I've seen full harvests / Over Mullach an Toil / I knew
all that, I knew it all / Before the living ones.

On the moor between Baile an Truiseil and Barabhas Uarach
is Druim nan Carnan – the ridge of the cairns – which is said to
have been a site of the last battle between the MacAulays of Uig,
under their leader Donald Cam, and the Morrisons of Nis. Donald
Morrison, the Sgoilear Ban, tells the story in his *Traditions of the
Western Isles*: [88]

> Judge Morrison's sons went from Ness to the Isle of Rona. When
> Donald Cam and his friends heard this, they went to Ness and
> plundered the cows of the Morrisons for none dare oppose them.
> But on the following night the Morrison sons returned. Strong ale
> etc. was drunk by the Morrisons and they and their followers, well-
> armed, went in pursuit of the MacAulays. The Morrisons caught up
> with the MacAulays between Shader and Barvas and a bloody battle
> ensued. The MacAulays got the worst of it and many of them were
> killed. They were buried on the spot, on a rise since termed Druim
> nan Carnan, so named for the heaps of stones placed on the graves
> of those who fell in the battle.

There is a sequel to this story, but we will keep it until we reach
its site at Cnoc Ruagan at Linsiadar.

Barabhas Uarach (Upper Barvas)

As you come into Barabhas Uarach from Siadar, the road takes a
wide bend to the left. It was not intended to do so; it was meant
to carry straight on through the old township of Barabhas Uarach
at Thangaigh, between the manse and the cemetery, and come out
at the shore end of Loch Mor Bharabhais, but the road-makers hit
deep peat, the line of the road had to be changed, and yet another
village had to be moved.

The old manse of Barabhas, now Morven Gallery, is the first
building on the shore side of the new road. Rev. Donald MacDonald
in the *Statistical Account* of 1797 notes: [89]

> The manse is small; was built about 28 years ago, and repaired last year at considerable expence. The church close by the manse is a perfect ruin and is to be rebuilt next summer.

Rev. William MacRae in the *New Statistical Account* of 1836[90] up-dates this:

> The church was built about forty years ago and has been lately well repaired. It is a long narrow building without gallery, and affords accommodation for 300 persons. The manse was built about sixty years ago, and has been also frequently repaired.

There is no sign now of the old church, though the old churchyard on the machair is still the main burial ground of the area; a still-older church, Teampall Mhoire, was situated in the cemetery. Machair land can be very productive, and its wild flowers are incredibly beautiful, but it does suffer from one great problem – sand-blow. If the surface is once broken – and rabbits can do great damage here – the wind can get in and cover acres of land with sand.

Iain Moireach – John Murray – from Barabhas Iarach makes this the theme of one of his small poems:[91]

a' ghaoth
a' siabadh na gainmhich
a' feannadh na machrach
ag isleachadh cnuic
ar n-eachdraidh
gu rannsachail gu fasach

rabaidean easgaidh
ag aiteach agus ag arach
far na thogadh ar sinnsir
is far an deach an caradh

a cinn-san an-diugh
a' sgaineadh uachdar
mo sheallaidh
aiseirigh na bochdainn
gun duil rithe

the wind / sweeping sand / flays the machair / reduces the hills / of our history / winnowing to desert / eager rabbits / cultivate and breed / where our ancestors were reared / and where they were interred / today their heads / crack the surface / of my vision / miserable resurrection / unforeseen

(What a relief to be able to use a poet's own translation!)

James Hogg, the Ettrick Shepherd, noted the incursion of the sand on his visit to Barabhas in 1803:

> The other things that we saw worthy of remark were the hills of sand contiguous to the manse. These are an insurmountable bar to improvement in that quarter, as a dry Spring always opens them, and lays the whole of the crops of grass or corn adjacent several feet deep in sand. These hills are accumulating from a sandy beach hard by, from which a strong north-west wind fetcheth immense loads of Sand. On the top of one of these hills is situated St Mary's chapel, an ancient place of Popish worship. It had formerly been on the very summit of the eminence, but the sand is now heaped up to such a height as to be on a level with the gables. Yet the eddying winds have still kept it nearly clear, so that it appears as a building wholly sunk underground. The baptismal font is still standing in a place in the wall prepared for it.[92]

In my time as project manager of a development project in the Islands in the 1980s, the reclamation of Barabhas machair from sand-blow was one of the major projects in this area, and attempts, of varying success, are still being made to stabilise the machair there.

Rev. William MacRae in 1836[93] notes the clarity of the sky:

> The luminous meteors, rainbow, halo and Aurora Borealis or polar lights, are very frequent and brilliant. The glare of the latter sometimes may afford light for reading, and their warlike motions are often interesting. As they advance, at their first appearance, slowly and majestically, the fertile imagination may fancy the cool and stately motion of two mighty hosts approaching to the onset, then the hurry and confusion of the thickening fight, then the rout, the fugitive and pursuer emerging one in another – until a third party shoots forth as from an ambuscade, ending the battle, and resigning the firmament to the stars and ancient night.

– indeed, a fertile imagination!

When George Atkinson visited the manse of Barvas in 1833, he was very taken with the hospitality of the manse:

> The Minister Mr MacRae proved a sensible good kind of man, and

put into my hands the manuscript of the Stornoway Cooper, of the legends of the Lewis, which proved to be very deficient in dates and data, as well as importance, though many of the tales were as wild and extraordinary as can be conceived.[94]

This was, of course, the Sgoilear Ban's manuscript, to which we have so often made reference in this book, and although I must agree that it is frequently infuriating in the detail it does not give, still it is an impressive collection of stories which could otherwise have been lost.

Atkinson also refers to a religious controversy of the day:

The family were out of spirits and depressed at the departure of their friend, the Minister of Ness, who had been driven away by the canting interference of one of the Methodists, though celebrated throughout Lewis for blamelessness of life, and the simple sincerity of his religious professions and practice.[95]

The minister of Nis then was Rev. Finlay Cook, later to be a stalwart of the Free Church. Atkinson is obviously wrong in blaming a 'Methodist', but one wonders what the particular controversy was about – perhaps it is better not to know.

As well as being the home of the parish minister, Barabhas Uarach also became the base for registration of births, marriage and deaths when this commenced in 1855. Some registrars were more diligent than others, and all had problems with keeping a register in English for Gaelic-speaking people. A girl named Raonailt in Gaelic might have recognised herself as Rachel – but hardly as Reginaldina!

Hector Barnett, who was registrar in 1887, was very lax in keeping up the register, and the inspectors at the end of the year found that only 46 births had been recorded, compared with 163 in the previous year, with the same position for deaths and marriages. Barnett, of course, lost his job, and the registers for the next few years contain back-dated entries as births, etc., were noticed which had never been registered. On one occasion when my wife Chris and I were researching in New Register House in Edinburgh, she noticed the registration of death of an eighty-year-old man – and his birth registration on the same day! – Barnett had missed him in his register, and no one had noticed until they came to register his death.

Of course, the registers can only be as accurate as the information given to the registrar – and his own memory of it. My friend Alex Murdo Morrison of Barabhas Uarach, whose father was registrar for the first half of the twentieth century, tells of an example in our *Croft History of Lewis,* vol. 9:[96]

> I remember a lady who was over from Canada and she came for her birth certificate in order to get her pension. Her name was Flora MacDougall, but she had been registered as Roderick MacDougall. My father and her brother had to go to the Court House in Stornoway to swear on oath that it was a mistake!

Barabhas Iarach (Lower Barvas)

The old township of Barabhas Iarach was down near the shore, above the storm beach of Croic, the noise of whose boulders being rolled by the high seas is a continuous background rumble on all but the calmest of days. From here the village was moved to three series of 'streets', running parallel to the present Loch Street, then, when the main road was made on its new line, the inner streets were changed to lines of crofts at right angles to the new road. Even then, the township was hardly in a settled form, for it was one of the last in Lewis to use the practice of suidhicheadh: every few years all the crofts and their houses were re-allocated by ballot – which incidentally is probably why a Lewis croft is referred to generally as a lot, whereas in most other areas, it would be cruit. Suidhicheadh gave every tenant a chance of getting a period on the best land, and there would have been little difference in the houses – though what the housewife thought of the change would surely have been a different matter. In later years, the allowance was made that if you had built a chimney on your house, you would not be required to move, but suidhicheadh continued to be the general rule in Barabhas Iarach until the 1860s.

At the junction of three roads – one to Carlabhagh, one to Steornabhagh, one to Nis – is the old Barvas Lodge, at one time also an inn. Abhainn Bharabhais winds it way from halfway across Lewis, down Gleann Mor Bharabhais to the Loch Mor and Croic. It is still reckoned as one of the premier salmon rivers of the island. At

40. Norman MacLeod, who emigrated from Barabhas to Lindsay Township, Ontario

one point, the estate altered the outlet to the sea, to great objection from the people of Barabhas, who claimed that it would cause the river to eat into their old graveyard. One old man offered to show where the problem was most acute, but digging at the spot uncovered only the skull of a sheep!

The local people had their own way of ensuring that the fishing in the river would be good, according to Martin Martin:[97]

> The natives in the Village Barvas retain an ancient Custom of sending a Man very early to cross Barvas River, every first day of May, to prevent any Females crossing it first, for that they say would hinder the Salmon from coming in to the River all the year round; they pretend to have learn'd this from a foreign Sailor, who was shipwreck'd upon that Coast a long time ago. The Observation they maintain to be true from Experience.

Barabhas was probably the last place in Lewis where the old-style craggan pottery was made. Arthur Mitchell in his *The Past in the Present* describes the process as used by one lady there:[98]

The clay she used underwent no careful or special preparation. She chose the best she could get, and picked out of it the larger stones, leaving the sand and finer gravel which it contained. With her hands alone she gave to the clay its desired shape. She had no aid from anything of the nature of a potter's wheel. In making the smaller craggans, with narrow necks, she used a stick with a curve on it to give form to the inside. All that her fingers could reach was done with them. Having shaped the craggan, she let it stand for a day to dry, then took it to the fire in the centre of the floor of her hut, filled it with burning peats, and built burning peats all round it. When sufficiently baked, she withdrew it from the fire, emptied the ashes out, and then poured slowly into it and over it about a pint of milk, in order to make it less porous. The craggan was then ready for use and sale.

The potter, anxious to show her abilities, also produced copies of table china for Mitchell, though even he had to admit that the likeness was only superficial. We had an exhibition in *Seallam!* Visitor

Fig. 25.—Lewis Tea-pot. Imitation of Staffordshire Ware.

Fig. 26.—Barvas Copy of a Tea-cup.

Fig. 27.—Barvas Copy of a Sugar-basin.

41. Barabhas craggan pottery

Centre in 2006 of articles collected by Miss Hope MacDougall of Oban, which included replicas of craggan pottery – more remarkable, I have to say, for their oddity than for their attractiveness.

Gleann Mor Bharabhais drains the whole of the western half of Mointeach Bharabhais – Barvas Moor – that great mass of undulating peatland in the centre of Lewis. To the north it rises to the hill of Muirneag at 248 m., and to the south Beinn Mholaich reaches 292 m., the highest of the Beanntan Bharabhais – the Barvas Hills. At one time, all the accessible areas were cut for peat for fuel – but peat was a cheap fuel only if time and labour were unvalued. For a full-time crofter it was part of the annual rhythm to allow so many days in the late spring for cutting the peat, and so many days through the summer – how many depending on the weather and how well the peat was drying – on lifting, turning and stacking, and finally in getting the peat home. Today, if you have a job and have to take time off all through the summer, you soon find that the lost wages would have bought sufficient coal or oil, without the back-breaking labour.

Working at the peats was a good time – out in the fresh air, in company, good exercise – but what if it was a wet year, and you were up to your knees in mud, trying desperately to salvage enough to provide your only hope of warmth for the whole of the coming winter?

Peat consists of the incompletely decomposed fibres of grasses, mosses and heather, and in the winter a peat moss is a mass of squelchy mud, with a thin topping of grass or heather. As the ground begins to dry out in the spring, this top layer has to be taken off with a spade, to expose the peat, and laid down again carefully at the bottom of the peat bank where last year's peats were cut, as in time this will be the new surface level and required for grazing. As the peat itself begins to dry, it is cut off in vertical slices with a taraisgeir, or peat iron – a pole with a step and blade set at right angles. Anything up to five levels of peat can be sliced off, depending on the depth of the peat and the skill and strength of the person catching them, for each peat has to be caught as it is sliced and thrown up behind the top of the bank to where it can dry – you have to throw carefully and far enough to accommodate almost all the peat to be cut, though the last depth is sometimes built into a honeycomb wall on the top of the bank if the peat is dry enough.

Then the time-consuming part of the task begins. Peat, when it is first cut, is slabs of mud. As soon as they have dried enough to handle, they have to be lifted off the ground and set in little stacks of three or four, to let the wind round them, to dry them further. Then, as they dry, they are made into larger and larger stacks until they are fully dry and hard. That assumes a good drying year. In a wet year, you may have to turn them many times, trying to find a dry spot on which to stand them – and remember, the wetter a peat, the heavier it is. As the autumn comes on, the ground begins to get wetter again, and you have to get the peats off, properly dried or not, before the bog becomes impassable once more. If your peat bank is near the road, or at least a good track, you could use a tractor today, or a horse in the old days if you had enough grazing to feed a horse. Otherwise, it was a creel or sack on your back, with the path getting wetter and the creel heavier on every trip back and forwards to the bank. Where there was a proper road close-by, the peats would be stacked in rough piles beside the road, then the day of the lorry came, when everyone gathered to throw the peats into the back of the lorry, where some of the more agile men made them into a stack that would hold together till they got them home. That could be a dangerous task, and I still have a slight scar on my nose where I was hit by a hard caoran, loading a lorry across in Liurbost thrown with a less-than-accurate aim – at least I hope it was!

Then, at last, to the end of the house and the building of the peat stack – a work of art, as the finished stack had to stand up to the wind and shed the rain, and yet be accessible for taking peats out without the rest of the structure collapsing. Usually, an oval-shaped foundation would be built, using the firmer peats as building blocks, building in a set pattern, sometimes diagonal, sometimes herringbone, and filling in smaller peats, then finally roofed with slabs of peat so set as to turn off the rain. Some finished peat stacks were a work of art – and there was nothing as shameful as a peat stack which collapsed!

The peat near the surface is full of fibres, lights easily and burns quickly, but that nearest the rock at the bottom of the pall is black, almost as hard as coal, and burns almost as well. The 'skinned

42. Peat bank

land' where peats had been cut could be fertilised, re-seeded with grass and clover and developed as good grazing, though infestation by rushes was always a problem. Re-seeding and peat-cutting are frowned upon today by the conservation bodies, though man's efforts could do little but nibble around the edges of vast bogs such as Mointeach Bharabhais. If you want to buy peat fuel in most parts today, you will find that it comes from Bord na Mona in Ireland, where they seem to realise that the proper management of a natural asset is preferable to outright prohibition. But then in Ireland they do not seem to have conservation bodies as powerful as ours, like SNH, whose initials are supposed to stand for Scottish Natural Heritage, but whose stance on any project in the Islands seems to be SNH – Shall Not Happen!

There are proposals for wind farms in Lewis, but the conservation bodies are vehemently against them, in any place and in any circumstances. Wind is certainly one of our natural assets, and one would think that it could be developed sensitively. Three towers have been built on Airinis moor, outside Steornabhagh, without any adverse effect that I can see on the environment, and one would think that there must be sites on Mointeach Bharabhais where groups of windmills could be accommodated, but the conservation bodies have banned the whole of the interior moor, so that the only places left are beside the townships, where, of course, people object.

It appears also that the birds here are much more likely than elsewhere in Scotland to fly into windmills – but the figures quoted for likely collisions have been revised so often and so dramatically that one can hardly place any credence in them.

Apparently all the species of bird-life on the island are of a subspecies – not *hebridensis* as one might expect, but *myopica*!

Barabhas was the home of the poet Donald MacDonald – Domhnall Chraisgean – though he was actually born in Gabhsann. No doubt his best-known song is 'Eilean mo Ghaoil' – printed in *Bard Bharabhais*:[99]

Eilean mo ghaoil! Is caomh leam Eilean mo ghraidh
Eilean mo ghaoil! Is caomh leam Eilean mo ghraidh
An Eilean an Fhraoich bidh daoine 'fuireach gu brath
An eilean mo ghaoil; is caomh leam Eilean mo ghraidh

Is toigh leam gach beinn, gach gleann, gach tulach is os.
Gach sruthan is allt gu mall 'tha siubhal gu lon.
Is toigh leam am feur 's gach geug a choinneas air blar,
An eilean mo ghaoil; is caomh leam Eilean mo ghraidh

O Island belov'd! The Isle to me ever dear! / O Island belov'd! The Isle to me ever dear! / O Heather Isle! Drawing sons of thine ever near! / O Island belov'd! The Isle to me ever dear! / I love every hill and glen and headland and bay / Each stream ever winding slowly sea-ward its way / The flow'rs that amongst her waving grasses appear; / O Island belov'd! The Isle to me ever dear!

The English version is taken from *Bard Bharabhais* also and is by Lieut. Col. Matheson, heir of Sir James and proprietor of Lewis until it was sold to Lord Leverhulme (and makes me feel there might be some merit in my doggerel translation!).

Another side to Domhnall Chraisgean's bardachd can be seen in his 'Oran an Radain'[100] – 'Song to the Rat'. It was an old tradition that the most effective way to get rid of rats was to make a satire on them, suggesting where else they should go.

O! radain a' bhalla.
'Bheil duil agad fantuinn gu brath!
Carson nach rachadh tu 'Ghallaobh.
A dh' iasgach an sgadain le bat',
An fhearr leat fuireach aig baile,
A' sgriobadh nam praisean air cach,
Na 'n gabhadh tu comhairl' do charaid,
Bhitheadh d' imrich thairis air sal.

Na 'n rachadh tu 'Steornabhagh 'dh'fhuireach
Gheibheadh tu beo-shlaint' na b' fhearr
Gheibheadh tu tea agus siucar
A mach as na buitean air dail
Ma chithear a muigh thu le daoraich,
A' mionnan 's a' caoch air an t-sraid,
Cuirear a stigh thu am priosan,
'S cumair fo chis thu gu brath

O! rat in the wall / Do you hope to stay there forever / Why don't you go to Caithness / fishing herring from a boat / would you prefer to say at home / scraping everyone's dishes / If you would take the advice of a friend / your journey would be across the sea. / If you went to Steornabhagh to live / you'd get a better living / you would get tea and sugar / out of the shops without delay / If they saw you out with a drink in you / swearing and shouting in the street / They would put you into prison / and keep you there forever.

Bru

Bru began on the shore of Loch Mor, beside Barabhas Iarach, but in the early 1800s the townships split and Bru moved to the west side of the loch, gradually extending southwards. Then, when Riof in Uig was cleared in 1851, the village was extended almost to the main road – the Newlands. The Riof people cannot have been very taken with their new crofts, for, when the Gabhsann people were offered free transport to Canada in 1863, all but one of the Newlands crofters took advantage of the offer too, and their crofts passed to families from Gabhsann.

I can remember my friend Eubaidh MacLeod, himself a crofter in the Newlands, telling of those who left in 1863: 'They all had to go, except my grandfather – he was a big strong man, and nobody would dare tell him where to go!' And then his face would crinkle into a smile: 'Well, to tell the truth, he had a hernia, and was the only one who wasn't fit to go and cut trees!' Eubaidh's own father was a bard:

Mheall thu, mheall thu mi, carson a mheall thu mi?
'S thu cumail fad' a gheamhraidh rium nach bitheadh ann ach mi.
Nuair thainig fear na b'shaoibhir na mi mheall thu mi 'nad chridhe
Gun toireadh e crodh-laoigh dhuit agus bainne 's annlan ti.

Nuair choinnich mis' an toiseach thu, 's ann aig a' mhanse ud shuas
Latha 's mi ri spealadh ann agus tu ri ceangal sguab
Nuair thainig am na dinneir, bu bhreagha leam do shnuadh,
Bha cota sgiobalt, grinn ort 's polca-doighri shuas.

Cha tug mi gaol cho mor dhuit 's nach gabh a thoirt air ais,
'S nach gabh a chuir a sgaoileadh cho fad 'sa iar fon ear,
Nach toir an druchd bhon suilean, co dhiu cha leig e las,
Oir gheibh mi te cho deigheil ruit bheir run dhomh anns a bhad.

You deceived me, why did you deceive me? / all winter you told me that I was the only one / when a richer man than me came along, you deceived me in your heart / that he would give you calves and milk and dairy produce. / When I first met you it was at the manse up there / one day when I was scything and you were tying sheaves / when it came to dinner-time I thought you looked so beautiful / you wore a lovely smart skirt, with a 'polka-doighri' above it. / I didn't give you so much love that it couldn't be taken back / that couldn't be spread around as far as east from west / that will not bring a tear to the eye, it need not do so / for I will find another as attractive as you who will fall in love with me immediately.

Arnol

Among the families of this township is a group of MacLeods known as na h-Ualaich, who claim to be one of the oldest branches from the main line of the old MacLeod chiefs, though what grounds this claimed is based on I do not know. They appear in old rentals under guises such as MacOylish and MacValich, before they finally settled as MacLeod in the early 1800s.

Arnol is probably the most-visited township in Sgire a' Chladaich today, as it contains the Black House, preserved by the National Trust as an example of typical Lewis housing of its date. Mitchell in 1876 gives a description of the basic Taigh-dubh of his day.

> The typical old black house on Lewis consists of a major block, of forty or fifty feet, with a small porch-like wing at one side in front and a larger projection or attachment at the other side behind, which last serves as a barn. Access to all is gained by one door. By this the so-called porch is entered, and on one hand there is frequently found that which is now seen in most museums of antiquities – the quern – not kept as a curiosity, but as a thing for daily use. Opposite this is the stall for lambs and calves. In passing from the porch to the major block, the byre is first encountered; and in the summer, after the planting of the crops, there is here a step down. In the early spring, however, instead of a step down, there are steps up, for the dung of the cattle, which rarely leave the house during the winter, is allowed to accumulate – there being only one annual cleaning of the byre. The peat-reek, with which the houses are always filled, and the soot in the thatch and on the rafters, both acting as antiseptics, combine to lessen the injurious effects which might be expecting to result from living on the edge of this heap of decomposing animal and vegetable matter.
>
> At the other end of the central or major range the human beings live; and their portion of the dwelling is not cut off from that belonging to the brutes by the faintest pretence of a partition. At a convenient point, about the centre of the part now reached, is the fire; and from the rough, undressed, soot-begrimed rafters above, there hangs a rope or bit of chain, on which the pot is suspended. On the woman's side, with its back to the cattle, there is occasionally a rude dresser, with shelving to hold such plates and basins as belong to the household.[101]

To be fair, such basic black houses were a rarity even in Mitchell's time, generally being replaced with houses of two doors, or at least with a partition between byre and house, though the fire in the middle of the floor was generally retained, since the soot in the thatch was a valuable manure – at least a part of the roof being taken off every year and spread on the land to be used for grain crops.

I suppose we do tend to look for the unusual and the extreme when we should be considering the average – my friend Calum Ferguson from Port Mholair was making the same point in a cartoon he drew for *Gairm* as long ago as 1959:

"A Dhòmhnaill, nach neònach gur h-e sinne an aon *typical house* anns a' bhaile"   (Calum MacFhearghuis)

43. 'Donald, isn't it strange that this is the only typical house in the township?'

Considering their housing conditions, the people of Lewis at that time were generally healthy, once they had passed the danger period for childhood diseases, which were, of course, killers, and so greatly feared.

Rev. Donald MacDonald commented on the general health of the parish in 1797:[102]

It is well-known that a great deal of rain falls in most parts of the west and north-west of Scotland; there is however less here than upon the mainland coast, or even in the adjacent parishes, the high hills, which collect the vapours and break the clouds, being at a considerable distance. The frost is seldom very intense; the snow, in general, not deep or of long continuance. The air, though moist, is salubrious. Rheumatism, the general complaint of all moist climates, is very common; it is rather a matter of surprise that it is not more frequent, considering their damp and dirty houses, how much the inhabitants are exposed to rain and cold, and their clothing poor. Flannel-shirts, which are in general worn by the common people, may be a good antidote against it. Fevers and fluxes are not uncommon; and many infants die of a complaint called the five nights sickness, from their dying of it upon the fifth or sixth night; there are no instances of any who have been seized with it that escaped, nor has the nature of this uncommon disease been as yet fully comprehended by the most skilful upon this island.

Rev. MacRae in 1836[103] also mentions 'a more uncommon ailment, for which no remedy has yet been discovered, the five or seven nights' sickness – a disease very fatal to infants, and so called from its attacking them on the fifth or seventh night.' Those acquainted with the history of the St Kilda islands will recognise this as neonatal tetanus, the scourge of St Kilda, often written about as though it were specific to that island only, but actually common enough in many other areas in the west of Scotland and Ireland.

While on the subject of disease, it is interesting that many writers about tuberculosis, that later scourge of Lewis, point out that it rarely developed in communities living in black houses, but more generally was brought back to Lewis by people who had been working on the mainland.

When Sir James Matheson bought Lewis in 1844, he attempted to improve the standard of housing by incorporating many conditions of this type as clauses in his leases. These were very unpopular – one old man from Nis pointed out that even the Commandments were only ten in number – and a reward was offered if they were kept. John Munro MacKenzie in his *Diary 1851* mentions cases where crofters had built new houses with chimneys and separate doors for humans and stock, only to revert to the old style when they thought the factor's eye had passed them. The needs for thatch as manure and to keep the cattle warm were used as excuses, but there was also a great deal of peer pressure not to differ from what the neighbours were doing.

Arnol, with its long line of black houses, all with smoke percolating through the thatched roofs, was described by one visitor as being like 'a reeking caterpillar', while another, seeing it from a distance, thought he had seen a railway train.

Arnol must be the stoniest part of the Hebrides – not bare sheet-rock as is found in the Bays of Harris, but rather boulders strewn everywhere on the surface of the ground. It is little wonder that there are so many stone dykes, built with stones cleared off the ground to permit cultivation.

Rev. William MacRae's comment[104] was:

Along the whole arable ground, the most striking feature in the surface, as well as the composition of the soil, is the multitude of stones with which it is overrun, rendering it equally injurious to vegetation as unfavourable to culture.

Bragar

There are two townships here – Bragar bho Dheas and Bragar bho Thuath (South Bragar and North Bragar) – which is complicated by the fact that the Labost area of Bragar bho Dheas is actually further north than Bragar bho Thuath.

The original villages would have been down near the shore, between Loch Ordais and Port Mhor Bragair, and in this area are the ruins of Teampall Eoin – referred to by Martin Martin as the Church of St John Baptist in Bragar. T.S. Muir in 1885[105] noted:

Down in a fearfully disordered burying ground near the shore, is the church of St John Baptist, a not-much-wasted building, consisting of a chancel and nave with flat-headed windows – one east and one south in the chancel, and one in the west end of the nave.

It is suggested that the church belongs to the fifteenth century, but the burial ground in which it stands is called Cill' Sgaire, Sgaire being a Norse personal name, still used in the MacAulay families in its Anglicised form of Zachary, which could suggest that there was a much earlier church on the same site.

44. Teampall Eoin

Although Bragar has the stone beach at the Port Mhor, it has
no harbour, and this was a continual matter of complaint from the
local fishermen.

Originally, the main type of fishing off the shores of Sgire a'
Chladaich was for bioraich – dogfish. Rev. Donald MacDonald
tells us in 1796:[106]

> There are a few cod, ling and haddock taken upon the coasts, but
> the principal fishing is that of dog-fish, from the liver of which they
> extract a considerable quantity of oil. Upon the average, there are
> about 8,832 Scotch pints annually manufactured of it, and sold to
> the Stornoway merchants at from 6d to 8d per pint. The season for
> it is from the beginning of May to the latter end of August, when
> the weather proves favourable; indeed it must be very moderate

before they can venture to sea, which makes them exceedingly cautious when the wind blows off the land, lest they be driven to the northern ocean. It is very astonishing how few accidents happen, considering the terrible seas they encounter and the badness of the creeks where they land.

According to Donald Morrison of Bragar[107] – they were still fishing for dogfish fifty years ago:

Thig an Fheill Pharuig mu'm paigh sinn na fiachan
Ri dorghach nam bioraich air slios an Taobh Siar;
Tha pris air an langainn an Sasunn am bliadhna
'S gheibh mi mo lion an ordugh.

Failte gu fearann air balaich an iasgaich
'G iomradh, is tarruing is gearradh a' bhiathaidh;
Coma leam leabaidh no cadal no biadh
Gu faigh mi mo lion an ordugh

Peter's feast will come before we pay our debts / fishing with a darrow for dogfish off the shores of the west side / there's a good price for ling in England this year / I'll get my lines ready. / Welcome ashore to the fisher-boys / rowing and hauling and cutting the bait / I don't care for my bed or sleep or food / until I've got my lines ready

The same author wrote the well-known song 'Eilean Beag Donn a' Chuain':[108]

Hi-ri-o-ri, togaidh sinn fonn
Air Eilean beag donn a' chuain
Eilean beag Leodhais, dachaidh nan seoid
A chumas a' chomhrag suas;

Eilean nan tonn, a dh' araich na suinn
'S chuidich an Fhraing gu buaidh,
Comhla ri cheile togaidh sinn fonn
Air eilean beag donn a' chuain

O 's laidir na bannan 'g am tharruing a null
Gu eilean beag donn Mhicleoid,
'S gu stiuir mi gu h-ealamh gu cala mo long
Nuair ruigeas mi ceann mo lo;

'S ma ghreimicheas m'acair ri Carraig nan Al
Bidh m'anam tighinn sabhailt beo,

Mo shiuil air am pasgadh am fasgadh Chill' Sgair'
Le m'athair 's mo mhathair choir.

Hi-ri-o-ri, let's raise a song / to the little brown isle of the sea / little
Isle of Lewis, home of the men / that will keep up the fight / Isle of
the seas, where heroes were reared / who helped France to victory
/ all together, let's raise a song / to the little brown Isle of the sea.
/ O, strong are the ties that pull me over / to the little brown Isle
of MacLeod / And I will steer skilfully to harbour my ship there /
when I come to the end of my days / If my anchor holds at Carraig
nan Al / my soul will feel safe / my eyes closed in the shelter of Cill'
Sgair / with my dear father and mother.

Strangely enough, one of my friends, no mean Gaelic scholar,
used to insist that the line in the first verse should be 'Cuidich an
Righ' – 'help the king' – the motto on the badge of the Seaforth
Highlanders. But helping the king would hardly fit with the socialist
principles of the Lewismen of the time, so it was changed to helping
the French – which, when you think of it, is a rather strange view
of the war!

At the roadside in Bragar, there is a gateway framed by a huge
whalebone arch – but not even a Siarach would try to convince you
that it was brought ashore at the Port Mhor on a dorgh!

On the moor side of Bragar is Loch an Duna and, on a low spit
of land projecting into it, a ruined dun, still standing to a height of
twelve to fourteen feet in places. Probably the dun was originally
on an island, and the causeway connecting it has silted up and
become dry land, for one of the folk tales of the area tells how John
Roy MacPhail had a fort in the loch, from where he was captured
by men of Donald Cam MacAulay of Uig – but more of that when
we come to Uig.

Bragar was one of the furthest south tacks to be held by a
Morrison – John Morrison – Iain mac Mhurchaidh 'ic Ailein –
author of a *Description of Lewis* by 'John Morisone, indweller there'
in the 1680s. John Morrison was a poet, and some of his lines were
noted by Rev. William Matheson,[109] such as his complaint about
his talkative wife:

Toiseach tus an anraidh
Am taigh am bi 'n toirm

45. Whalebone Arch at Bragar

An coileach tric 'na thamh
's a' chearc a ghnath ag gairm

The very beginning of trouble /in a house filled with noise; / the
cock often silent / and the hen forever crowing.

Again, on a poor landless man:

Is buidhe dhuit fhein, Dhomnhnaill a' Chuain
'S tu 'nad laigh' air do chluain thaobh;
Cha tog pracadair do gheall,
ni mo tha thu 'm taing nam maor

You are a lucky man, Donald of the Ocean, / lying at ease on your
side; / no teind-collector will exact what you owe, / nor are you
beholden to ground-officers.

Strangely enough, Martin Martin appears to refer to the same person:[110]

> Donald-Chuan, in a Village near Bragir, in the Parish of Barvas, had by accident cut his Toe at the change of the Moon, and it bleeds a fresh drop at every change of the Moon ever since.

Although 'a' Chuain' translated as 'of the Ocean', it must have been a family by-name, as there is a 'Donald Ochone' in a rental of Bragar bho Dheas in 1780.

John Morrison was the father of Roderick Morrison – Ruairidh Dall – the Blind Harper – who was harper to the MacLeods of Dunvegan for a period, and more can be found about him in Rev. William Matheson's book of that name.[111]

One of Ruairidh Dall's best known poems is 'Oran Mor MacLeoid'[112] lamenting the changes that had come over Dunvegan Castle since the death of his patron Iain Breac MacLeod:

> Chaidh a' chuibhle mu'n chuairt;
> Ghrad thionndaidh gu fuachd am blaths
> Gum faca mi uair
> Dun ratha nan cuach 'n seo thraigh;
> Far 'm biodh tathaich nan duan,
> Iomadh mathas gun chruas, gun chas;
> Dh'fhalbh an latha sinn uainn,
> 'S tha na taighean gu fuarraidh fas.

> The wheel has come full circle, / warmth has suddenly turned cold. / But once I saw here a bountiful castle, / well-stocked with drinking cups that have now gone dry, / a song-haunted place abounding in good things, / given without stint or question. / That day has gone from us, / and the buildings are chill and desolate.

You can tell from the quality of the translation that it is not mine, but comes from the late Rev. William Matheson, as does this version of the verse.

Bragar also saw its share of emigration to Canada in the 1800s. *Old Timers' Tales – a History of Stokes Bay and Area* tells of two families, one going first to Huron in the 1850s and only later to the Bruce Peninsula, and another going there direct as late as 1887.

'Malcolm-the-Bone' McIver was a real crusty old Scot, full of years and rheumatism, which didn't help his disposition any. His cabin was much the same as those of the old timers in the land of the heather whence he came. A fireplace of field stone filled one end of the cabin, and in the iron pot that hung over the flames most of the cooking was done, even the bread was baked there. McIver was a truly courageous, if a stubborn old man. He sold his first farm and all their belongings of his first farm in the Stratford area. He was determined to pioneer again in a more rugged section of Ontario, and he was equally determined not to spend a penny more than was necessary for doing it.

The McIvers' family were grown and on their own when their father and mother made this move. Their daughter Jessie had left home and gone to work in Detroit, where she met and married Robert Gray, a handsome officer in the army. Robert Gray came only once to visit his in-laws on the Peninsula, and once was enough. He was so terrified of the rugged bush country that he sat up all night with pistol drawn, ready for the wild animals that he felt sure would come crashing through the cabin door. He left the next day and never returned for another visit.[113]

The name Malcolm-the-Bone is interesting, as there is a family of MacIvers, based in Carlabhagh, known as muinntir nan Cnaimh – the Bones. Presumably Calum nan Cnaimh was related to them, though he himself came from Bragar and his wife Margaret Graham from Siadar Uarach. They were both in their sixties when they went to Stokes Bay; Calum may have enjoyed being a pioneer again, but I wonder what Margaret thought about it!

Mrs Eber Burley has the distinction of being the only person living in Stokes Bay (1959) who came directly from Scotland. Mrs Burley was the former Henrietta 'Effie' MacIver and was born in 1882 at Braegar, Lewis Island. When five years of age she and her sister Johanna, emigrated from Scotland with their parents, Mr & Mrs John MacIver (Big John). They came by steamer to Montreal and then by rail to Southampton, where they visited with relatives, the Dan MacKays. They resumed their journey to Stokes Bay in company with Mrs Burley's uncle, Kenneth Smith 'Kenny the Buckle'.

One incident stood out in her, Mrs Burley's, memory about the trip from Scotland. She remembered going from their stateroom with a very small pail to another part of the ship to get some water. The ship took a very sudden roll and she almost went through a porthole, but a sailor grabbed her by the clothes and saved her life.

It was certain Mrs Burley was not to die of water. Early in their married life, she and her husband were to take a trip on the ill-fated steamer 'Jones' which sank in 1906 with all on board. It was not until some days later that anxious friends and relatives found out that they had not gone on the trip.[114]

Iain Mor MacIver was mac Dhomhnaill Mhurchaidh Thormoid – son of Donald son of Murdo son of Norman – from Bragar bho Dheas, and he was married to Ann Smith of Bragar bho Thuath, an aunt of Roderick Smith, later provost of Steornabhagh.

There were emigrants leaving Bragar long before the MacIvers. The passenger list of the *Friendship* sailing for Philadelphia in 1774 includes a 'Norman Morison' aged fifty and his wife 'Cathrin McKenzie' aged forty, and the reason for their emigration, and that of all the other passengers, being 'in order to procure a Living abroad, as they were quite destitute of Bread at home' – but we shall hear more of the *Friendship* when we reach Steornabhagh.

PART THREE – SGIRE CHARLABHAIGH (CARLOWAY)

The area from Siabost to Cirbhig formed in historical times a part of the parish of Lochs, although it was geographically quite separate from the main part of that parish – there does not appear to have been any good reason for the link, except in order to make Lochs parish about the same size as the other parishes on the island in terms of population.

Rev. Alexander Simson, in his notes on the parish of Lochs in the *Statistical Account* of 1797 does not even mention the separate part of his parish, but Rev. Robert Finlayson, in the *New Statistical Account* of 1833[115] does refer to it:

> a part of the parish situated on the north-west side of the island, between the parishes of Uig and Barvas, a distance of eighteen miles from the parish church of Lochs, where the minister of Lochs is bound to preach every three months. This district is named Carloway, and stands more in need of the labours of a missionary than any other place in the Long-Island. The inhabitants of Carloway have no opportunity of attending divine service except when the minister of Lochs preaches there. The population of Carloway is 910.

When we look at the Old Parochial Registers of Lochs, we can see that the minister paid only occasional visits to Sgire Charlabhaigh, when he appears to have baptised every child within sight, then gone home to write up as many as he could remember – for there are many cases of a few members of a family not appearing in the register – and others appearing there more than once!

Siabost (Shawbost)

Here again we have a composite township – Siabost bho Thuath and Siabost bho Dheas, on either side of Loch a' Bhaile. Forty-four joint tenants appear there in a rental of 1726, with their names in phonetic patronymic Gaelic, such as MacWunlay and MacWurchie, which a bit of practice allows us to translate as MacFhionnlaidh and MacMhurchaidh. A name which is not in the rental of 1718 but appears in 1726 is Kenneth Gow – Kenneth Gobha or blacksmith; the family appears in later documents as Murray – so this shows the arrival in Siabost of one of the descendants of the Gobha Gorm whom we first met at Eoropaidh.

Malcolm MacPhail, of Siabost bho Dheas, giving evidence to the Napier Commission in 1883[116] complained:

> the people of the township have no land worth calling land. It is stony ground, that cannot be worked by a horse. I introduced a horse and plough and I had to give them up. They were of no service to me. We must work it with spades because of the stony character of the soil. Whereas my father and grandfather lived upon milk and butter, and flesh and meal, I live upon meal, hot water and sugar. My father had a croft of £5, and such was the produce of it that not only did we not buy anything, but we were scarcely able to consume the produce at that time. I am quite certain that the land was better when I was a young man. The old land that was cultivated by our fathers has got exhausted.

The call from most crofter delegates was for more land, but as John Munro MacKenzie had reported in 1851, that by itself did not solve the problem. New crofts had been made in Siabost bho Thuath for tenants evicted from Riof in Uig – some on the Gearraidh Buidhe road between Siabost bho Thuath and Loch a' Bhaile, and others on the moor at Pairc Shiaboist:

> North Shawbost is one of the largest townships in the Lews, a portion of it is occupied by people removed from Uig who I hope will do better here than in their former holdings, they have much more arable land than they occupied at Uig and intend to establish a fishing here. Upwards of 100 acres of new land drained and trenched was lotted out to the small tenants here, but they are not doing well, their crops have been very bad, not being able to give the land so much manure as it would require, several of those who took the lots emigrated and a large proportion of the new land is now vacant. Two people who took 10 acre lots wished them to be reduced the first year to 8 acres and last year to 4. One of them now wishes to give up the land.[117]

There was little point in just giving land to people who could not afford to stock it, and after the bad years of the potato famine, there were very few who had such a stock. Other help was necessary also.

The drained land was in Pairc Shiaboist, and the drainage never worked properly, as John Nicolson explained to the Napier Commission:[118]

> The drains are of no service now. They are choked up. We were obliged to open up afresh the upper portions of the ground of late years, in order to allow the water to run off, because the drains were useless. They have not been re-opened, but they never worked well. They never drained the ground so well as by the process we use ourselves – that is gathering the soil together, and allowing channels to run between the various patches.

Sir James Matheson spent a great amount of money on land drainage, as we shall see at Loch a' Ghainmhich, but little of it was successful in the long term.

Donald MacLeod explained about the fishing from the township in his evidence, here put into narrative form:

> They fish for cod and ling, which the curers take from them. They buy boats and lines from the curers, and get credit till they pay them in fish. They get 1s. for ling and 6d for cod. They fish with long lines, and use eels and herring for bait. In the year before last, they bought some old boats – 25 feet long, for a crew of seven to eight men, and they paid them within that year. There was once a sort of quay, but the sea washed it away. It was not much worth and it was in a bad place. If a new quay was built, it would be built in a different place. There is great need of it. There is certainly no good safe place for boats.[119]

Although there had always been fishing from Siabost, the life at sea was not to everyone's liking – as Murdo MacLeod tells in his 'Oran Neibhi':[120]

> An teid thu leam air bharr nan tonnan
> No 'n toir thu dhomh-sa gealltainn
> An teid thu leam dha'n an long chogaidh
> Gus an tog thu m'intinn.
>
> Saoilidh balaich bhios a ceilidh
> 'G eisdeachd ris na chluinn iad
> Nach eile ceard as fhearr na'n Neibhi
> Gus an teid thu innte.
>
> Innsidh mise ladh an Neibhi
> 'G eiridh feadh na h-oidhche

Mur a freagair thu cheud eubha
Ceusaidh iad fo chuing thu

Chunnaic mis' am bruadar cadail
Mo leannan a bhith laimh rium
'S an uair a dhuisg mi as mo shuain
Bha 'n deice chruaidh fo m' uilnean

Will you come with me over the wave-tops / or will you give me your
promise / will you come to the war-ship / to lift my spirits. / The
boys at the ceilidh would think / from what they hear / that no trade
could be better than the navy / until you are in it. / I'll tell you the
law of the navy / getting up in the middle of the night / if you don't
answer the first shout / they'll crucify you under their yoke. / I saw
in my sleep a dream / my love was at my hand / when I wakened
from my dream / the hard deck was under my elbows.

Siabost was at one time a centre of the Harris Tweed industry,
which has fallen on hard times recently. The mill there has now been
reopened, and it is certainly to be hoped that this will be successful,
as the tweed industry was the mainstay of this and many other parts
of the island – it is hard to imagine now the incessant clack-clack
of the looms which at one time could be heard throughout every
village.

On the moor west of Siabost, quite close to the road, is a 'Norse
mill'. At one time every community in the Islands would have had
its own mill, but when the estate built modern mills, most of the
old ones were destroyed or fell into disuse – the difference with the
Siabost mill is that it has been painstakingly restored by a local
group, under the leadership of Dr Finlay MacLeod of Siabost, and
is now in working order.

The working of the Norse mill was described in my earlier book
Harris in History and Legend:[121]

On a timber platform over the lade sat the two mill wheels, each
about three feet across. Each had a central hole, and the upper stone
also had a cross-shape cut into its upper face. An iron spindle passed
through the eye of both stones: at its upper end was a cross-piece
which fitted into the cross-shape on the upper stone and at its lower
end flanges, dipping into the water of the mill-lade. When the
sluice was opened, and the stream poured down the lade, it struck
the flanges, turning the spindle, which turned the upper stone. A

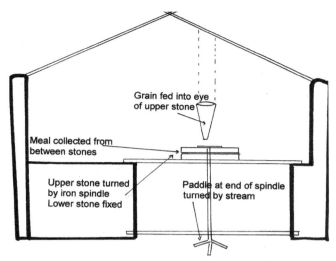

Grain fed into eye
of upper stone

Meal collected from
between stones

Upper stone turned
by iron spindle
Lower stone fixed

Paddle at end of spindle
turned by stream

46. Diagram of Norse mill

timber hopper suspended above the stones dribbled grain into the
eye of the upper stone, and it was ground between the stones, and
came out around the rim of the lower stone. It was a primitive way
of grinding grain, but it worked, and any repairs could be done
from local materials.

Dail Mor and Dail Beag (Dalmore and Dalbeg)

The anomalous position of the part of Lochs parish in the Carlabhagh
area has been rectified, for civil purposes at least, and the area
divided between Barabhas and Uig parishes, with the boundary
running between these two small townships.

John Munro MacKenzie in 1851[122] writes of Dail Mor

> Dalmore is a most unhealthy place, every male head of a family
> having been twice married, and several have lost their second
> wives – there does not appear to be a healthy man in it except
> an old pensioner who served in Egypt – all seem consumptive. I
> advised them all to emigrate, but found them very reluctant tho'
> they themselves told me of the above fact. They are also much in
> arrear of rent. This farm should be cleared & added to Dalbeg being
> a good sheep grazing would add much to the value of Dalbeg which
> is now rather contracted in its boundaries.

When I check our own genealogical records at *Co Leis Thu?* I cannot find the Dail Mor families in the state MacKenzie gives – I wonder whether the Dail Mor people were trying to make the point that the township was not worth clearing, or was MacKenzie just making a good case for clearance to the landlord?

Both villages had originally been farms, broken into crofts only in the 1820s. Dail Beag was made into a farm in the 1840s, and in 1851 Dail Mor was cleared and added to Dail Beag, and it was only in 1921 that the townships were broken into crofts again, mainly for families from Carlabhagh.

Dail Mor and Dail Beag both have beautiful little beaches, with that at Dail Beag now being promoted as one of the best beaches in Lewis for surfing.

Laimsiadar

This township, on the headland to the west of Carlabhagh, was one of the first places to be cleared in Lewis, in 1796. Murdo MacLeod of Borghaston gave evidence to the Napier Commission[123] about the clearance.

> Leimshadder was at one time inhabited by eight crofters, but these were removed and the place given to a tacksman. About twenty-seven years ago we offered a rental of £50 for Leimshadder, promising to pay the rent before entering into possession, but our offer was refused, though the place was afterwards given to a tacksman for a rental considerably less than what we offered. Four or five years ago it was let to its present holder, who has large possessions of land elsewhere in the island. We are still willing to take Leimshadder at a reasonable rent.

Laimsiadar was given first to the minister of Barabhas as part of his glebe, then later added to the farm of Linsiadar.

Carlabhagh (Carloway)

Loch Charlabhaigh was known to Martin Martin, but only just so:

> About 24 Miles South-west lyes Loch Carlvay, a very capacious, tho unknown Harbour, being never frequented by any Vessels: Tho' the

Natives assure me that it is in all respects a convenient Harbour for Ships of the First-rate.

Carlabhagh consists of five townships, na Gearrannan (Garenin), Borghaston (Borrowston), Cnoc Charlabhaigh (Knock Carloway), Mullach Charlabhaigh (Upper Carloway) and Cirbhig (Kirivick) – six if you add Laimsiadar – all contiguous around the shore of Loch Charlabhaigh.

Na Gearrannan was the home of a family of MacNeils – a most unusual surname for Lewis. It is sometimes claimed that they were of the MacNeils of Colonsay in Argyll, but I wonder whether that was because they did not want to belong to the MacNeils of Barra! Anyway, the first of the family seems to have been Finlay MacNeil, who had a son Donald, who had a son Finlay born in about 1770, still remembered as Fionnladh a bha 's an Arm – Finlay who was in the army. One wonders what inducement was used to persuade Finlay to enlist, as he was a married man with a young family.

Finlay was with the 78th Ross-shire Highlanders in the Java campaign, and when they were being shipped home in September 1816, their ship sank off the shore of an uninhabited island, where they were marooned for over three months. The survivors were eventually rescued, and reached Portsmouth again in June 1817.

Finlay managed to make his way home, but news of the shipwreck had preceded him, and he and his companions had been officially given up for lost. Finlay's wife, Mary MacDonald, had found another husband to support her and her young children, and when she heard that Finlay was still alive she threw herself off a cliff rather than face him.

Details of the campaign and shipwreck can be found in Col. David Stewart's *Sketches of the Highlanders of Scotland*,[124] which also has a delightful footnote about the discipline of the regiment:

There were in this battalion nearly 300 men from Lord Seaforth's estate in Lewis. Several years elapsed before any of these men were charged with a crime deserving severe punishment. In 1799 a man was tried and punished. This so shocked his comrades that he was put out of their society as a degraded man, who brought shame on his kindred. The unfortunate outcast felt his own degradation so much that he became unhappy and desperate; and Colonel Mackenzie, to save him from destruction, applied and got him sent to England, where his disgrace would be unknown and unnoticed . . .

I make no comment!

Murdo MacLeod from Borghaston included Laimsiadar in his complaint to the Napier Commission.[125]

> The peat moss connected with our township was exhausted upwards of twenty years ago. Our peat banks are now 3 miles distant from our homes. For half this distance there is no road, though we have to carry all our peats on our backs. We have further to cross a river which, being without a bridge, is, after heavy rains, often dangerous and impassable. Our peats being so far away from us, and to relieve ourselves somewhat of the hardship of carrying them the whole way on our backs, we sometimes have resource to the expedient of floating them on the river for a certain distance, but as the river is let by the Estate for fishing purposes, we are not allowed to float our peats on it till the beginning of January. We could get a supply of peats for twenty years or more in Leimshadder within a short distance of our homes.

Norman MacPhail of Mullach Charlabhaigh complained to the Napier Commission about the thirlage of Carlabhagh area to the mill at Breascleit:[126]

> For the last thirty years we have been compelled by the estate to send all our grain to be ground at Breasclete mill, six miles distant. We had two mills of our own at Carloway, but the estate ordered them to be destroyed. We, in common with the people of the surrounding townships of Borrowston, Knock and Garenin, who also send their grain to Breasclete mill, are thus deprived of about the eighth part of our grain, between mill dues and our own trouble and expense in going to Breasclete. The old mills ground our meal as well and much better than the new one.

Loch Charlabhaigh was the point of embarkation for the emigrants who left Lewis on the *Barlow* in 1851, and the final details of the embarkation are given in John Munro MacKenzie's *Diary 1851*:[127]

> Wednesday 18th June – The steamer arrived & by her Mr Morison with the Emigration Contract tickets. The Owner of the *Barlow* with a surgeon for her also arrived.
>
> Thursday 19th – Proceeded to Tolsta Chailish and went on board the *Barlow* off that place, remained on board till 11 p.m. arranging

47 Loch Charlabhaigh

with passengers, inspecting stores with Comptroller, berths etc. The greater number of the passengers are now aboard.

Friday 20th – Went on board the *Barlow* at 10 a.m. and was engaged in making up lists of the passengers and Contract tickets. Mustered the whole of the Emigrants and examined them by families & individually in presence of the Custom House & Medical Officers, the owner giving them Contract tickets as they passed along. After this was finished the Revd. Mr Campbell of Uig gave them a long address and baptized a number of children young and old. I thereafter distributed some clothing to the poorest of the emigrants who were very ill off, being some of what had remained unsold – the Emigrants with the exception of a few families were very respectably clothed and seemed very happy and contented. The number on board is 287 souls equal to 221½ Statute Passengers.

Saturday 21st – On board the *Barlow* & having got all ready she weighed anchor at 6 a.m. I took leave of the passengers which was very affecting – They thanked me over & over again & tho' sorry to part seemed pleased with the change they were about to make & with the ship & captain. Left the *Barlow* off Carloway where we landed at 7 a.m. We soon lost sight of the ship, she having a fair wind and plenty of it.

Even allowing for MacKenzie's bias, it is clear that a lot of trouble was taken for the safety and comfort of the emigrants, as was noted on their arrival by the Canadian Emigration Department's chief agent at Quebec, A.C. Buchanan, in a letter of complaint about the condition of emigrants from South Uist:

> These parties (from South Uist) presented every appearance of poverty; and from their statement were without the means of leaving the ship or of procuring a day's subsistence for their helpless families on landing and many of them were very insufficiently supplied with clothing.
>
> I cannot close this letter without referring to the wholly different circumstances under which a party of 986 persons were sent out in the past spring by Sir James Matheson, from the Island of Lewis. These emigrants were provided with a passage to this port, food and clothing, and on arrival were supplied with a week's rations and a free passage to their ultimate destination.

Probably the embarkation at Carlabhagh had been arranged to avoid the troubles which had arisen the previous month with emigrants on the *Marquis of Stafford*.

From MacKenzie's *Diary*[128] again:

> Friday 16th May – On board the *Marquis of Stafford* in the Sound of Bernera – The greater part of the Emigrants in the upper part of Uig have already shipped their luggage. Sent John MacKenzie ground officer over the Carloway district to tell the emigrants from that quarter to be on board with their luggage tomorrow, and all north of Galson to be at Port of Ness all ready to come on board at 3 a.m. Tuesday. Sent notice to Tolsta that the Steamer will call off that place early on Tuesday and the emigrants all to be ready.
>
> Monday 19th – Had to refuse the greater number of emigrants from Bernera to keep room for those from Ness and Tolsta – Having got all on board who had sent their luggage last week sailed from the Sound of Bernera at 12 p.m. with 400 emigrants on board.
>
> Tuesday 20th – Arrived at Port of Ness at 3 a.m. having had rather a disagreeable passage from Loch Roag. Had considerable difficulty in getting the fishermen to get out their boats and put the emigrants on board the steamer, but after losing much time & using entreaty & force by turns got the Emigrants with their luggage all in boats, but observed the first boat sent to the Steamer returning with her cargo without getting it on board. On proceeding on board the Steamer found that the Uig People had rebelled against allowing any of the Ness people on board, saying that there were quite enough on

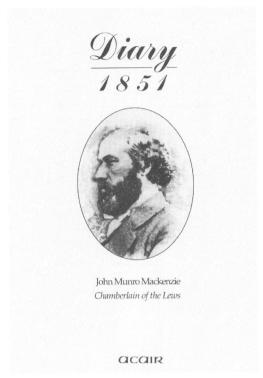

Diary
1 8 5 1

John Munro Mackenzie
Chamberlain of the Lews

acair

48. Frontispiece of *Diary 1851*

board – that there being fever and smallpox at Ness they would not allow a man on board at this place. I remonstrated with them, but to no effect, and the Ness men having taken fright returned to the shore – Seeing that no good could be done here, ordered the Captn. to proceed on his voyage. Told them that if they did not object we would call at Tolsta and take on board the Emigrants there, which was done without the least trouble, making up the number on board to 450 full Statute passengers.

What I find fascinating here is that the emigrants stood up to the factor – and won their case! We hear so much today about the poor oppressed people, driven about by the whim of the factor, and I always wondered what could have happened to them on the way across the Atlantic, where they became such successful pioneers.

Perhaps they were not as broken-spirited as we are asked to believe, after all.

Carlabhagh was also the port of embarkation of the Gabhsann emigrants on the *Elizabeth* in 1863, as described by John Graham,[129] who settled in the Eastern Townships of Quebec:

> 'S ann bho Loch an Dunain a sheol sinn
> Air ar fogradh a Alba
> 'S iomadh neach a bha tuirseach
> 'Nuair a chaill sinn Muirneag 'san anmoch
>
> Am bata iarainn gu sunndach
> Null leinn gu fairge
> Dh'ionnsuidh Baile Doire an Eirinn
> Far an d'fhuair sinn t'eile gu falbh leinn
>
> *Ealasaid* bhoidheach 's i an ordugh gu guanach
> Le cuid chroinn agus ropan dol a sheoladh a' chuan leinn
> Dh'ionnsuidh fearann Cholumbus air an turus bu luathe dhi
> Far an sgap sinn uile mar bhucas chuileagan dheidh fhuasgladh

> It was from Loch an Dunan that we sailed / on our exile from Scotland / everyone was sad / as we lost sight of Muirneag in the evening. / The sturdy iron ship / taking us over the sea / to Derry in Ireland / where we met the other ship for our departure. / Bonny *Elizabeth* in sprightly order / with every rope and mast for sailing the ocean / on a fast journey to the land of Columbus / where we scattered like flies from an opened box

Carlabhagh became a major fishing port, and was the centre of one of Lord Leverhulme's schemes, which, like so many others, ultimately failed.

Alasdair Alpin MacGregor,[130] writing in 1933, laments the decay of Carlabhagh:

> Today there is about Carloway little to remind one of the industry and activity that distinguished this remote Hebridean township some years ago, when that part of the harbour known as the Dunan was the centre of busy-ness and prosperity. In its palmy days Carloway was famous for the ling and salmon cured at the Dunan, and despatched in huge quantities at regular intervals to Stornoway, wherefrom they were shipped to distant buyers. Half a century ago a fleet of some seventy fishing boats operated from Carloway,

49. Dunan, Carlabhagh

landing at the Dunan the herrings caught on the once prolific grounds between the Flannan Isles and the Butt of Lewis. Foreign vessels used to come all the way to Carloway to load consignments of cured fish.

The fleet of sail-boats now owned locally has declined to about half a dozen vessels of the smaller type. Almost any day they may be seen lying at anchor in the Loch, a little to the landward of the pier. Only occasionally do their owners use them. It was one of the dreams of the late Viscount Leverhulme to revive the fishing industry on the west of the Long Island, and to convey the fish landed at Carloway by a light railway across the moors of Lewis to Stornoway. But alas! Fate and the obstinate herring thought otherwise.

Carlabhagh is the terminus of the Pentland Road across the moors from Steornabhagh. Apparently it is named after Sir John Sinclair, later Lord Pentland, who officially opened one section of the road; there had been many hold-ups in the making of the road – and many more still to come!

J.P. Day in his *Public Administration in the Highlands and Islands of Scotland*,[131] gives the history of the road:

The history of the Carloway Road is not without a significant interest. It may be compared with that of the Ness Harbour Works as another example of the difficulty in translating the goodwill

50. Iain MacAulay, fish-curer, at Carlabhagh

of the State into effective action in these outer isles. Carloway is
the centre of the Loch Roag fisheries, and what the people really
wanted was a railroad to carry the fresh fish to Stornoway. They
already had a fairly good, though indirect, road twenty-three miles
in length. Since, however, there was no prospect of local financial
support, the Government declined to consider the railroad project.
The District Committee then asked for a direct road to save seven
miles, and for this purpose £15,000 was considered by their engineer
an ample sum and was granted by the State in 1891. By 1898, £1485
remained unspent, less than half the distance had been completed,
the engineer dismissed, and the contractor – found only with the
greatest difficulty – had become bankrupt. The Congested Districts
Board had spent the £1485 and another £500 by 1902, when it was
estimated that another £10,000 would be required to complete the

51. On Pentland Road

unfinished central portion. In 1910 £8000 was granted by the Board, and the work should now, more than twenty years after its start, be approaching completion. A sixteen-mile road costs £23,500, and takes over twenty years to construct!

Arthur Geddes, usually a good friend to the Islands and their people, was uncharacteristically critical about the local input: [132]

The figures alone might not condemn the work done – or rather not done – by the local labourers; for deep peat has misled road engineers elsewhere. But impartial observers have left no doubt that the work was shirked – partly from the labourers' lack of will, in other words from laziness, and partly from the not unnatural desire that further grants might continue, offering easy money. Inspection revealed deliberate and combined concealment of bad work, road metal being thrown on to give a surface which had no foundation. The Carloway Road, which was to help the Loch Roag fishermen by rapid transport of fresh catches, was never completed. The bad work of many contributed to the undoing of all.

Lord Leverhulme's projected plans for the fisheries involved a reopening of the railway proposal:

Leverhulme marked out the routes which the railway was to follow. Stornoway of course was to be the main terminus, and from it three separate lines were to radiate. One was to the south through Balallan to Aline on the Harris border, with a later extension to Tarbert. A second was to serve the west-coast fishing harbours of Callanish and Carloway and return to Stornoway via Barvas. The third was to branch northwards from this line at Barvas to serve the group of townships near the Butt of Lewis and return down the east coast through Tolsta to Stornoway. The total track required for the three lines amounted to over a hundred miles.

His power was to be hydro-electric, rather than steam. 'We shall gain the immense advantage of leaving the beautiful valleys and lochs and rivers of Lewis without a pall of black smoke polluting their fair surface,' he claimed, in terms more than slightly reminiscent of present-day arguments against any development.

When the project was fully costed – more than £1.5 million for the lines alone – the whole idea of railways was shelved, and all that remains to show of the plans are the rebuilt bridges on the Pentland Road, and the fly-over – or rather under – which was to take the rail line to the pier in Carlabhagh itself.

Carlabhagh too had its bards – such as Robert MacLeod of na Gearrannan: [133]

Tha ceol air mo bhilein 's mo chridhe ri leum
Luiginn gun cluinneadh an saoghal mo sgeul;
Tha 'm forladh seo agam 's mo chead agam fhein
'S mi gabhail mo cheum gu Carlabhagh.
Aite mo ghaoil, tha mise dol ann.

Mur a b'e 'n cuan 's nach urrain dhomh shnamh
Cha leigeadh mo shubhachas dhomh bhith 'n am thamh
Bhithinn ri siubhal 's mo chas air a barr
Thar monadh is sal gu Carlabhagh
Aite mo ghaoil, tha mise dol ann.

There is a song on my lips and my heart leaps / I would wish that the world heard my tale / I'm on holiday and I can please myself / and I'm taking my steps to Carlabhagh / Place of my love, I'm going there. / If it wasn't for the ocean and I can't swim it / My joy would not let me be still / I would be travelling with my foot on the crests / over moor and sea to Carlabhagh / Place of my love, I'm going there.

Dun Charlabhaigh (Doune Carloway)

Dun Charlabhaigh and neighbouring Tolastadh a' Chaolais were at one time a part of the tack – long lease – of Bearnaraigh Bheag – it is so easy to forget that the sea was the highway then, and that these places, now far apart by road, were so close by sea.

Dun had a particularly changeable history. In our *Croft History of Lewis* vol. 5,[134] we traced a part of this history:

> From a Judicial Rental in 1754 we have details of the rents paid in Dun Charlabhaigh then –
> Compeared Alexr. McGilechalum Tenent in Dune, a married man aged fourty six years . . . Depones that Dune and Sandwick consists of eight farthings land and is possest by eleven tenents, That each farthing payes one pound one shilling and eight pence yearly money rent, so that the eight farthings payes Eight pounds thirteen shillings and fourpence sterling, Depones that each of the above tenents payes a weekly days services etc . . . and that the said towns of Dune and Sandwick is thirld to Carlway Mill.
>
> The result of the Judicial Rental was that Dun and Tolastadh were changed to being held directly of the Seaforth Estate, so by 1766 we find eleven tenants in Dun, but by 1807 the picture is quite different – Dun and Sandwick have become a farm, let to the heirs of Major MacIver of Pabail Uarach and Aignis, Dun remained a farm until 1828, when it was broken down again into sixteen crofts, mainly from tenants evicted from Tacleit on Bearnaraigh. Dun did not remain long in crofters' hands, for it was cleared again in 1853 to create a farm. It remained in this form for twenty years, until it was re-crofted in 1873, mainly for crofters from Mangurstadh in Uig.

The late Duncan MacKenzie – Donnchadh Toggan – of Tolastadh a' Chaolais, a good friend of mine and a great source of oral tradition for the area, commented on the people of the Uig settlement in an interview he gave for the same book:[135]

> 'S e bh'ann daoine ur dhan an sgire, daoine ann an doigh eadar-dhealaichte ris a' chorr dha na bh'anns an sgire. Daoine abhcaideach, lan dibhearsain, lan gearra-ghobaich. Tha beagan dhan an fhreumh ud ann fhathast ach tha e gus ruith a-mach.

> These were new people to the district, and people with different ways from what we had in this district – sporty people, full of fun and full of sharp wit. There is a little of that in them still, though it is running out now.

Dun Charlabaigh is, of course, most famous for the dun itself, with which we started this book. Historic Scotland, in the booklet *The Ancient Monuments of the Western Isles*[136] describes it thus:

> Dun Carloway is one of the finest brochs in Scotland. It still stands in part almost 9m high, close to its original height. The collapse of part of its wall provides a cross-section showing the typical double-skinned wall with two tiers of internal galleries formed by flat slabs, which also serve to tie the wall together. As with all brochs, the plan is almost circular. At ground level the wall is pierced by a narrow entrance, provided with checks for a wooden doorframe. A small cell in the thickness of the wall opens from the right-hand side of the entrance passage, perhaps to house a guard or a dog. At this level, the wall is part-solid and part-hollow, but about 2m above ground the continuous galleries begin. On the inside of the face of the wall at the level of the lower gallery is a stone ledge or scarcement, which may have supported a raised floor, or the edge of a roof. The main weight of this floor or roof, however, would have been carried by a ring of timber posts.

Ian Armit, in his *Towers in the North*[137] suggests that the ground floor was probably used for cattle and storage, and that the living quarters were on the upper floor supported by the scarcements and timber posts. The living quarters would have been protected from the weather by a conical thatched roof, supported by beams set into the outer walls at a point below the wall-head. This suggestion would explain the inter-wall cavities as a form of 'cavity wall', and the window-like opening in the inner walls as a means of allowing warm air from the home to percolate through the cavity – a suggestion which, if it cannot be now proved, would certainly fit with the structure of the building and the comfort of its inhabitants.

Armit also makes the point that the broch is not basically dissimilar to the Atlantic wheelhouse type of architecture, except in its height and dominance, and suggests that the brochs were built as a statement of power, the ability to organise sufficient material and its carriage to the site, and the money to employ an experienced 'architect'.

Iain Armit is co-author with Noel Fojut of a definitive booklet[138] – *Dun Charlabhaigh and the Hebridean Iron Age* – about the dun, and it cannot be bettered as a survey of the dun and the whole of the Iron Age in the Hebrides.

Such a dominant building as Dun Charlabhaigh could hardly fail to become the basis of folk tales, such as the one told by the Sgoilear Ban – Donald Morrison of Steornabhagh – about Domhnall Cam, the folk hero of the MacAulays of Uig:[139]

> Donald Cam and the Gow Ban went on a trip to the Flannan Isles. The Morrisons of Ness came across the moor to Uig and stole all the cows belonging to the MacAulays. When the men came back from the Flannans, their wives told them what the Morrisons had done. Donald Cam and all the men in the boats set off immediately across the channel in an attempt to overtake the stolen herd. As they came in sight of Dun Carloway, they spotted the cattle beside a loch. Guessing that the Morrisons must be inside the strong fortification of the Dun . . . Donald Cam began to climb up the walls of the Dun, using a pair of daggers to help him climb. When he got to the top, he discovered that it was closed by a large flagstone. He then called down to his men to pull heather from the moor and to pass it up to him. He made bundles of this heather and filled the top room of the Dun with it. This done, he set the heather on fire and replaced the flagstone. The smoke and heat from the blazing heather smothered the men inside the Dun. Now Donald Cam and his men demolished this old Dun at Carloway built in the fourth century by a giant called Darge MacNuaran. There are two similar duns in Uig and they were built by Darge's brothers, Cuoch and Tid MacNuaran, who lived in them. One Dun is at Uig, the other at Kirkibost.

There would certainly have been some foundation of truth in the story, but the structure of the dun makes it impossible that it could have had a stone roof, and the last part of the story is, of course, complete fiction – but one wonders what folk memory it was drawing on?

PART FOUR – SGIRE UIG
(A) TAOBH LOCH ROG (LOCH ROAG-SIDE)

In the old days, the boundary between Lochs and Uig parishes was between Dun Charlabhaigh and Tolastadh a' Chaolais, so all the rest of the area of the volume is properly in Uig parish, but this is too large an area for handiness, and I propose to divide it in three – Taobh Loch Rog (to Calanais and Linsiadar), Bearnaraigh (with the mainland opposite) and Uig proper beyond Scalascro.

Tolastadh a' Chaolais (Tolstachulish)

Tolastadh is a strange but very attractive little township, spread along the shore of Loch a' Bhaile, a little off the main road to Carlabhagh, with an off-shoot to the north around the head of Loch Siadar. Donnchadh Toggan remembered the village of his youth in the 1920s:[140]

> There was hardly a house in this district in my young days except the old black-houses. I think that the west side of the island was far behind the east side and Ness. There were plenty there who had concrete houses. It was in 1932 and 1933 that they started to build the white houses here. It was after the war that they started to move out of the black-houses. There were still two or three black-houses quite a while after the war. I can remember two houses with fires in the middle of the floor, and I remember one or two with the bare stone walls – some had them papered or even timbered.

Tolastadh a' Chaolais was the scene of a rather bizarre occurrence narrated by James Shaw Grant in his *The Gaelic Vikings:*[141]

> On Sunday morning an old lady, who lived in a little timber house, was having a cup of tea. Two of her grand-children were spending the weekend with her. As she sat in the bedroom, which also served as living room, sipping her tea, the caorans [small peats] began to jump from beside the very large cast-iron stove which stood in the corner of the room. One caoran hit her on the cheek. Another plopped into her cup of tea. Then there was a crash, and half the

glass chimney of the hanging lamp lay in fragments on the floor . . .
It was then discovered that a row of cups, which had been hanging
by their lugs from nails near the sink had all been broken. The cups
had fallen to the floor, but the lugs were still dangling from the nails.
The plates on the sink were also cracked clean across.

The incident gave rise to all sorts of stories in the village. There
were many who were afraid to pass the house after dark. The old
lady herself, however, had a clear mind and strength of character.
She continued to live there alone. 'I don't understand it,' she said.
'But I know there is an explanation!'

The story appeared in the press as 'The Lewis Poltergeist' but
James Shaw Grant's own explanation was that it had been the result
of an electrical storm, of which there were several that week.

Breascleit (Breasclete)

Breascleit is a large township in Lewis terms, with forty-four crofts,
many of which are split into halves and even thirds. Even in the hard
times of the 1850s, John Munro MacKenzie notes: [142]

The tenants of Braesclate & Garynahine are very industrious &
their rents well paid up. They have also plenty of room; as none
volunteered in these two townships, I did not ask them to emigrate.
They generally pay their rents if work can be had in the Country and
at kelp making. The kelp from this district not having been shipped
yet I could not settle with the people, which when put to their credit
will clear the greater part of the arrears against them.

Despite this, John MacIver, giving evidence to the Napier
Commission in 1883,[143] stated that the number of crofter families
in Breascleit had increased from thirty to forty-four, together with
twenty-five squatters, children and grandchildren of crofters. Five
new lots had been taken out of their grazing, and a further £7 of
land had been taken for the mill. He himself sent only a boll of oats
and a boll of barley to the mill every year, and had to buy in any
further meal required. When asked what stock he had, his answer
was: 'Two cows, a stirk now and again, six or seven sheep, sometimes
perhaps only four, no horse. Though we keep two cows, what is the
use of that? The one only eats up the other.'

Breascleit was the site of one of the major investments of the old

52. Flannan Isles Shore Station, Breascleit

Highlands and Island Development Board, who built a large fish-processing factory there, together with landing facilities, wharves etc. With deep water access through Loch Rog, it seemed the ideal place to encourage the commercial fishery in the area, but after a number of years it failed, and after lying empty for a time, became the centre of a fish-oil company, selling oil capsules under the name of Callanish. In time this also failed, but just recently the factory, or a part of it at least, has been opened again by the family of the former owner. It is to be hoped that this time it can be made a commercial success, not only for the sake of the local fishermen, but as a source of employment for the many university graduates in appropriate subjects from the Islands.

Na h-Eileanan Flannach (Flannan Isles)

Breascleit was the shore station for the light on the Flannan Isles, and I must immediately declare that they are the one part of the area covered by this book on which I have never set foot – I have been at sea off them several times, but never as yet in weather when the swell had dropped enough to allow us to land. The islands lie some twenty miles to the west of Gallan Head in Uig, and are seven in number – which gives rise to an alternative English name of the Seven Hunters. On Eilean Mor, the largest of the group, is a lighthouse, for which the islands are probably best known. The light was made operational in October 1899, and only a year later, in December 1900, the tragedy occurred.

A passing ship reported that there was no light on the island, and the Northern Lighthouse Board ship, the *Hesperus*, was sent to see what was wrong. What they found is given in Francis Thomson's *St Kilda and other Hebridean Outliers*:[144]

> In a mounting fit of alarm, the party climbed up the concrete steps and ran up over the inclined path over the brow of the cliff to the lighthouse. There was an uncanny silence which was accentuated when they entered the living-room. The fire was dead. The clock had stopped. On the table lay a meal which had never even been touched. There was cold meat, pickles and a dish of potatoes. An overturned chair lay a silent witness on the floor. The men then went up the spiral steps to the sleeping quarters. There they found the beds made up in the clean, clinical way of sailors. A search carried on outside the lighthouse revealed no sign of the keepers. Nothing was found which could account for the disappearance of the three men.

The head keeper's log recorded that there had been a severe storm, as was witnessed by a great amount of damage to the shore gear, and to the island itself, but the last note was that the storm was abating.

The explanation usually given is that the men were caught by a freak wave in the aftermath of the storm, but the lack of certainty has given rise to many literary efforts, including that of Wilfred Wilson Gibson:

'Three men alive on Flannan Isle, who thought on three men dead' – which I am sure was learned by most schoolchildren of my age group, even though they had no idea where the Flannans were!

Dean Munro knew where they were in 1549:[145]

> Fiftie mile in the occident seais, from the coist of parochin of Vige in Leozus, towards the west north-west lyis the 7 Iles of Flavain . . . Within thir saidis Iles is infinite wild scheip . . . The flesh of thir scheip may not be eittin be honest and clene men for fatnes. For

53. Access stair on Flannan Isles

thair is no flesh on thame but all quhyte like talloun, and wild gustit thairwith.

Martin Martin in 1703[146] also knew of them:

To the North-west of Gallan-head and within 6 leagues of it, lyes the Flannan-Islands, which the Seamen call North-hunters; they are but small Islands, and six in number, and maintain about 70 Sheep yearly. The Inhabitants of the adjacent lands of the Lewis, having the right to these Islands, and visit them once every Summer, and there make a great purchase of Fowls, Eggs, Down, Feathers, and Quills . . . It's observed of the Sheep of these Islands, that they are exceeding fat, and have long Horns.

He also gives great detail of the superstitious practices followed by Lewis people visiting the island, though he also added that:

These remote Islands were places of inherent Sanctity; and that there was none ever yet landed in them but found himself more dispos'd to Devotion there, than anywhere else.

But the best description of the quantity of sea birds on these islands comes from 'John Morisone, indweller in the Lewis':[147]

The way they kills the fowls is, one goeth and taketh a road 10 or 12 foot long, and setts his back to a rock or craig, and as the fouls flieth by, he smiteth them continuallie; and he hes ane other attending to catch all that falls to the ground; for the fouls flee there so thick that those who are beneath them cannot see the firmament.

John MacCulloch, the geologist, was impressed by the number of birds also:[148]

The most numerous is the puffin. These literally cover the ground, so that when, on the arrival of a boat they all come out of their holes, the green surface of the island appears like a meadow thickly enamelled with daisies. On any alarm, a concert of a most extraordinary nature commences. It requires no effort of imagination to trace the sound of the flute, the hautboy and the bassoon, in the cries of the several birds; the upper parts being maintained by the terns and the gulls, the tenors by the auk tribe, while the basses are occasionally sounded by the cormorants. Separately considered, the individuals cannot be esteemed peculiarly melodious, yet the total effect is no less pleasing than extraordinary.

Extraordinary indeed!

Calanais (Callanish)

Calanais is, of course, best known today for the Tursachan – standing stones – but to the average Leodhasach of a hundred years ago, it was much more important as the ferry point to Uig and to Bearnaraigh. At that time there was no road into Uig, nor to Iarsiadar, where the Bearnaraigh Bridge is today. Anyone wishing to go to Uig had either to hike through the hills or take the ferry from Calanais – even Seaforth himself in 1793 when he visited Uig in order to enlist recruits for his 78th Highlanders, and was not amused when the Uig people, as a protest, sent a boat crewed by women.

A road was made as far as Iarsiadar in the 1930s, though the

people of Bearnaraigh still required a ferry to take them across to
Barraglom. The doctor for Bearnaraigh was based on Miabhag
in Uig, and until the Iarsiadar road was built the only official
way for him to get to Bearnaraigh was to drive the thirty miles to
Calanais – and not on the best of roads – and then take the ferry
from there to Bearnaraigh, though I am sure that many times
he took an unofficial lift on a local boat across the narrows from
Miabhag to Tobson.

Alasdair Alpin MacGregor was with the doctor, Dr Grant, on
one such occasion:

> Early in the morning we drove off from Miavaig in his car, hoping
> to arrive at Callernish by 9.30 a.m., at which time the late Duncan
> MacRae was supposed to leave with the ferry-boat for the Great
> Bernera . . . Fears that the ferry-boat might have left Callernish
> ere we reached that township urged us to slip down the Grimersta
> road to Linshader, where we had hopes of being able to attract the
> attention of old Duncan MacRae, the ferry-man, as he steered out
> from the pier at Callernish, less than half a mile across the loch.
>
> For long enough we stood in the rain at that jetty, waiting and
> waiting, and wondering when Duncan's assistant would be able to
> start up the 20-horse-power Kelvin engine that for the last twenty
> years or so has propelled this old and clumsy ferry-boat through the
> treacherous channels of Loch Roag. At length we heard the engine
> give a kick or two, and watched the ferry-boat moving astern from
> its concealment behind the pier at Callernish. We hailed Duncan
> from Linshader; and in a few minutes he brought his craft alongside,
> though at first he pretended to be neither heeding our bawling nor
> seeing our frantic gesticulations.
>
> Up till the Spring of 1928 Duncan MacRae used to steer his ferry-
> boat right on to Miavaig; and not seldom would he be encountering
> heavy seas in following the exposed route between the fairly large
> islands known as the Bhuidha Mhor and the Bhuidha Bheag, ere
> the ferry-boat slipped into quieter water behind the long tapering
> peninsula at Uigean. Now one of the light, red 'G.R.' motorvans
> runs all the way to Miavaig from Stornoway, thus depriving the
> ferry-boat of the latter part of the voyage.[149]

A note in the Seaforth Papers in 1827 states that Alexander Stewart,
who had studied law at Glasgow for three years, and was then the
factor for Lewis, was building a new house for himself at Calanais.

No doubt it was this house which became the old inn at Calanais –
the taigh seinnse or changehouse – where travellers changed from
one type of transport to another – or more realistically waited to
make the change! Later it became a farmhouse once again and has
recently passed into the ownership of a locally based community
trust, though what their plans are for the area are not yet clear.

The inn had not the best of reputations. Rev. George Hely
Hutcheson describes it in his *Reminiscences of the Lews*:[150]

> It was a queer place that said Callanish Inn, then – the dirtiest
> little den it was ever my misfortune to locate in. It was an exertion
> to hold on to the hard, slippery, black horsehair chairs; the beds
> not inviting; the food, when you arrived without notice, not of
> the first order. But it is of the chickens that I have the strongest
> remembrance. We had a couple for dinner the day of our arrival.
> We tried our hands and teeth on one; no impression. The next day,
> the remaining untried gentleman was sent out for our luncheon.
> We tried him cold, with the same success as the day before. We
> handed him over to the Highland keeper, who, after various futile
> endeavours, passed him on to Snow and Muggro, our two dogs.
> They had been refusing porridge in disgust for days, and, though
> half famished, could not break up that singular bird.

Luckily, Hely Hutcheson was there for the fishing, so he did not
starve!

Today, Calanais is best known, the world over, for the Tursachan,
the great cruciform pattern of standing stones, dating back to over
four thousand years ago. Visitors come from all over the world to
see the Stones – for all sorts of reasons – but the local people seem
to view them with a certain ambivalence – a sense of their being
present beside them, but not belonging to them.

Here is the official description from *The Ancient Monuments of
the Western Isles*:[151]

> The main site at Calanais stands on a low ridge, visible for many
> miles around. The plan is unique. A circle of standing stones is the
> terminus for a double row, or avenue, of stones leading north. To the
> east, south and west single rows lead off from the circle. The circle
> consists of thirteen stones, up to 3.5 m. tall, with a central single
> stone over 4.7 m. high.
>
> Until 1857, only the upper parts of the stones could be seen. In

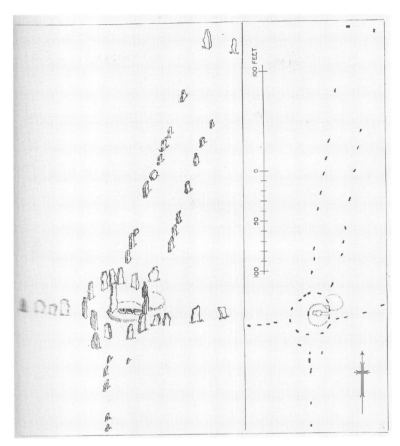

54. Diagram of Calanais Stones

that year, however, a thick layer of peat was removed on the orders of the landlord, Sir James Matheson, and a previously unsuspected feature was revealed; the remains of a small chambered cairn within the central circle.

What was the significance of these great stone monuments, and why were they sited where they were? Although self-styled experts on the meaning of stone circles abound, in fact no one knows! There is no doubt, however, that some, though not all, of the stone circles contain alignments which correlate with the positions occupied by the heavenly bodies at certain specific times of the year. Whatever their original purpose may have been, today's visitors can only stand, ponder and speculate for themselves in the presence of these inspiring monuments.

Lesley Riddoch, the broadcaster, on a visit to the Islands last year (2007) went to Calanais at the time of the 'moonwalk': [152]

> My friend Douglas Scott had calculated the precise time the moon will be at its lowest point in the heavens for eighteen years. If we get to the Callanish stones at 3.45 a.m. tomorrow, and if it's a cloudless night, we'll see the moon walk across hills shaped like a woman lying on her back before setting into the middle of the stone circle.
>
> We wander up the path and suddenly hear ethereal chanting. Sure enough, silhouetted against an iridescent sky is the unmistakable shape of druid-like gowns. Seconds later, the reassuring sound of drums floats across from the stones on a wave of incense. Out of the darkness we bump into a Jethro Tull lookalike carrying a set of bagpipes. 'Something happened half an hour ago and all the pagans started howling – you know that ululating stuff. Then this Free Church choir started singing something in Gaelic, and for a crazy moment they seemed to be trying to outdo one another, so I thought the pipes will sort this out and started playing *Amazing Grace*. It was so loud it kind of drowned them out and they all sang along – Magic.'

The Gaelic choir – psalmody group to be more precise – sang again for Lesley:

> Anna's high, clear tones soar above the deeper voices around her – I have a strong impression of the Young Mermaid statue in Denmark with the waves swirling around but never quite overwhelming her. The effect is electrifying – and strangely, a more fitting tribute for the natural phenomenon happening above than all the earlier pagan ululations.

The Calanais Stones are believed to belong to the Neolithic period, some two to three centuries BC. The Islands then were in a predominantly easterly, drier air stream, but this changed to westerly, wetter winds; more moisture was falling on the land than it could breathe out again by transpiration, and the peat began to grow. Sir James Matheson had about five feet of peat cleared away from the Stones in the 1850s, and I think I can remember when you could see the tide-mark on many of the Stones – until some officious person

55. Calanais

gave them all a scrub and destroyed a couple of thousand years of evidence – or am I merely remembering an old photograph?

The Calanais Stones seem to mean so many different things to so many different people. Elizabeth Ogilvie, herself of Lewis descent, gives her own impressions in the prologue to her romance *The Silent Ones*:[153]

> Here at the Stones the Priest-King had walked in his cloak of feathers, with wrens flying about him, so long ago that he was only a dream, a myth, to the first Celtic and Pictish Christians who built their chapels and bee-hive cells on Leodhas: a dream, a myth, but still they called the place pagan and accursed, believing the turf to have been nourished by the blood of human sacrifice.
>
> Over the centuries the peat built up around the Stones, but their power never lessened. For they could hide themselves from those who had no right to see them; sometimes they spoke. They saw the Beltane fires each May, and at the Midsummer sunrise the Shining One walked the avenue, proclaimed by the cuckoo's call.
>
> The peat was cleared away. The scholars came and went as they will always come and go. And the Stones will stand, impervious to interpretation. All their successive mysteries will never be told. Those who believe they feel the emanation of mystic forces here are like the child who holds a shell to his ear and believes he hears the sea; it is the salt tide of his own blood that echoes there.

There is a visitor centre there now, between the Stones and the old farmhouse, with a very informative, if slightly over-technical, description of the site, but you really have to go the Stones yourself – and, to my mind, preferably on a day of dark storm-clouds – and decide for yourself!

Calum MacLeod was thinking of his home there from the war in North Africa:[154]

'Se nochd oidhche bhatail mhoir,
'S tha gach aon againn air doigh,
Le rifle 's biodag thruis nar dorn
Air bruachan ciuin El-Alamein.

'S beag mo chail bhith 'n so an drasd;
'S mor gum b'aill leam a bhith tamh
An Eilean Leodhais le mo ghradh
Fo sgail Fir Breige Chalanais.

Ach sud am Fifty-first an sas'
Seoid na b'fhearr cha deach gu blar,
Na Siphorts, 's Camronaich 's EarrGhaidheal
Cur smuid ast' le'n cuid bhiodagan

Cha robh buaidh bha sud gun phris,
Phaigh sinn oirr' le fuil ar cridh';
Tha sinn fagail miltean sint'
San uaigh an uir El-Alamein.

This is the night of the great battle / every one of us ready / with rifle and bayonet in hand / on the gentle braes of El Alamein. / Little do I want to be here now / I would far rather be living / in the Isle of Lewis with my beloved / under the shadow of the False Men of Calanais. / There go the 51st / heroes as good as ever went to battle / Seaforths, Camerons and Argyles / steaming in with their bayonets. / That was not a battle without its price / we paid for it with the blood of our hearts / we left thousands behind there / in their graves at El Alamein.

When the Stones were being cleared, the tenants of some of the crofts beside them had to leave; some of them went to Bruce County, Ontario, including a family of MacDonalds:

Donald MacDonald (15 June 1824–1914) son of Angus MacDonald and Catherine Campbell, was born at Callenish, Parish of Uig, Ross-shire, Lewis Island. He came to Canada with his wife

Christena MacLeod. Their first child died at sea, near the end of the almost ten-week voyage. Donald's parents, sister and two brothers accompanied them.

The MacDonalds went to Toronto, to Galt, to Goderich for the Land Sale, and then to claim their land in the Queen's Bush. They had had a daughter Christena born in Galt in 1852. They carried this infant, the first white baby to be seen in this area, to their new home. Donald MacDonald played an important role in the development of municipal government. He served on the council, as bailiff, warden (by-laws) and postmaster. He was known as Councillor Dan.[155]

Gearraidh na h-Aibhne (Garynahine)

This is a little township at the junction of the roads from Carlabhagh, Uig and Steornabhagh, and at the junction itself is a building which at one time rejoiced in the name of the *Prince Arthur Hotel* – named, I assume, after one of Queen Victoria's numerous progeny – but I have no idea why!

There was an old crofting township there – though not so very old, as you can tell from the fact that it has a Gaelic name, whereas the oldest townships have Norse names – but it was destroyed by fire in 1865 and most of its tenants relocated to Acha Mor and Calanais. There is a folk tale that the fire was started by an old bodach trying to light his pipe, and a spark set alight to his own roof and all the others in the township, but that does sound rather too good to be true. The land was made into a farm for the hotel and a shooting lodge, and only in 1935 was the village resettled.

Gearraidh na h-Aibhne has the honour of being the site of a modern ghost-story. Men going around there at night, no doubt in connection with the salmon in the river, were seeing a white ghostly figure wandering around the river-banks – which eventually turned out to be the owner, Mrs Perrins, who had found that wandering about at night in a white nightdress was a very effective way of protecting her salmon!

Mrs Perrins is remembered also for her 'Ceemo' lightweight tweeds. She was one of the first to try to convert tweed to a fashion fabric, and I have a copy of *Gairm* from 1963, with not merely an advert for Ceemo, but a sample of the cloth fixed onto the page. I remember too that we used to be able to buy headsquares and scarves, some with a Lurex thread through them, which made

56. Garynahine Lodge

excellent small presents for the ladies – a marketing idea which has only recently been taken up again by some of the tweed-makers.

The salmon fishings in this area were famous, and as early as 1718 there is a separate entry in the Seaforth rental for the 'River of Ranol's Fishings', let to the MacIvers who then had the farm of Calanais.

Loch a' Ghainmhich (Lochganvich) and Deanston

In the old rentals, Loch a' Ghainmhich appears as a grazings let, tenanted by Major MacIver of Aignis and Pabail and his heirs, though no doubt they had resident shepherds in the area. By 1851 it consisted of five crofts. Although Loch a' Ghainmhich is in the parish of Uig, the neighbouring township of Acha Mor is in the parish of Lochs, and records for each township frequently appear in the records of the other parish.

The Forestry Commission planted an experimental area of forest at the roadside near Loch a' Ghainmhich, but growth proved to be too slow to make it commercially viable. A number of years ago, the forests here and at Ath Linne were decimated by an infestation of Pine Beauty Moth – they say that on a calm night you could hear the caterpillars munching! – and though the forest has recovered to some degree since, the dead trees are still a depressing sight.

Deanston was a new village created on the Gearraidh na h-Aibhne side of Loch a' Ghainmhich in the 1850s for tenants evicted from the Riof area of Uig. It was an experiment, whereby a Mr Smith of Deanston in Perthshire expected to be able to create good farmland by draining deep peat. Sir James Matheson at this time was creating new croftlands by draining moorland on the edges of many townships, and Deanston was to be the prime example of what could be done on the most difficult of sites. The experiment was an utter failure, and by 1853 all the tenants had left, many of them for Cape Breton in Canada. Today, a few traces of the lines of drainage are all that remains of this vastly expensive experiment – I am afraid that Sir James, though he spent a great amount of effort and money in trying to improve the economy of Lewis, was an expert at picking losers!

Strangely enough, the fishings in the Abhainn Dubh at Gearraidh na h–Aibhne and its tributaries went with the lodge at Sobhal, on the east coast, south of Steornabhagh. Hely Hutcheson had these fishings as part of his lease of Sobhal:[156]

> At that time there was no Inn, as there is now, at Garrynahine; therefore I was constrained to build myself a bothy, kennel and stable on the top of Diensten Hill, about seven miles from Soval, whence I could get at the heart of the shooting, and which was about three miles and a half from the best river; and in this said bothy I located a keeper. Diensten Hill – where, as I said, I built my bothy – commanded one of the finest, if not the finest, view in the country. The whole line of Park, Lewis, and Harris, and the Uig Hills, lay like a panorama before it, and of a fine day it was truly such a view as was seldom looked at; but it had its disadvantages. This same hill, when it was not fine – which it is not always in the Hebrides – was about the windiest spot in that very windy country. Diensten bothy did not originally cost a great deal, but its repairs did. In roofs and windows I hardly know what it did not cost – they were continually blowing off or in.

Scapraid

This was a shepherd's village in the moor to the south of Loch a' Ghainmhich. It was on the boundary between the MacAulay tack of Linsiadar and Major MacIver's grazings at Loch a' Ghainmhich, and the MacLeods who were shepherding for him there acquired the nickname of 'Maidsearan' from the Major. Scapraid was a resting place for travellers on their way across the moor from Acha Mor to Uig, but nothing now remains of the village except a green mark on a hillside, visible in the springtime from the Loch a' Ghainmhich road. Older folk may remember a lady who was born there – Peigi Scapraid, who ran the Sailors' Home in Steornabhagh for many years.

Linsiadar and Griomarstadh (Linshader and Grimersta)

Linsiadar in historical times was a tack held by a branch of the MacAulays of Breanais in Uig. The tacksman there in 1726 was Angus MacAulay, brother of Rev. Aulay MacAulay of Harris who made himself famous (or infamous) by trying unsuccessfully to arrest the fugitive Prince Charles Edward on Scalpaigh Island in Harris – the only man known to have tried to collect the £30,000 prize-money offered by the British government.

Another brother, Donald, was the grandfather of Alderman George MacAulay in London, whose diary of the year 1796 has been published under the title of *The War Diary of a London Scot*.[157]

This Donald MacAulay was tacksman of Linsiadar at the time of the judicial rental of 1754:[158]

> Compeared Donald McGilechaulm tenant in Linshadir, a married man aged Thirty two years . . . Depones that the said town consists of four farthing lands and that two farthings thereof is possest by eight tenants and the other two by the Tacksman . . . Depones further that the pendicle of Cnockrougan pays to the said tacksman Two pound yearly rent and was possest last year by two tenants . . . Depones that the tacksman of Linshadir pays Twenty Four Marks yearly for the Salmon Fishing of the Water of Grimirstey . . . Depones further that the pendicle of Keanhulavick is two farthings and a half land.

Cnoc Ruagan was where the moor track from Acha Mor by Scapraid reached the shores, and Ceann Thulaibhig at the head of Loch Rog.

Donald's son George obtained the tack of Calanais also, and his grandson Dr MacAulay probably did more to try to clear Lewis of its tenants than any landlord ever attempted! When tacksman of Ranais, Liurbost and Crosbost, he tried to evict all the tenants there, only foiled when his lease ran out before his plans could succeed. He then took a lease of Bhaltos, Riof and Cnip, and was thwarted in his plans to clear them only by the sale of Lewis to Sir James Matheson, who bought him off.

Dr MacAulay seems to have thrived on lawsuits, both against the subtenants and against the Seaforth trustees: his ploy with the latter was to take a lease, and then to bombard them with claims for compensation for minor breaches of the lease, often to more than the value of the lease itself. Why the trustees continued to lease to him is hard to see, but eventually he was forced to leave Lewis, to settle in Liverpool, with which he, like most tacksmen in the time of the kelp industry, had commercial contacts.

The salmon fishing of Grimersta is famous; to quote Hely Hutcheson again:[159]

> The Grimesta, with its different lochs, take it all in all, is the best fishing in the Lewis for sea-trout; and the different salmon-casts in the lochs, where the stream runs from one to another, are very good. The river itself, between the first loch and the sea, I never thought much of; for, though you may, and do, catch fish in it (by fish I mean salmon), yet, as a rule, fish do not rest in these short rapid rivers. I attribute the superiority of the salmon-casts in the Grimesta lochs to those of any of the other lochs in the Lews, to their being supplied with a very large body of water, as they form the outlet of the extensive and fine Loch Langavat, that receives all the waters of that side of Harris that run into Glen Langan; and the Grimesta has this advantage, that there is spring fishing in it, provided the weather is not too cold, and there is no snow on the hills or in the water.

I am not a fisherman myself, but even I have to admit to a thrill when I see the salmon thronging in the bays of Loch Ceann Thuilibhig and the mouth of Abhainn Ghriomarstaidh.

At Siadar, earlier, we told the story of the last battle between the MacAulays and the Morrisons at Druim nan Carnan. Donald MacDonald – Dolaidh Dotair – completed the story in his *Tales and Traditions of the Lews*:[160]

Only three of the MacAulays managed to escape – Zachary, one of their strong heroes, and two of his near relations. The Morrisons pursued these as far as Carloway, but on the point of giving up the chase they met an illegitimate brother, who persuaded them to follow on to Callernish as he knew the exact place they were sure to be hiding. When they got to Callernish, he led them to the brink of a rock below which there was a scooped-out hollow like a bed-place, and there were Zachary and his companions sleeping deeply from exhaustion. It is still called 'Leabaidh Sgaire' or Zachary's bed.

The Morrisons were for leaving them unharmed to sleep on, but when the brother from Carloway heard this he was very angry, and taking a dagger in each hand, he jumped down with all his powerful weight on the chest of the sleeping Zachary, staved in his ribs, and quickly stabbed the other two before they could gain consciousness. Thus died all the MacAulays who took part in that raid.

The Sgoilear Ban[161] tells a less detailed version of the same story, but says that it was the glint of their swords in the moonlight that betrayed Zachary and his companions to the Morrisons.

According to tradition. Cnoc Ruagan was the home of the Cochull Glas – the grey-cowled one – said to have been of the Clann MhicGill-Eadharain, one of the buffer tribes settled between the MacAulays and the Morrisons. That may be so, but the Cochull Glas was usually to be found on the side of the MacAulays. On one occasion, as Rev. William Matheson tells:[162]

The Morrisons invaded Uig when the MacAulays were away on a sea-foray. The Cochull Glas was prostrate with fever, and his sons, who were but youths at the time, allowed the plunderers to get by into Uig. The Morrisons rounded up the Uig cattle and drove them away, halting with the spoil at Ceann Thulaibhig on the first night. When the lads told their father what had happened, he is said to have gone berserk, with the result that his fever left him. He seized his bow, and wrought such havoc among the Morrisons that they took to flight, leaving the cattle to be driven back to their pastures in Uig. According to some versions, this happened in the time of Donald Cam MacAulay, and the following salutations were exchanged between him and his trusty lieutenant when he returned home to see his herds being driven safely back:

A Chochuill chaoimh Ghlais
Co thill an creach?
A Dhomhnaill Chaim bhrais
Thill mis' a chreach.

Gentle Cochull Glas / Who turned the raid? / Rash Donald Cam
/ I turned the raid.

The descendants of the Cochull Glas in Lewis today are MacDonalds,
and it is sometimes claimed that he was a MacDonald refugee from
the Massacre of Glencoe, but if so, the dates would not allow him
to have been a contemporary of Domhnall Cam. Rev William
Matheson suggests that the Glencoe story results from a confusion
between Glen Coe and Glen Quoich, where the MacDonalds of
Glengarry had tenants of the name of MacGill-Eadharain. This
could explain why some of the Clann MhicGill-Eadharain later
took the surname of MacDonald – but why did then do some of
their descendants in Nis have the surname Campbell today?

A genealogist becomes used to the vagaries of surnames in
the islands, but the reasons for some of the changes are hard to
fathom!

PART FOUR – SGIRE UIG
(B) BEARNARAIGH (BERNERA)

The Isle of Bearnaraigh has in its day contained six townships – Crothair (Croir), Bostadh, Tobson, Breascleit, Circeabost (Kirkibost) and Tacleit (Haclete) – seven, if Barraglom, between the two last, is counted separately – and along with it we will include the mainland opposite, with townships of Lundal, Crulaibhig, Iarsiadar, and the sites of Tornais, Drobhanais and an t-Srom.

In many ways Bearnaraigh, though part of Uig parish, had closer connections with Carlabhagh, especially in the Circeabost area. Though they are far apart today by road, they were no distance by sea, and the sea was the main highway in the old days. The same families are found in Circeabost, before the clearance there, as in Carlabhagh, and it was from Tacleit that most of the families came to settle in Dun Charlabhaigh in 1828.

MacArthur was one of the common names in both areas, but you are quite likely to find it as Campbell today, for there was a period when the registrars refused to accept MacArthur as a proper surname. The explanation I was given by one old man, and it seems as good as any, is that Arthur was used as a Christian name in the family, so the registrars thought MacArthur was a patronymic and wouldn't accept it as a surname. The MacArthurs of Argyll are connected to the Campbells there, so Campbells the Bearnaraigh MacArthurs became!

Eventually the name reverted to MacArthur, but if a family had left the district in the meantime, Campbell they remained. There were MacArthurs who had gone across to Ath Linne in Lochs and then emigrated to Englishtown in Cape Breton, but they were Campbells when they arrived there, and they still are!

On the other hand, there are MacDonalds in Bearnaraigh, especially in Tobson, who are 'MacGolligan' – presumably mac Dhomhnaill 'ic Iain – whose connections are strongly with Uig. According to Dr MacDonald of Giosla – and he belonged to the family himself – the Golliganaich claimed descent from Clan Ranald in Uist, though Rev. William Matheson thought that they were of the same people as Clann MhicGill-Eadharain and descended from the Cochull Glas.

And, of course, there was a strong branch of the MacAulays of Uig in Bearnaraigh – so far as I know the only ones still to use the name Sgaire.

As you come across the 'Bridge across the Atlantic' you come to Barraglom, at one time a township in its own right, then added to the farm of Circeabost and now crofted as part of Tacleit, though to reach the rest of Tacleit you have to head into the next township, Breacleit, and then turn back to the south-west. To the west of the bridge-end is a set of standing stones, guarding the access to the island, though I am told that where they are now is not their original site.

A road along the shore takes us to Circeabost and one of the first crofts you come to is that of my old friend Finlay MacDonald Fionnlaidh Thormoid Dholl – better known in most of the island as 'Dan Dare' because, I am told, of the way he used to drive his old lorry! Finlay and his lorry could not be missed out of this book, for in a way they are responsible for my writing it. On my very first visit to Lewis, as a student, I stayed in Liurbost with Finlay's mother-in-law, and one day Finlay arrived, with the offer of a lift down to

57. Circeabost

Harris. Finlay then had a croft at Luachair, on the Harris boundary with Uig at Ceann Loch Reusort, and a sheep straying from there had been picked up at a faing in Harris. Off we went, and I was so taken with Harris that I now live there.

Finlay was wanting company on the road to Harris – and the journey up the Clisham was not quite so easy then as it is today – but he also had a hidden motive – the windscreen wiper on the lorry had broken, and a string from the wiper was passed right through the cab and back to the wiper – and my job was to pull it to and fro to keep the windscreen clear – no word of MOTs in those days! Finlay had an old flop-eared sheepdog then called Fly, and it was with him that I had my first try at working sheep with a dog – disastrous, of course, as Fly answered only to Gaelic, and I had none at that time!

Finlay, of course, turned his hand to any work that came along, and I remember one time when I was on Easter holiday from university and came up to Circeabost. Finlay was then cutting seaweed for the factory at Ceos, so there we were, cutting weed, up to our ankles in the cold sea, trying to shelter from sleet under the lee of a little cliff, when Finlay smiles at me; 'Aren't you sorry for these folk who have to go to the Bahamas for a holiday?' I do not remember my answer, but that is probably just as well!

58. Fly

Finlay's people had had the shop at the crossroads in the middle of Circeabost, and near them were clann-nighean Scotaidh – Eilidh and Catriona MacLennan – who were the first to try to teach me how to use a creel properly, bringing the peats home to the house. I could load and carry the creel all right, but I never got the hang of tipping the peats out to the side – I either got my arms fankled up in the chest-rope, or I got my hair full of smuir – peat dust – and I had a head of hair then!

Circeabost was an old township, but was cleared in 1826 to add to Linsiadar farm. Most of the tenants were relocated in Braigh na h-Uidhe and Siulaisiadar in an Rubha. In 1879, the crofters of Bostadh, at the north end of Bearnaraigh, asked to be relocated, mainly because their peat moor was running out, and they asked for, and obtained, the farm of Circeabost instead.

Circeabost was also the centre of fishing, with an excellent harbour at the Dubh Thob. The MacAulays had the fish-curing business, and at the time when I was working in Glasgow they had a distribution base there. I had to organise a weekly run to Blochairn to collect boxes of thick, juicy kippers for most of the other staff – and for one of the bosses too!

A surprising, and unfortunately short-lived, industry in Circeabost was diatomite, dug from Loch na Cuilce, and used in polishes. The

59. Fly and friend

60. *Mormina* at Circeabost Pier

page from *Gairm* in 1960 shows the work-squad, and one of the adverts for the polish (see opposite).

Breacleit is the next village to Circeabost, and sits in the middle of the island, with roads radiating to the other townships. Although it is the smallest of the townships, its central position means that it has the church and school, and now the museum of the local Comann Eachdraidh – History Society. I remember one time I had been asked to give a talk there on local history, and I decided to hitchhike there from my friends in Barabhas. On the road through the open moor between Griomarstaidh and Lundal a car stopped to offer a lift. The driver was the schoolmaster in Bearnaraigh, and as we talked, he realised that I was interested in history, and started telling me all about the speaker who was coming to the hall that night – realising just too late who it was he had in the car!

North and east of Breacleit is Crothair, once a part of the farm of the offshore island of Bearnaraigh Bheag – Little Bernera. Bearnaraigh Bheag was an important tack – at one time it included Breacleit, Lundal, Crulaibhig, Tolastadh a' Chaolais and Dun Charlabhaigh. In 1776 the island part of the tack passed to Neil MacDonald of Iarsiadar and Drobhanais, along with Sandibhig and Cirbhig in Carlabhagh area. The MacDonalds later moved

So agaibh, air Loch na Cuilce, iadsan a chladhaich a' chiad earrann a chaidh air falbh, maille ri fear na factoraidh Mgr. Rollo. So an ainmeannan: Tormod MacIllinnean (Tormod a' Ghaidheil), Alasdair MacIllinnean (Alasdair Iain a' Mhaighistir), Mgr. Rollo, Tormod MacDhòmhnaill (Tormod Spung), Eachann MacAmhlaidh (Eachainn Firidh), Fionnlagh, bràthair Alasdair, agus Murchadh Dhànaidh.

Polish Your Car
with DI-ATOM
Highland Polish

MADE AT KINLOCH RANNOCH USING DIATOMITE FROM THE ISLAND OF BERNERA, LEWIS

10 oz. TIN PRICE, 4/6

Di-atom Polish has been tested and approved by the Rootes Group, Makers of Hillman, Humber, Commer

If you have any difficulty in obtaining supplies write to:

ROLLO INDUSTRIES LTD.
BONNYBRIDGE

DI-ATOM!

An liomhadh Gaidhealach air a dhèanamh le ROLLO

61. Diatomite workers at Circeabost

62. Crothair

to Caolas Bhearnaraigh, and later took over the township lands of Crothair.

John MacDonald of Caolas Bhearnaraigh was the prototype of one of the main characters in William Black's novel *A Princess in Thule*[163] as the 'King in Borva'.

> As he drove through the town of Stornoway, the children playing within the shelter of the cottage doors called to each other in a whisper and said 'That is the king of Borva'. But the elderly people said to each other, with a shake of the head 'It iss a bad day, this day, that he will be going home to an empty house. And it will be a ferry bad thing for the poor folk of Borva, now that Miss Sheila iss gone away and there iss nobody left in the island to tek the side o' the poor folk.

Miss Sheila was the daughter of the king of Borva and had married Frank Lavender and gone to London:

> so faa away that no one will see her no more – far away beyond ta Sound of Sleat, and far away beyond Oban, as I hef heard people say. And what will she do in London, when she has no boat at all, and she will never go out to the fishing, and I will hear people say that you will walk a whole day and never come to ta sea, and what will Miss Sheila do for that?

Sheila was unhappy in London and Lavender was bad to her, but it all ends up with a happy ending as they return together to live in Borva. I can tell you the beginning and the end of the story, but I have never been able to read it all through – it is awful! Just off the coast from Crothair is Bearnaraigh Bheag, of which T.S. Muir[164] tells us:

A rough hillocky island about one mile in length, lying off the north end of the greater Bernera, from which it is divided by a caolas only a few yards in breadth. At about its middle it is picturesquely hollowed into four or five little valleys close to each other, running north and south, the eastmost one leading to the Traigh Mhor, a lovely crooked expanse of sand near the north-east point of the island. Overlooking a smaller but equally beautiful traigh, at the east side, there is an open burying-ground, containing a few slabs, plain but of ancient form; and elevated on a rocky mount, close by, are some remains of the chapel of St Michael. Part of another chapel – that probably mentioned by Martin as having been dedicated to St Donnan – was till not many years since standing on a lower part of the shore; of it no traces remain.

A mile or so north and west of Bearnaraigh is the island called Seana-Bheinn – the old hill – a noticeable landmark from the shores from Carlabhagh north. Between them is Bearasaigh (Berisay), at one time the shelter place of Neil MacLeod, one of the many illegitimate sons of Roderick, the last MacLeod chief of Lewis. He was much involved in the struggles in which the MacLeods lost Lewis to the MacKenzies, as will be told in the second volume, when we come to Steornabhagh. Here, we can tell the story of Neil MacLeod and the English ship, or rather we can let him tell it himself. First, the charge by Sir Alexander Hay, in a letter of 3 September 1610:[165]

You haif heard no doubt of the pirate ship takin by Neill McCloyde of the Lewis, This English capitane, wanting men, desired some supplie from Neill, and he willingly yieldit to it. Neill is feasted aboorde of him, and will nocht be so vnthankfull bot will repay him with a bankett on land. The captane and his company for most pairt being all invited, whatever there faire wes, the desert wes sour. Whither it wes that thay refused to pay there rekneing, or that now by there deliverye he thoght to gett his pardoun, he deteynis them,

hes putt of his owne men in the ship, and hathe sent advertisement
to the counsell, whereupoun my L Dounbar hathe directed Patrick
Grieff with a ship to bring her aboute.

Neil, of course, denied responsibility:

I ressavit your letter from this beirair, Patrik Greve, desiring me to
delyuer him the Inglishe Pirott which wes taen by my men with all
her equipage and apparelling. Suirlie, my Lordis, I wes not at the
taking thairof, for had I bene thair, I sould haif sent the said Pirott,
as she wos tane, to his Majestie and Counsell; for suirlie I delyverit
hir to the said Patrik with all her munitioun, as I ressavit hir myself,
to wit, with all hir saillis, towis, and tua ankeris, with xiiij peele of
grite cairte peeleis, with hir captane and nyne of his. As for the rest,
thay war slayne at the taking of the said Pirott; and foure Dutcheis
that wer tane by the capitane aucht dayis befoir the hulk, past to the
Meane-land, for I wald nocht hald thame as prisounairis, in respect
they were takin perforce be the capitane, with twa that deceissit, and
I did keip ane Scootis man in my awin company to forder aduise.
So I rest, Neill McCloud.

According to the Sgoilear Ban,[166] Neil MacLeod, when finally
captured and taken to Steornabhagh:

stood on the top of that hillock about half-way between Uig and
Stornoway known as Toum MhicLeiod – MacLeod's hillock. Neil
looked behind him in the direction of the Island of Berneray and
said 'In that two riggs now in view, there is a vast deal of treasure
buried.' He then told some of those present to set a mark on those
two riggs in Kirkibost and try for the treasure, for it surely would be
found. And he spoke the truth! Two hundred years later, in the year
1813, two tenants of the farm of Kirkibost, with determination and
resolution trenched the ground for this treasure – and succeeded in
finding it. They found a blackened clay pot full of pieces of unminted
gold. They handed the treasure to Thomas MacKenzie, a merchant
of Stornoway, and he gave them the current price for their find. The
two men who found this treasure are still alive, one of them in the
Parish of Uig and the other in this Parish of Stornoway.

Back on Bearnaraigh, and to the west of Crothair is Bostadh,
the site of the present-day cemetery, and of a recently restored Iron
Age House. Bostadh was once a crofting community, but in 1879 its
tenants asked to be relocated to Circeabost.

63. Circeabost Pier

There was a considerable emigration from Bostadh in the 1850s, with people leaving for all sorts of reasons. One of the tenants there was a Zachary MacAulay, four of whose sons emigrated to the Eastern Townships of Quebec, though Zachary himself and one son, Angus, remained on the croft in Bostadh. We were doing genealogical research for a lady in the USA who was descended from one of the brothers, Malcolm, and she was asking us what would have been the reason for his leaving Lewis, and was rather surprised when we told her it was because he was crossed in love. She could not think how we would have known that, but, of course, it is in the song – 'Oran Chaluim Sgaire'. Like most songs of its type, it tells a story, so we will give it in full as it appears in *Bardachd Leodhais,*[167] unlike some singers nowadays who select verses, and so miss out the whole point of the story.

Och hi-ri gur trom m'osna
'S fhada bho mo luaidh a nochd mi
Tha mise Tuath aig ceann Lochluinn
'S is' aig Loch-an-fhir-mhaoil.

Dh'fhalbh i ghluais i leinn dhachaidh
Chuir i 'chuairt ud air Arcamh

64. Circeabost

Siuil ura 's croinn gheala,
Tide mhara 's i leinn

Fhuair mi nise lan ordugh
Air an t-soitheach a sheoladh
'S ann a stiuireas mi 'n t-sron aic'
Gu Macdhomhnuill an Fhraoich.

'Nuair a nochdas mi faire
Bi' mo leannan-sa 'g raitinn
'So an soitheach aig Cragam,
Calum Sgaire tha innt',

Tighinn a nuas dhomh aig Barabhas
Thainig osn' oirr' bho 'n earra-dheas,
'S ann a shamhlaich mi falbh i
Ri earba air tir.

'S ged is math a' bhi seoladh,
Cha n'eil e 'g a mo chordadh
'S mor gu'm b'fhearr leam bhi 'm Bostadh
'Cur an eorn' anns an raon.

'Nuair a rainig mi dhachaidh
Bha mo mhathair 'n a cadal

'Us m' athair 's e 'spealladh
Air machair a' mhaoir.

'S 'nuair a dhirich mi 'chruallach
Thug mi suil air mo ghuallainn
'S ann a chunnaic mi 'ghruagach,
Dol mu'n cuairt air an spreidh.

'S 'nuair a dhirich mi 'bhruthach
Thilg i 'bhuarach 's an cuman
Thuirt i ''S uaibhreach an diugh mi
So cuspair mo ghaoil'.

Ach na 'm bithinn-s' ag baile
A gheamhradh 's a dh' earrach
Cha leiginn mo leannan
Le balach gun strith.

Na 'm bithinn-sa lamh ruit
'Nuair a thug thu so lamh dhi
'S ann a dh'fhaodadh do chairdean
Dhol a charadh do chin.

Och-hi-ri my sigh is heavy / far from my love tonight / I am north off Norway / and she is at Loch an Fhir Mhaoil. / She set off to head us home / set her course for Orkney / with new masts and white sails / and the sea tide with us. / I now got the order / to sail the ship / and I steered her prow / to MacDonald of the heather. / When I came into sight / my love would say / 'There's a ship at Craigeam / Calum Sgaire is on her.' / Coming down past Barabhas / with a wind from the south-east / she was to my mind / like a roe-deer on the meadow. / Though it is good to be sailing / it is not to my liking / I would rather be at Bostadh / planting barley in the field. / When I reached home / my mother was sleeping / and my father was scything / on the ground-officer's machair. / When I climbed the brae / I threw a glance over my shoulder / and I saw the maiden / making her way among the cattle. / When I climbed the brae / she threw away the tether and milk-pail / and said 'It is proud I am today / here is the one I love'. / But if I had been in the township / in the summer and the spring / I wouldn't relinquish my girl / to another without a struggle. / You there! If I had been at hand / when you gave her your hand / your family would have needed / to bury your head.

There are two versions of the story. Anne Lorne Gillies in her *Songs of Gaelic Scotland*[168] says that Calum and his girlfriend – Margaret MacLeod – ni'n Chaluim Neill – from Breacleit had decided to elope at night, but missed each other in the darkness. Calum decided that she must have changed her mind and headed off on an emigrant ship the next morning. The story as I heard it in Bearnaraigh was that she had been persuaded to marry Angus MacDonald during Calum's absence at sea, and he arrived home too late to prevent it. The last two verses of the song would seem to bear this version out, but the late Rev. William Matheson, whose copy of *Bardachd Leodhais* I have, had made a note querying whether these two verses were authentic, or had been added from another poem – and indeed the second-last verse appears as part of 'Oran a' Mharaiche' in Sinclair's collection *An t-Oranaiche*!

When we check genealogical sources, we find that Margaret was married to Angus on 5 January 1855, and Calum emigrated later that year. The song says that Calum would not have allowed the marriage if he had been at home in the winter or spring, suggesting that he only arrived home in the spring, by which time she would have been married – but what was his father scything in the spring? Yet another version of the story was told in Bearnaraigh to my friend Angaidh Eubaidh – Calum Sgaire and his brothers had bought a boat in Orkney, and had sailed her down to Bearnaraigh. They were tired when they got there, and instead of taking her ashore they had left her moored in the bay. Overnight a storm blew up, and she was wrecked on a sgeir. The brothers had been relying on the takings from the following year's fishing to pay for the boat, so they decided that the best way to avoid the debt was to emigrate – fast!

And there you have one of the fascinations of oral tradition – stories change in the telling, and songs have different verses added in different places, so you can never be sure that you have the original version.

Another fascination is that songs and stories take place within a historical context. When Calum was sailing south from Norwegian waters, Margaret was at Loch an Fhir Mhaoil, which is on the mainland, south of the present-day road from Gearraidh na h-Aibhne to Uig, in the area where the Bearnaraigh people at one time had their summer grazings.

Tha'n t-uisge an nochd air Roineabhal
'S tha ceo aig Beinn a' Chuailein

There's rain tonight on Roineabhal / and mist on Beinn a'
Chuailein

This couplet appears in one of the waulking songs of Cairstiona
Sheadha[169] in Harris, but it must have come originally from the
Bearnaraigh shielings, which at one time extended from Loch an
Fhir Mhaoil right across the moors to Loch Langabhat. In 1872
these grazings were taken from the crofters to form part of the
new sporting estates of Morsgail and Scalascro, and in return the
crofters were offered the old farm of Iarsiadar and its hill grazings.
These were reckoned to be smaller and less valuable than Beinn a'
Chuailein, but they were closer to Bearnaraigh, so the crofters agreed
to the exchange, and to build a dyke between their new grazings and
the deer forest, under the promise that the new grazings would be
theirs so long as they held their crofts on Bearnaraigh.

Hardly had the crofters finished the task of building a seven-
mile turf dyke, when they were told that their grazings were to be
changed again, to the former farm of Tacleit on Bearnaraigh itself,
and they would have to leave Iarsiadar.

I.M.M. MacPhail in his *The Crofters' War*[170] – a book much
undervalued to my mind – tells the next stage:

> The Bernera men were naturally very much aggrieved, not merely
> because of all their labour on the dyke and the promise given to
> them but because they considered the new grazings offered to be
> inferior. Donald Munro, the Chamberlain, himself went over to
> Bernera in order to persuade them and, when he failed, he foolishly
> threatened to bring the Volunteers from Stornoway to prevent them
> putting their cattle across to Earshader, although he afterwards
> maintained that he had intended the remark only as a joke. He
> finished his harangue by telling them that he would have them all
> evicted from their crofts in Bernera, even although there was none
> of them in arrears.

The danger of this threat was that Munro held so many public
offices in Lewis that he could virtually do what he liked without
any legal recourse; and indeed he did follow up his threat, and
sent sheriff officers to Bearnaraigh to serve notices of eviction on

all the crofters there. There was a fracas in which one of the sheriff officers threatened, 'If I had a gun with me, there would have been some of the women in Bernera tonight lamenting their sons.' As the sheriff officers left Bearnaraigh they were confronted by a group of Bearnaraich, including an Angus MacDonald from Tobson, and in the argument, one of the sheriff officers had his coat torn.

Two weeks later, Angus was arrested in Steornabhagh. When word of this got back to Bearnaraigh, men were gathered from all over the island and the surrounding districts, and a group of 150 men began a march on Steornabhagh, with the aim of breaking into the jail to release Angus. By this time, the sheriff had released Angus on bail, and he headed back home, only to meet the marchers, who then decided to continue to Steornabhagh and seek a meeting with Sir James Matheson. A small group met Sir James and gave him their complaints, which he promised to look into, while Lady Matheson entertained the others to tea!

Angus MacDonald and his colleagues were brought to court, but found not guilty, and in the course of the trial Munro attracted so much adverse publicity that he was relieved of many of his public offices. When asked if Sir James had authorised the removal notices, Munro had replied that he was not accustomed to consult Sir James about 'every small detail of estate management'. While the summonses of removal in Bearnaraigh were allowed to lapse, Munro's abuse of his power had been so clearly shown that he was removed from the post of chamberlain in 1875.

While the details of the dispute are important, far more important was the fact that the Bearnaraich, by their decided and restrained action, had shown that the factor was not invincible and that people could successfully stand up for their own rights – a moral that was not lost on crofters in other parts of the island. It always surprises me that so little is made of the action of the Bearnaraigh men, which achieved its aim, compared with the Pairc Deer Raid, Aignis Riot, etc, which had little practical effect at the time, however much they may have influenced public opinion in the longer term.

To return to Calum Sgaire – he and his brothers sailed for Quebec, where they settled in Whitton Township, in an area still called Bosta Hill, and there he married Mary MacIver, who had come with her brother and sisters from Suaineabost. He was more fortunate than

Margaret, who died in the year following her marriage – of a broken heart, according to oral tradition – but according to the register of deaths, she died in the birth of her first child, who died also.

Although we think of Quebec today as wholly French, there was a Gaelic-speaking community of over 3,000 in the Eastern Townships area in 1891. The Lewis settlement in the Eastern Townships was in the hill country, east of Montreal and above the alluvial plain of the St Lawrence, near to the boundary with Vermont and New Hampshire in the USA.

Chanell's *History of Compton County*[171] tells of the first Lewis settlers:

The British-American Land Company had in 1836 set up a village for English emigrants at Victoria, west of the present Scotstown, but the land there was poor, and by the following year, all but one family had left. Some of the Scotch settlers were later tempted to settle in Victoria, but when they saw the poor soil, after a few weeks residence, the ill-fated village was for the second time deserted. It is said that when the Scotch settlers wanted nails they would go to Victoria, burn down one of the houses and, after cooling off, pick the nails out of the ashes.

The first Scotch immigrants were eight families who came from the Isle of Lewis in 1838 and settled in Lingwick. The next Scotch settlers came in 1841 and for fifteen or twenty years after, these were increased by accessions from Scotland, until today (1896) there are upwards of four hundred and fifty families, distributed over the townships of Lingwick, Winslow, Hampden, Marston and Bury.

The first eight settlers were brought over by the British-American Land Company, but the rest paid their way. The settlers lived the first year principally on oatmeal, advanced by the BAL Co. They paid for this the following summer at the rate of $5 for one hundred pounds, by grubbing out a road from Bury to Gould. These Scotch families were all housed in four cabins the first winter. They were chopping all the time, and kept a fire going night and day. Each family had been given a sap kettle by the Company and after leaching the ashes the lye was made into potash. In this way it helped to get seed grain and potatoes in the spring. In 1841 the second crew of Scotch settlers arrived in Lingwick, twenty-seven families in all. They were instructed by the first settlers, profiting from their experience.

The first settlements were on the Scotch Road, leading north-east

65. Derelict Lewis settler house in Quebec

from Bury to Gould, and the side roads to Fisher Hill, North Hill
and Red Mountain. The main road north of Gould passed through
Galson and Tolsta on its way to Stornoway. In 1849 the first store
was opened at Stornoway, and in 1851 Rev. Ewen MacLean was
sent from Scotland by Sir James Matheson to minister to the new
community, first in a log shanty, and then in a church a mile or so
out of Stornoway.

Letters from Quebec at that time are full of praise for that country.
John MacKenzie, writing to Norman Matheson, Barvas:[172]

> It seems, as far as we can understand, that all from first to last
> is a preparation for the poor of the Lews, as provision is cheap
> and plentiful, and the people that have labourers can get through
> without much hardship. All the railroad is going on at Sherbrook,
> and all who are able to work are working at it and welcome. Dear
> Norman, I hope you will come; and if you will not, send me John to
> prepare for you, by Sandy Morrison, as I hope that Sandy will come
> anyway, who would do well here. Wages are from 4/6 to 5/- per day.
> I was very sorry when I saw the rest coming, that you were not along
> with them, and I cannot describe how sorry I am; and if I was near
> you, as I am far from you, you might not be in such hardship.

66. Presbyterian Church at Stornoway, PQ

Or Donald MacIver to his father Alexander:[173]

I have to say about this country, anyone who wishes to work can get
plenty, and good wages, from 4/6 to 7/6 per day; and I would advise
young lads and young women to come here. I am sure the country
will not please you at the beginning; but there is no fear of any man
who can work, although he came here without one penny.

Of course, it would only be those who were successful who would
write home, but these writers seem to have been realistic about the
difficulties as well as the prospects.

The main road south-east of Stornoway led through Druim
a' Bhac to Lac Megantic, but a side road to the south led to Baile
Shiadair, Baile Bharabhais and Giosla on the way to Marsden,
later renamed Milan, and on to Balallan, where another side road
joined from Dell, and carried on to Scotstown, then past the ruins
of Victoria and back to Bury. But the land was poor once the
leaf-mould and lumber had been exhausted; the settlers moved
on to the west and the USA, and the forest and the French took

over. Of all that great settlement, little remains today except the placenames.

Stornoway, PQ, still exists, though the last time we were there, there was only one lady with a little English – the rest of the community was wholly French-speaking.

And other things have changed there too, since the days of the Presbyterian Scots:

67. Bar in Stornoway, PQ

Back on Bearnaraigh, to the south of Bostadh, comes Tobson, at the head of the long narrow sea-inlet of Tob Bhalasaigh, and at the mouth of the Tob, a part of Tobson called Bhalasaigh. The last time I was there, there was no road access to Bhalasaigh – the road stopped on the other side of the Tob and a pedestrian bridge was all that connected it with the houses.

South of Bhalasaigh again, on the southern shore of Bearnaraigh is Tacleit, at one time crofted but made into a farm in 1820 for Kenneth Stewart, previously at Eireastadh, with a few cottars left on the shore at Druim a' Gharraidh, but in 1851 some of these were sent to Canada and others resettled in Breacleit, and the shore added to the farm.

Despite this Kenneth Stewart could not make the farm pay and

68. Bhalasaigh Bridge

in 1853 he and his family emigrated to the Whycocomagh area of Cape Breton. Tacleit remained a farm, let to Stewart's son-in-law John MacDonald of Caolas – the King in Borva – but it was broken into crofts in 1880 for families from Crothair.

An Tir Mor (Mainland)

From the point of view of the Bearnaraich, the little villages on the opposite shore, from Lundal to an t-Srom were an Tir Mor – the mainland.

Nearest to Linsiadar was Lundal, which was at one time part of the tack of Bearnaraigh Bheag but by the 1760s was a small farm in its own right. By 1804 it was divided into four units; it was cleared in the 1820s to add to the farm of Linsiadar. In 1893 it was broken into the present six crofts, and I remember Mairi, my late mother-in-law, talking of sailing from Calanais to Lundal to visit her sister Etta, who was the schoolteacher in Crulaibhig for a time. The northern part of Lundal is Peinthinndalein; there were one or two families there in the 1820s, but they were soon moved on to Acha Mor and their lands added as grazings to the farm of Linsiadar.

69. Bearnaraigh Bridge

Crulaibhig (Crulavig) had also been part of the tack of
Bearnaraigh Bheag, but by 1819 it had been divided among crofters.
Two families left from Crulaibhig in 1851 for the Eastern Township
of Quebec, one of them a Neil Ruadh Buchanan. Neil settled first
in Bury Township, on land belonging to the British-American Land
Company, but free government land soon became available further
into the forests and many of the settlers moved there, including
Neil, who moved to North Whitton, near the town of Lac Megantic.
His great-granddaughter was Mrs Gladys Taylor, who first visited
me with her family in my days as a lecturer in Paisley. She lived
latterly in Drummondville, PQ, and many a visit we paid to her
there, talking of Quebec families, and poring over the voluminous
scrapbooks she had gathered – I wonder what has happened to them
now she and her husband Kelly have gone.

70. Margaret Buchanan, Kenneth-John Smith, Kelly and Gladys Buchanan in Quebec

At the mainland end of the bridge to Bearnaraigh is Iarsiadar, originally a tack occupied by a Widow MacLeod and Donald MacLeod, then by Duncan Smith of Drobhanais.

Widow MacLeod is thought to have been the widow of John MacLeod – Iain mac Thorcaill – of the MacLeods of Pabaigh, and Donald was most likely her son. Donald in turn had a son, John, who made his fortune in Jamaica, where he had the estate of Colbecks. John of Colbecks claimed to be the heir of the old MacLeod chiefs – a claim which, though spurious, was accepted by the Lord Lyon of the day. John of Colbecks had a son, John, who was married with a large family, all of whom died young except his son, Barlow, but he also died without issue, so the Colbecks claim died with him.

John of Colbecks had a brother Donald, tacksman of Baile Ailein, who was much involved in organising emigration from Lewis to the USA in the 1780s.

Some years ago we had clients in the USA who had a historical connection with Lewis, though its details had been lost. What they did have, however, was a copy of a sworn affidavit from 1837 that their ancestor John MacLeod had come to America with his father Malcolm in 1773, and that his father was Malcolm, son of John, son of John MacForth. Unfortunately the original affidavit had been lost in a fire, but they had a typed copy. I had no idea what the name MacForth could mean, nor why anyone would bother to go to the courthouse to swear such an affidavit. Then it dawned on me that MacForth was probably not the original name, but was what an English-speaking typist had made of the original handwritten word.

What if the original, instead of MacForth, had been MacTorkle? Could their ancestor have been Calum mac Iain mhic Iain mhic Thorcaill and so a relative of Donald, brother of Colbecks – Domhnall mac Dhomhnaill mhic Iain mhic Thorcaill? Could he have been preparing to claim the chiefship of the MacLeods, on the expiry of the direct Colbecks line, which could explain why he was prepared to go to the trouble of swearing the affidavit? If so, nothing ever came of it.

By 1851 the eastern part of Iarsiadar had been broken into the present four crofts, but the western part remained as a farm for Farquhar Smith, son of Duncan Smith of Drobhanais. Most of the crofters in Iarsiadar were Smiths also, but Rev. William Matheson used to argue that they had taken the name of the farmer, and that some of them at least were Morrisons from west Uig.

Among the Smiths there in my younger days was Coinneach-Iain Smith – the kindest of men, though perhaps a little accident-prone. He had never seen his father, who was lost on the Iolaire in 1919 when Coinneach-Iain was only an infant, but he had a large photograph of him on the wall – a very serious looking man, dressed in his Sabbath best, including a very fancy winged collar, of a type known in my Ayrshire youth as a 'Go-to-heaven' collar. His eyes were rather protuberant in the picture, probably because of the long exposure, but I liked Coinneach-Iain's explanation: 'Well, you see, nobody here had a collar like that. It was the photographer who brought the collar with him, and if he brought a size 8 and you took a size 10, that was why your eyes were popping out in the picture!'

Coinneach-Iain, who wrote several books of religious verse, is gone now, but his elder sister, Mor, is still living in Bru – a great source of information about old times in the area.

West of Iarsiadar was Tornais, where the Bearnaraigh faings are still, and west again the ruins of Drobhanais (Drovernish), where the Smiths farmed before Iarsiadar. I remember one time when I was at Drobhanais, I noticed a lot of madaidhean – horse-mussels – like ordinary mussels but bigger, brown in colour, and even tastier. I have a memory that they were not at Loch Drobhanais itself, but in a little bay nearer to Tornais, but I am not sure. Anyway, I gathered as many as I could carry, and took them back to Finlay's house at Circeabost where I was staying. Catriona and I had to go out somewhere that evening, but Finlay was left to cook the madaidhean for our return.

71. Swimming cattle from Bearnaraigh to the shielings

When we got back, Finlay had taken to his bed – as he was cooking them, he kept tasting them, and by the time we came back, he had finished the lot and had taken to his bed with a mixture of stomach-ache and embarrassment. So I never got to taste the Drobhanais madaidhean!

Beyond Drobhanais, at the mouth of Loch Rog Beag, was the village of an t-Srom (Strome) – hardly a village, just the houses of a shepherd and his family. At one time the shepherd here was an Angus MacIver, known as Aonghas Og bu Shine – the older young Angus – which seems nonsense in English, but makes perfect sense in Gaelic. Aonghas Og was the father of Donald – Domhnall Ban an t-Sroim – who was the ancestor of a great many MacIvers in Lewis today, including the Sobhal family.

Capt. J.T. Newall,[174] writing about an t-Srom at the time of the land raids by crofters from Bearnaraigh in 1889 has an argument which is certainly logical – so far as it goes:

> I am not aware that the men of Bernera, who hold the grazing on the other side, or others there, could establish any right to this, for it must have belonged to the now deserted village of Strome. It is the inhabitants of that village, wherever they may now be, who have suffered, and not Bernera, an island wholly disconnected with

72. Faing at Tornais

it; and no doubt, were the village resettled, its inhabitants would themselves have resisted any such attempt on the part of the Bernera men to dispossess them. I cannot see that they actually possess any sort of abstract right to inherit the ground from which others have been ousted.

I suspect there is a fallacy in that argument somewhere!

PART FOUR – SGIRE UIG
(C) UIG

If Nis was Morrison country, Uig was MacAulay land, and perhaps before we look at Uig proper we should have a quick glance at the different generations of MacAulays we shall meet there. Strangely enough, the first story we have of the MacAulays is their massacre by the MacLeods, as we shall see when we reach Pabaigh. John Roy MacAulay was the only survivor, and we shall hear of his revenge at Bhaltos and at Baile na Cille. John Roy had a son Dugald, who in turn had a son Donald – Domhnall Cam – one-eyed Donald – the subject of many of the folk tales of Uig.

In his youth Donald Cam fought as a mercenary in Ireland, but in his adult life there was enough fighting to do at home, without going overseas! He returned to Lewis at the time when King James VI was trying to encourage the Fife Adventurers to take over Steornabhagh from the old MacLeod chiefs. That story belongs to the second volume of this set, but you can be sure that Donald Cam was to the fore in the fighting, especially if there was a chance for revenge on his Morrison enemies.

On one occasion Donald Cam was taken prisoner on board Brieve Morrison's ship, largely through the assistance of John Roy MacPhail, whom we met coming ashore at Eoropaidh, and who was now settled in the dun at Bragar. Donald Cam escaped, and his first thought was of revenge against John Roy MacPhail. John Roy was captured at Dun Bhragair and taken to Circeabost, where he was killed, the hill where this occurred still being known as Cnoc na Mi-chomhairle – the hill of bad advice.

The Sgoilear Ban tells of John Roy MacPhail's death:[175]

> The following strange thing happened. Men began to thrust their swords at MacPhail, and it is said that no fewer than fifty blows were struck to MacPhail's body. But they had no effect. His body appeared invulnerable. Then a pedlar who was looking on said: 'Let the grass between MacPhail's feet be cut, and that charm now making him proof against every weapon will thus desert him.' This

73. Ceann Loch Rog

was done and MacPhail's body was no longer proof against the sword thrusts and blows. He was killed and his body was slashed to pieces by the swords of all those present at the execution.

It was after another raid by the Morrisons that Donald Cam destroyed the Morrison band hiding in Dun Charlabhaigh, but he was not always the winner, and we shall see how at times he had to skulk on a stac off the shore at Mangurstadh.

Donald Cam had at least three sons – Angus of Breanais, John of Cnip and William of Islibhig, and we will mention each of them in their own townships.

Scalascro

Scalascro on the shore of Loch Rog formed part of the tack of Carnais in 1754, but by 1807 it had been taken over by James Chapman, the estate factor. By 1851 it had passed to the Mitchells of Timsgearraidh, then to Alexander MacRae from Lochalsh, then became a shooting lodge for the estate, and latterly a hotel. The present proprietor is Cristin MacKenzie, a great-great-grandson of John Munro MacKenzie, the factor of *Diary 1851*, and it is to him and his father, Jock MacKenzie, that historians must be grateful for

74. Scalascro

the preservation and publication of that most interesting journal, on which we have drawn so largely in this book.

One of the tenants of Scalascro as a shooting lodge was Captain Newall, whose *Scottish Moors and Indian Jungles* contains his own sketches of the area.

There is no trace today of the next farm in line, and even its proper name is far from clear. The first reference I have found to it is in 1754, as 'Cleithoge', a pendicle of the tack of Pabaigh. In 1780, Norman and Donald MacLeod have a joint tack of 'The Isle of Pabay and Cletihog'. In 1807, 'Kenlochroag, Clettichog and Skalliscroe' are held jointly by James Chapman and Peter MacKinlay, while by 1819 the sole inhabitants of Cletehog are a shepherd, John MacNaughton from Balquhidder, and his family, who later moved to Circeabost. Cleite h-Oig then becomes part of the farm of Scalascro. But was the first part of the name Cleite – a rock – or was it Clettich – a subdivision of a farthing-land – who can tell now?

The name Peter MacKinlay does not sound a Lewis name, but his son Daniel MacKinlay was the author of a booklet *The Isle of Lewis and its Crofter-Fishermen*[176] written at the time of the Napier Commission of 1883, giving backing to the case of the crofters.

75. Morsgail Lodge

At the very head of Little Loch Rog, a road leads to the fishing lodge of Morsgail. The old lodge at Morsgail was destroyed by fire a number of years ago, but it was quite an impressive building in its day.

To the east of the road are the hills of Coltraisal Mor and Coltraisal Beag, where Captain Newall stalked deer:[177]

The stag was standing half-turned from us on the farther side of a gully, and was more than two hundred yards off. He looked very dim and ghostlike against the hill. He was aware, I think, of our neighbourhood, or, at any rate, suspected something, and seemed to be listening. He certainly had not the wind of us. I aimed and fired. He started off at once, not skirting the hill, as one would have expected from a wounded stag, but faced the steep acclivity above him, and got along at a fair pace. He had not ascended far when he exposed his broadside fully to me, and I took the opportunity of letting him have my left and pet barrel, not certainly expecting much result. Down, however, he came, rolling down the hill without a kick till brought up by being lodged in the bottom of a small hollow. We all agreed that the distance could not be less than two hundred and fifty yards, and taking all the circumstances into consideration, and that the stag was moving at the time, I put it down as the best shot I ever made, and I think so still.

Captain Newall has my admiration, not for his skill with the gun, but for his pluck and determination:

> Many years ago in India, a horse I was riding reared, fell back, with me underneath, and left me with a fractured spine. I eventually recovered my health to a great extent, but remained quite paralysed in the lower limbs; and from that day to this have been quite unable to walk or even to stand.
>
> After considerable cogitation I devised a sort of little iron framework chair, without hind legs, which would receive my cushions and myself, and be capable of being placed in an ordinary chair, or transferred, with me still sitting in it, to carriage, cab or railway carriage. Having succeeded so far, it occurred to me that, by attaching this chair to poles, and placing men between these poles, I might, by means of their legs, in some measure provide substitutes for my own, and be carried to places unattainable by chair.
>
> With one man in the shafts, so to speak, in front, and one similarly placed behind, with two, one on each side, to assist the latter, he having the principal weight, I can manage to ascend high hills, and get carried to places and over ground which would have been quite inaccessible to a pony. In fine, I shoot over dogs, and even stalk deer with success, though of course it is shooting under difficulties.[178]

76. Stalking at Morsgail

Not only Captain Newall has my admiration, but also the men who carried him over hills and rivers in pursuit of game!

Giosla

Giosla is on the west shore of Loch Rog Beag, and was originally also a part of the tack of Pabaigh. In the judicial rental of 1754 Murdo MacLeod 'tenant in Gisly, a married man aged 64', gives evidence of the rental of Pabaigh, but states that Giosla is by that time a part of the farm of Riof.

By 1780 there is a separate tack of 'Ghisla and Keanresort' let to a John MacLeod. In 1804 there was a dispute about the boundary between Lewis and Harris, and various witnesses were called to testify. There was no great dispute about the boundary at the Uig end, but one of the witnesses was a John MacLeod, whose testimony begins with establishing his own family history:[179]

> John MacLeod, cooper and ship-owner in Stornoway, aged sixty-six years, a married man, depones, That he was born in the parish of Uig, and lived there until he was twenty-six or twenty-seven years of age; Depones that his father Murdo MacLeod took the farm of Kenresort from the family of Seaforth in the year 1752 and occupied it for twelve years; that his father was succeeded in the possession of the farm by Donald MacLeod his son, brother to the deponent, who held it for seven years; that his brother having gone to America, he, the deponent, entered into possession of that farm, and held it until Whitsunday 1796.

A note in a Seaforth rental of 1780 queries whether John MacLeod is to have any salary as forester of Uig – the answer was 'No'! According to Rev. William Matheson, Murdo MacLeod was mac Iain mhic Thorcaill, so his son Donald, who went to America, would have been a first cousin of John of Colbecks whom we met at Iarsiadar – is this the missing link with the MacForths?

By 1819 Giosla had been made into four crofts, three of them let to members of a MacDonald family – Norman MacDonald, known as Tormod Laghach, and his sons. In 1855 Giosla was made into a farm for Angus MacLean, formerly at Scalascro, and the MacDonald sons were given crofts in Einacleit and Breacleit, apart from John, who decided to emigrate to Quebec.

John MacDonald settled in Winslow Township, near the town of Stornoway, PQ, but his son Angus moved further east, nearer to the town of Lac Megantic, though his family, as Duncan MacLeod tells in his *History of Milan*,[180] scattered all over Canada and the USA:

> One of the earliest settlers in the Milan area was Angus 'Iain Luachd' McDonald. He lived on the 13th Range of Marston. A son Donald A bought a farm farther down the range, but in 1911 he was accidentally killed by a train near his home. A son John A lived at McLeod's Crossing and later moved to Saskatchewan. Archie was single and lived in Vancouver. Katherine was married to Walter Murray and they lived for awhile in Milan, later moving to Portland, Maine, and Edmonton, Alberta. Annie was married to Norman McIver from Winslow, and they lived for a few years in North Dakota, later moving to Vancouver. Christie was married to Allen Iain Tormud McLean and they lived on the home farm.

I do not think that there are any of the Laghaich left in the area, which is mostly covered now by secondary forest, but there is still a graveyard among the trees, and among the burials there is that of the Megantic Outlaw – but we will come to him when we reach Cnip!

Angus MacLean, a mason from Steornabhagh who had married Ann MacRae, daughter of the farmer at Scalascro, became the farmer at Giosla in 1855. His son William went to Canada with the Hudson's Bay Company and is remembered there as 'Big Bear'.

According to a newsletter in the Hudson's Bay Company Archive:[181]

> W.J. McLean was born in the Isle of Lewis, Scotland. He joined the Hudson's Bay Company service on 1st June 1859, sailing for York Factory on the ship Prince of Wales, whence he was transferred as apprentice clerk to Fort Garry. During his charge at Fort Pitt post in 1885, the Northwest rebellion had broken out. Mr McLean and his family were made prisoner by Chief Big Bear and carried in to northern Saskatchewan by him and his hostile Indian following. He retired from the Company's service on 18th October 1892, with the rank of chief trader. W.J. McLean was familiarly known among his friends as Big Bear, a name given him at a dinner in his honour after the '85 rebellion, and commemorates his captivity with the Indian chief of that name.

77. Giosla

More recently, Giosla was the home of Dr Donald MacDonald – Dolaidh Dotair – whose *Tales and Traditions of the Lews* is a goldfield of nuggets of history about Lewis.

Einacleit

The shores of Loch Rog Beag were the main focus of the kelp industry in the parish. The *Statistical Account* of 1797[182] tells us:

> There are about 140 tons of kelp annually made at Loch Roag, which is superior in quality to any other kelp in the Highlands of Scotland; this is sufficiently evinced by its selling for at least a guinea a ton more than any other kelp.

By the time of the *New Statistical Account* of 1833, the amount of kelp made had increased to 226 tons, but the market for kelp was declining. A little kelp was still made, and John Munro MacKenzie in his *Diary 1851*[183] mentions that the tenants in these villages 'have not yet delivered the Kelp made by them this season & they have not been Cr(edited) for the same' – which explained why they were in arrears, but should be able to pay in due course.

The townships along the shore of the loch appear in 1754 as part of the tack of Berie, but by 1807 they were let directly to crofters.

Because of the kelp, the tenants of the villages were able to earn money, and although the bulk of the profits went to the landlords, enough was left for tenants to gather a little capital. Kelp-working was back-breaking work, and bad for the eyes, and many used their savings from the kelp to get away from the enforced labour, pay their passage across the Atlantic and develop new lands for themselves in Cape Breton.

Three of the tenants of Einacleit emigrated to the Eastern Townships of Quebec in the 1850s, including Donald Campbell and family. Donald was a son of Malcolm MacArthur, who had come from Tobson in Bearnaraigh, but, as we mentioned already, many of the MacArthurs of that area were registered as Campbell in the early 1800s; it was as Campbell that Donald was recorded in Einacleit, and as Campbell that he arrived in Quebec, where he eventually became the town clerk of the township of Winslow.

Ungsiadar

Ungsiadar village was off the road, on the shore of Loch Rog, but is now deserted. It was on the narrows of the loch, a trip down which is described by Captain Newall:[184]

> The narrows which separated our land-locked fiord from the outer loch were only negotiable, generally, at those states of the tide which admitted of our exit or entry with it in our favour, or when the tide was slack. There was no pulling against the race in the full flow or ebb. We were soon in the race, amidst the little bubbling and breaking waves outside the entrance to the narrows. Oars were got out to steady the boat if necessary, and then we were among the little whirlpools. Round we slowly spun, as a great swelling roll of the water somewhat lifted the boat and took us into the vortex, all the time hurrying us rapidly forward. This was repeated once or twice, and then we had passed the narrowest part at the entrance, and swept along in more equitable fashion. Stack Glass (the green rock) now submerged on our right, we shot past, and also another dangerous rock on the left, and gliding along the winding channel by pretty broken little crags on our right, with a sheltered bay or two, we neared Stack Alister, so called from the circumstance of one Alister having managed to get his boat jammed between the two points which formed the top of the rock. There he had to remain

high and dry aloft till the rising tide floated him off. After that the
narrows opened more, and the pace at which we had been hurried,
decreased.

Between the Ungsiadar road and that which leads to the next
township, Geisiadar, is Loch Chroistean, on the shore of which
is the old school of the area. Captain Newall describes fishing on
the loch:

> The Uig road passes along one side of the loch, and on the other
> there is a high hill which somewhat screens it from westerly winds.
> At the ends, however, to north and south, it is more open, and it
> takes a good deal of surface disturbance to make the salmon take,
> though I caught sea-trout with the slightest ruffle of the water. Very
> pleasant memories I have of that little loch.
>
> I had seen a fish rise, and backed down to the spot. He came at
> the first offer, ran out about forty yards, as hard as he could spin,
> and then allowed me to manoeuvre him close to the boat, when
> he was gaffed before he had considered what next to do. It was not
> five minutes. He weighed nine pounds. I got another the same day,
> and he very nearly saved us the trouble of gaffing at all, by almost
> jumping into the boat. Beside these two fish, I had fifteen sea-trout
> that day, from three pounds downwards.

78. Loch Chroistean

Geisiadar

Geisiadar also is off the main road, with houses running from the head of Loch Geisiadar to the seashore at Grasabhig. It was from Geisiadar that one of the later emigrants went to Cape Breton. Murdo MacDonald and his wife Mary appear in Geisiadar in the census of 1841, but they must have died soon thereafter, and their children decided to go to Cape Breton where they already had relatives. Their son Donald, later known as Domhnall Ceisdear, had married Jane MacLean from Lacasaigh in 1840, and with his brother Neil and sister Peggy, they headed for Cape Breton.

A rather romantic view of Donald's journey and later life is quoted in *The Road to Tarbot* by Bonnie Thornhill:[185]

> After being buffeted by wind and waves for six long weeks, enduring countless hardships, the good ship John Walker sailed into the harbour at Sydney Mines, with as nostalgic a company as ever crossed the broad Atlantic. No sooner were the brave little ship's company landed on the sandy shore than they proceeded to hold family worship and offer up to God heartfelt thanks for a safe voyage. Bivouacs were then erected, supper spread, a fire built on the shore to scare away any prowling wild beasts, and they and their dear ones commended to the care of the Almighty Father, these pioneers slept soundly in 'New Scotia' with not even a dream of Auld Scotia to break their rest. Soon after sunrise next day, the party started on the long picturesque trail, winding over mountain and glen to North River St Ann's. All the heartaches, all the privations, all the loneliness was more than compensated by the first glimpse of this beautiful country, so new as to be virgin, so like the old land it made them forget the salty miles that intervened.
>
> Fourteen years earlier several of Donald MacDonald's relatives had settled at Oregon, North River. He had planned to make his home there also, but not being fully satisfied with the state of religion there (he was a most pious man) and being greatly interested in the religious work of Peter MacLean, whose headquarters was at lovely Whycocomagh, Donald MacDonald proceeded to establish his family there. In 1843 he started out again over the rough but beautiful trail. When he reached Middle River the news met him that his friend MacLean had returned to Scotland. Whycocomagh had no attraction for him, so turning aside, he took a farm at Middle River. He lived there for two years, preaching, teaching

and catechizing, under the leadership of Reverend Alexander Farquharson. In 1845 he returned to North River, where he spent the rest of his life preaching and teaching.

The area where Domhnall Ceisdear finally settled had been named Tarbert by its original settlers from Harris, but when a Post Office was established there in 1888, it was under the name of Tarbot.

Unfortunately, Cape Breton shares some of the same problems as Lewis, as Dan Alex MacDonald of Framboise there tells:[186]

Latha dhomh 's mi thall aig Tuath
Chualas fuaim a bha faisg dhomh,
Dhubh an iarmailt cho luath,
De an truaighe bha tachairt?

Ma 's e cuileagan a tha ann
Gu bheil grunn dhiubh mu m'amhaich
'S e 'Kilmarnock' bha 'd a' seinn
Agus roinn 'ga phresentadh

Nuair a dh' amhairc mi dh'an speur
Le mo lamh air mo mhala
De bha tighinn ach plaigh
Chuileagan grannda 'gam chreachadh.

Iad bha casan fada caol,
Bha iad a' stiuireadh air m' amhaich,
Dh'fhalbh mise 's mi bha leum,
Bha mi 'g eigheach nan creachan.

Dan Alex gave his own English version:

One day I happened to be travelling in the North Shore and a noise was heard nearby me; suddenly the sky darkened; what calamity was about to occur? Then there were mosquitoes landing in hordes about my neck, singing to the tune 'Kilmarnock' and precenting it in parts. When I looked towards the sky, with my hand shielding my brow, what was coming but a plague of monstrous mosquitoes to wreak havoc on me. They had long narrow legs and they headed straight for my neck. I took off immediately and those that were with me made me scream 'blue ruin'.

Midges or mosquitoes – you can take your pick!

Cairisiadar

Cairisiadar is on the main Uig road – and what a road! As one of the worst parts of the old road, it was one of the first to be brought up to standard, but it did look rather incongruous with wide pavements and street-lights while the main road on either side was still single-track. As the other parts of the road were upgraded, Cairisiadar looks less out of place.

Cairisiadar was the home of one branch of the 'MacGolligan' MacDonalds from Bearnaraigh, and it was to this branch that Dolaidh Dotair belonged, who later moved to Giosla, and whose *Tales and Traditions of the Lews* has been quoted many times in this book. Dr MacDonald was married to Emily Paul, a niece of Lord Leverhulme. After his death, she published a book of her reminiscences *Twenty Years of Hebridean Memories* with many photographs of the area, some of which we have used in this book.

Miabhag (Meavag)

Miabhag was the centre of Uig in the old days, yet paradoxically it was not a crofting township. It was its geographical situation which made it central to the whole parish. In the census of 1861, there was only one household – James MacRae, postmaster and Inspector of Poor, and later tacksman of Ardroil. James MacRae was actually born in Losgaintir in Harris, where his father, Alexander MacRae, had come from Lochalsh as a shepherd, then to Scalascro.

James A. MacKay in his *Islands Postal History Series*[187] gives the history of the post office:

> Uig did not get the benefit of a postal service till October 1857, when a foot-post was established along the road to the west, via the townships of Achmore, Garrynahine and Enaclate and terminating at Miavaig. In the summer of 1885 a mail-car service was introduced between Stornoway and Miavaig, reflecting the greatly increased importance of the west coast with the boom in the fishing industry. This conveyance ran thrice-weekly along a new road (now the A8010) from Stornoway to Breasclete at the junction with the Garrynahine-Carloway Road, then it ran south along this road through Callinish to Garrynahine where it rejoined the original Miavaig road.

79. Miabhag Bridge

In the late nineteenth century Miavaig was second only to Stornoway itself in the importance of its post office, which had savings bank, money order and telegraph departments. The decline in the fishing industry, and the gradual increase in the number of other sub-offices in the parish of Uig, diminished the importance of Miavaig post office, though its relatively long history is reflected in the fact that it has had more postmarks than any other Lewis office except Stornoway.

Miabhag church was also the centre for weddings in Uig – as many generations of children have sung:

Morag Bheag nighean Mhurchaidh an t-Saoir
'S aotrom a dh'fhalbh i, 's aotrom a dh'fhalbh i,
Morag Bheag nighean Mhurchaidh an t-Saoir
'S aotrom a dh'fhalbh i a phosadh,

De ni mi ma sheideas a' ghaoth
'N oidhche mus fhalbh sinn, an oidhche mus fhalbh sinn,
De ni mi ma sheideas a' ghaoth
'N oidhche mus fhalbh sinn a phosadh?

Dh' fhalbhainn leat a Mhiabhaig an Uig
Ged bhitheadh e anmoch, ged bhitheadh e anmoch,

Dh' fhalbhainn leat a Mhiabhaig an Uig
Ged bhitheadh e anmoch is ceo ann.

'S ann theid mise le mo ghaol
Gu Caimbeulach Uige, ge Caimbeulach Uige,
'S ann theid mise le mo ghaol
Gu Caimbeulach Uige a phosadh.

Little Morag, Murdo, the carpenter's daughter / blithely she sets off
for her marriage/ What will we do if the wind blows up / the night
before we leave for the wedding? / We'll leave with you for Miabhag
in Uig / though it be late and misty. / I will go there with my love
/ to Campbell in Uig to marry.

Now there is a challenge for a genealogist – who was Morag
Bheag? There were two Campbell ministers at Miabhag – Rev.
John from 1846 to 1879 and Rev. Nicol from 1889 to 1897. The
only Marion, daughter of Murdo, I could find in the Uig marriage
register for these periods was a Marion MacAulay of Tobson who
married Donald MacDonald of Bosta in 1856, and they would have
sailed to Miabhag from Bearnaraigh, so they would have been
worried about the wind. But neither her father nor her father's father
were carpenters so far as I could see. And somehow the style of the
song seems wrong for as early as 1856. So have I found the subject of
the song, or was she perhaps wholly fictional, with a name made up
because it fitted the rhythm? Perhaps someone in Uig can tell me.

Miabhag was the base chosen by M.S. Campbell for her *Flora
of Uig*:[188]

One of scenic features of Uig – Valtos Glen – is an extended rift
a mile and a half long through which the road runs west from
Miavaig. The northern side of the glen provides a fine scree on which
grow abundant ferns. On the south side the zig-zag path of the peat
cutters and, in front of it, the peat chute shows the steepness which
further down, round the corner, becomes precipitous.

Miabhag pier is the base for my friend Murray MacLeod's '*Sea-
Trek*' tours around the Islands at the mouth of Loch Rog. Martin
Martin in 1703[189]merely lists the islands:

Near to the North-west Promontory of Carlvay Bay, call'd Galan
Head, are the little islands of Pabbay, Shirem, Vaxay, Wuya, the
Great and Lesser.

80. Gleann Bhaltois

Of these, only Bhuaidh Mhor and Pabaigh had permanent populations.

Bhuaidh Mhor (Vuia)

In the judicial rental of 1754 Murdo Smith tells that 'Wia' is a part of the tack of Pabaigh, and is occupied by himself and one other tenant. The Pabaigh tack was broken up in the late 1790s, and in 1807 'Viavore' is occupied by four tenants. One of these was a Neil MacLeod, who had a large family of sons, all of whom emigrated to the Little Narrows area of Cape Breton except one, John, who went to Baile Ailein as a boat carpenter.

The Bras d'Or is almost an inland sea, in the centre of Cape Breton, and most of the earliest settlers in that country took advantage of the more fertile shorelands and the fishery potential. The road from Whycocomagh to Sydney used to make two ferry crossings over arms of the Bras d'Or, at Grand Narrows and at Little Narrows, though the former of these now has a bridge. Little Narrows was originally called Caolas Silis – Julia's ferry – after an

81. Gravestone at Little Narrows, CB.

early proprietor, but much of the land in this area and across on the south shores of Whycocomagh Bay was settled by families from Uig – Mathesons, MacRitchies, MacAulays, etc.

In the 1841 census there are six households on the island, but by 1851 it is unoccupied, some of the tenants having moved to Loch Rog-side, and others having followed their former neighbours to Cape Breton.

Pabaigh (Pabbay)

The island of Pabaigh was the base of a family of MacLeods known as Clann Thormoid – Norman's family – descended from a brother of one of the MacLeod chiefs, probably Roderick, the 7th chief.

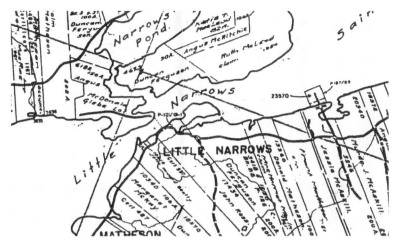

82. Land-grant plan of Little Narrows, CB

John MacLeod of Colbecks, whom we mentioned in connection with Iarsiadar, claimed that his great-grandfather was a brother of Roderick the 10th and last chief, but that could hardly be so, on chronological grounds alone.

The Sgoilear Ban[190] tells the story of the feud between the MacLeods of Pabaigh and the MacAulays. Apparently the MacLeods had the tack of Baile na Cille at that time, as well as Pabaigh, and their stock was ferried to and fro across the MacAulay lands at Riof and Bhaltos. On one occasion a MacAulay cow got mixed up with the MacLeod cattle on a boat, and in the subsequent tussle old Norman MacLeod fell and broke his two front teeth. Norman himself did nothing more about it, but his wife persuaded their sons to take revenge, which they did by slaughtering every one of the Riof MacAulays, except one son, John Roy, who was being fostered at Mealasta. Much of the early folk history of Uig concerns John Roy and his revenge on the MacLeods.

Rev. William Matheson points out in an article in the *Stornoway Gazette* that another tradition is that the MacLeods, who were probably on Bearnaraigh rather than Pabaigh at this time, were acting along with the Morrisons of Ness, the hereditary foes of the MacAulays. This was the period when the MacLeods of Lewis had become involved in the last rebellion of the Lords of the Isles, and Lewis was invaded by a force under the command of the earl of Huntly in 1506. The MacAulays of Uig were staunch supporters of the MacLeods, but the Morrisons were not, and for some reason the MacLeods of Pabaigh seem to have taken the opposite side to their chief in almost every dispute, even in their later dispute with the MacKenzies. When Huntly destroyed the MacLeod army at Allt an Torcan, near Acha Mor, that must have seemed a golden opportunity for the Morrisons and the MacLeods of Bearnaraigh to get their revenge on the MacAulays.

It does seem to have been later that the MacLeods went to Pabaigh, for the tacksman of Pabaigh in 1718 was Angus MacAulay of Bhaltos, though by 1740 the island had passed to John and Murdo MacLeod, who appear to have been sons of John MacLeod – Iain mac Thorcaill. The tack had at one time included Bhuaidh Mhor, Giosla and Cleite h-Og, but in the 1750s the tack was divided, with one brother taking the island of Pabaigh with Bhuaidh and the other Giosla with Ceann Reusort, and with it the post of forester of Uig.

By the early 1800s, Pabaigh had passed to a Sergeant Evander MacIver. The first part of the story is told by Rev. William Matheson in an article in the *Stornoway Gazette:*[191]

> Sergeant Evander MacIver of the 78th Highlanders returned from the wars in the first quarter of the last century with an Irish wife named Susannah Boyd, by whom he had two daughters, Ellen Ann and Dorinda. The Customs authorities appointed him receiver of wrecks in Uig, and Seaforth gave him the island of Pabbay in appreciation of his military service. In 1847 he was awarded a General Service Medal, with a clasp for Maida. The ruin of his house is still to be seen on Pabbay.

But why did he leave Pabaigh? The answer may be in a tale told by Dr MacDonald – Dolaidh Dotair – of Giosla:[192]

> It seems a ship put into the shelter of Pabbay, and the sailors, on coming ashore, disclosed to the islanders that she was loaded up with whisky, and that the captain was doing a roaring trade in this smuggled whisky. After the ship set sail the members of the boat's crew on Pabbay saw that she was becalmed in the Sound of Bernera and they set off in pursuit armed, and the seannachie says that the sergeant shot the captain through the head. We are not told what

they did to the others aboard, or to the ship's cargo of whisky, but
we can understand that they did not pour it all into sea!

A good many months afterwards the rumour reached Uig that
the relatives of the dead captain were coming to wreak vengeance
on the dwellers in Pabbay. A panic set up in the island, and they
hurriedly gathered all their wordly possessions and made for the
mainland, where they got pieces of land from the Valtos people.

The 1841 census shows the sergeant and his family living in Riof,
but they cannot have considered this safe enough, for a few years
later they emigrated to Melbourne in the Province of Quebec.

Dolaidh Dotair has another part to the story:

One woman, whom the storyteller knew as a boy in Valtos, was
only one year old when she left Pabbay and was known to her
contemporaries as Bliadhnach Phabaidh – she was a sister of Mairi
Dhall (MacIver), the authoress of the song 'Och nan och, tha mi
fo mhulad'.

Och na och, tha mi fo mhulad,
Dhomhsa tha mo chomradh duilich
'S cruaidh an cas, ach 's fheudar fhulang
Nach fhaod mi fuireach ann ad choir

Tha mi nis an so gle chianail
Falt mo chinn gach la a' liathadh
'S e bhith cuimhneach Leodhas riabhaich
A tha leagail sios le bron

'S iomadh madainn bhoidheach shamraidh
Bha mi ruith nan cnoc 's nan gleanntan
'S beag a shaoil mi anns an am sin
Thighinn a-nall an seo rim bheo

Nuair a ruigeas tu na cairdean
Gabhaidh iad dhiot naidheachd Mairi
Chan urrain dhut ni eil' a radh riu
Ach gun d' dh'fhag thu i fo bhron

Ach theid mis' air ais do Leodhas
Elilean comhnard, seasgair, boidheach
Fanaidh mi gu crioch mo lo ann
Is gheibh mi solas ann rim bheo

I have used here the version given by Anne Lorne Gillies in

her *Songs of Gaelic Scotland*:[193] for the sake of the translation she has given:

> Oh, alas, I am so depressed, / it's difficult for me to speak, / hard is my lot, but I have to endure it, / that I wasn't able to stay with you. / I am here now and so forlorn, / the hair of my head greying every day, / it's remembering dappled Lewis / that is destroying me with grief. / Many a lovely summer's day / I ran over the hills and glens, / little did I think back then / that I'd ever in my life come over here. / When you reach the kith and kin, / you'll bring them news of Mairi; / you can't say anything / except that you left her full of sadness. / But I'll go back to Lewis / the smooth, snug, lovely island; / I'll stay there till the end of my days / and be happy there as long as I live.

Dr Gillies unfortunately gets the story wrong, and confuses Pabaigh in Uig with Pabaigh in Harris – and then quotes me as her source!

Oran Mairi Dhall is often quoted as the quintessential song of the exiled family, but in fact it is much more personal. Mary's family came ashore from Pabaigh to Cnip and then to Bhaltos, where her father died in 1891. Mairi lived at Cnip until she was in her twenties, then left her family home, presumably to find work overseas. She returned to Bhaltos in the 1880s and died there in 1927. Her entry in the census of 1901 shows her as blind, but that of 1891 does not, and she must have lost her sight between these years, apparently because of the number of tears she had shed during her time away from Lewis. Traditionally, it was to North America that she went, but I cannot find her in Canada in the census of 1881; there is a Mary McIver of about the correct age in New Hampshire in the USA, but the remainder of the household does not seem to fit.

Na Ceithir Peighinnean Deug

The fourteen pennylands was the old name for the peninsula containing the townships of Cliof, Bhaltos, Cnip, Riof and Uigean, though Uigean is now officially reckoned as a part of Cnip, and Cliof as part of Bhaltos. This area nearly suffered clearance in the 1840s, as John Scobie told the Napier Commission[194] in 1883:

When Sir James Matheson bought the Lews there were arrears of £1417.18.1 due by the crofters to the Seaforth management, which he paid rather than disturb his tenants, no part of which was recovered by him, owing to the severe years that followed. A considerable part of the said arrears was due by the tenants of Reef, Valtos and Kneep, which may have induced the said management to set these townships, the year previous to the purchase, on 15 years' lease to a Dr MacAulay, along with the adjoining farm of Ardroil, formerly possessed by him. This being brought before Sir James as a hardship on the part of the crofters to be evicted, and represented to the Hon. Mrs Stewart MacKenzie of Seaforth, she handsomely came forward and arranged with Dr MacAulay to renounce said lease, for which he was paid upward of £4000, to which Sir James, on the score of goodwill, contributed £500, and besides took over the stock of Ardroil from Dr MacAulay at a cost of £933.4.10 in the hope of improving the condition of these crofters.

We know that pressure against MacAulay was also being expressed by the British Fisheries Society, and we can doubt whether all the motives were quite so clear-cut as Scobie suggests, but the fact remains that the Ceithir Peighinnean Deug were saved from clearance by Sir James Matheson.

Riof (Reef)

In the forfeited estate rentals of 1718 and 1726, Riof, under its alternative name of Berie, is one of the many tacks tenanted by a MacAulay, but by 1754 it has passed to Duncan MacLennan, of the family known as na Cleirich, who had come from Lochbroom to Bearnaraigh in the late 1600s. At that time the tack of Berie included all the little townships along the west side of Loch Rog Beag, Cnip and 'Teyva' – the southern part of Riof as opposed to Berie, to the north.

In a loch on the west side of Riof is one of the most important Iron Age broch sites in Lewis. Ian Armit introduces the area in his *The Archaeology of Skye and the Western Isles*:[195]

Before excavation, this structure was visible only as an unobtrusive mound in a sand-choked marsh. On excavation it transpired that this was indeed the site of a broch tower of quite exceptional preservation, the surrounding peat, and sand blown in from the coast, having swamped it almost completely. The Loch na Berie broch tower was built using the same architectural techniques as Dun Carloway, and its proportions suggest that it would have stood at least as high. Once the upper parts had been excavated it became apparent that the present-day ground surface was in fact the first floor level in the broch tower, and that the first floor gallery was intact, with a set of steps leading up to the now vanished second floor. Two doorways opened from this first floor gallery into the central area, where a timber floor would once have rested on the scarcement edge. A further set of steps led downwards into sludge which had filled the ground floor galleries.

Berie remained as a tack until 1804, when the township was divided among seventeen tenants; by 1814 it is referred to as 'Berie & Reef', but by 1819 the township appears in a note of the State of Education as Reef, with a population over the age of twelve of forty-five men and forty-eight women, of whom three men were educated (however that was defined – probably by the ability to write their own names). In the census of 1841 there were thirty-one houses in Reef, but the township was cleared in 1850 and its people scattered among other townships: 'Newlands' at Bru, Siabost, Calanais, Deanston, etc., and others sent to Canada. As Donald Matheson put it, in his evidence to the Napier Commission in 1883,[196] 'They were scattered here and there, and some were sent abroad, some to other places where hardly a snipe could live' – he had no great opinion of the 'Newlands'.

The clearance of Riof was well recorded, and it is interesting to read the varying records, from the different points of view, as expressed in evidence given to the Napier Commission in 1883.

William MacKay, chamberlain of Lewis:[197]

Reef was cleared in 1850 or 1851. The people were offered their passages to America – such as were willing to go. A ship was engaged to carry so many of them. There were twenty-seven tenants at that time. A good many would not go, so to fill up the ship people were taken from any other part of the island, and those who did not go got the lots of those who went from other places, and a number were sent to reclaimed lands, and there are some I believe in the Parish of Ness.

The reason for clearing the township of Reef was that it was not suitable for crofters. The ground being sandy, and the potato crop having failed, they could not raise enough of other crops to support them. There were no peats in the township and they had to go a distance of eight miles to cut peats. Their summer pasture was also a distance of eight to ten miles from them and they were very much in arrear of rent. They got two years to remove. Six of them took advantage of free emigration to America, and the rest of them were provided with vacant crofts in other townships.

Further details are given by John Scobie, who had been factor from 1845 to 1850:[198]

> The Reef tenants complained of being far from their hill pasture and peats (being about 8 miles by water) saying they would be glad of any holdings where these would be convenient. The arable land at Reef was light sandy soil and from constant tillage was apt to be blown away by every gale, being much exposed to the full force of the Atlantic, from which cause their fishing was anything but prosperous.

A totally different account of the events leading up to the clearance is given by Neil MacLennan of Breascleit Park:[199]

> We are now thirty-three years in Breasclete Park. We were formerly in Reef, where we were born and brought up, as also our fathers and grandfathers. The land there was good, and was quite convenient to the sea for fishing, and therefore we lived pretty comfortable. A stranger who wished a sheep farm then fixed upon Reef as a suitable place for that purpose. The result was that we got notice of removal from Mr Scobie, the then factor. We had no arrears of rent, and therefore we refused in a body to do this, and stood out against it for three years, when Mr Scobie's term of office expired. We then naturally expected justice from the next factor; but, on the contrary, he took up at once the work his predecessor had begun, and at last got us forcibly ejected. Four families, of whom my father was one, came to our present holding, and some of the rest had to go to America.
>   So far as my own recollection goes, and the testimony of the only old man now living who came from there at that time, there were works going on – roads and so on – under Government, and it was by these works that they were in the habit of providing for their families, and paying their rents. So when they were turned out in

this way and refusing to leave the place, each foreman having charge of the works got notice that no work was to be given to the people of this place. They then fell into arrears of rent when they did not get work, and so, when this additional hold was got on them, go they must, because the rent was not paid.

John Scobie's account of the relief work is again completely different:[200]

> There was no attempt at clearances during my five years of office except at Reef, in the hope of their doing better. They did not attend the works going on in the island as they should have done. Latterly there was a road made beside them at Glen Valtos and a lake drained at Kneep, each work more with the view of giving them employment than any hope of remunerative benefit. At Whitsunday 1848 the Reef tenants were £141.17.9 in arrears, their yearly rent being £89.14s. They were summoned, but were not removed until 1850, by my successor as factor Mr J Munro MacKenzie. They were then £231.8.6 in arrears of rent, besides a large sum for meal and seed given them. These tenants were then removed to crofts vacated by such as took advantage of free emigration, or to land not otherwise occupied, and were not crowded into other townships.

So what is the truth about the clearance of Riof? It has become the accepted view in some quarters that the crofters' evidence to the Napier Commission was always true and that of the estate not, but history is rarely so clear-cut as that. The actual figures quoted for arrears seem convincing – and it is hard in any case to believe that the Riof tenants had no arrears, when everyone else did! On the other hand there could well have been some underhand work going on about the relief work, and one is still left with the result that the township which was cleared was the one most suitable for a farm. One can well imagine that the township made enquiries about a move, as Mangurstadh did later; the estate realised that this would suit them nicely and matters were allowed to proceed, but I doubt if we will ever know for sure.

Cnip (Kneep)

We saw already that Iain Ruadh MacAulay, son of Donald Cam, was tacksman of Cnip in the 1640s. This was the period when Seaforth

83. Uigean

called out the Lewis families to support the Covenanters in their battle against Montrose and Charles I. It is said that over sixty men from Uig responded to the call, and all but one were killed at the battle of Auldearn in 1649, Iain Ruadh being the only survivor. It was noted afterwards that all the Uig men except him had embarked from a rock at Riof still called Laimrig Fir Uige – the Uig Men's Quay – avoided by boatmen ever since as a place of ill omen.

In his escape from Auldearn, Iain Ruadh had wounded an enemy soldier pursuing him, and it was said that many years later a blind beggar came to Cnip, and was given hospitality by Iain Ruadh. On asking the blind man how he came to lose his eyesight, he was told that it was after the battle of Auldearn, when he was pursuing one of the fleeing enemy.

Cnip remained as a tack until 1807, when it was shared between fourteen tenants.

One of the tenants there in the 1820s was a Norman Morrison, pensioner of the 78th Regiment. He was among those enlisted in 1804, a group known as Saighdearan mac a' Mhinisteir, because John Munro, son of Rev. Hugh Munro, was among those who enlisted. The battalion was in the Egyptian Campaign, when many of the soldiers, including Norman Morrison, fell victim to sand-blindness. With a cash pension, however small, the blind pensioners

84. Donald Morrison, the Megantic Outlaw

were considered eligible bachelors, and Norman married and had at
least nine of a family. Among his sons was Murdo, who decided to
emigrate to the Eastern Townships of Quebec in 1842. There he met
and married Sibla MacKenzie – Sioblag a' Bhreabadair – daughter
of a weaver from Barabhas, who had emigrated along with her
brother James. Murdo and Sibla had seven of a family, and their
youngest son, Donald, became famous as the Megantic Outlaw.

   Many books have been written about the Megantic Outlaw, some
of them more romantic than factual. One tells the story of how
Murdo and Sibla went to Steornabhagh to get a ship to Canada,
but had to wait so long there that they had used up all their capital,
and by the time they finally got to Quebec, they were penniless.
Unfortunately for this story, Murdo and Sibla both left Lewis single,
and only married in Quebec in 1844, though one could be forgiven

for not recognising them in the marriage register there – the Lewis registrars had enough difficulty with the name Sibla, but in the marriage register in Quebec, she appears as 'Chiefly MacKenzie'!

Anyway, Murdo and Sibla settled first at Red Mountain, in the main Scottish settlement, but later decided to join many of their neighbours in a move to free government land to the east, in an area known as Ness Hill. In turn each of Murdo's sons helped him with the farm, but in turn each of them tired of the old man's overbearing ways, and left to set up on their own. Eventually he sent for Donald, who was at the time working as a cowboy in the west, to come and help with the farm. Donald was willing, but only if the farm was put in his name. Murdo grudgingly agreed, but did not tell Donald that he had taken out a loan on the farm from a fellow Lewisman, Lt Col. Malcolm MacAulay (whom we met already in Suaineabost).

When Donald and his father eventually fell out – as they were bound to do – MacAulay claimed the farm in payment of his loan. Donald tried to resist MacAulay's claim but the law was on MacAulay's side, and the farm was eventually sold to a French-Canadian family by the name of Duquette. Donald took this badly, and began to harass the Duquettes, on occasion firing so close as to break the living-room clock beside Mme Duquette. Then the house was burned down, though Donald claimed this was not his doing, and a warrant was issued for Donald's arrest. The Lewis community hid him for a time, but eventually he was noticed on the main street of the town of Lac Megantic. An attempt was made by Jack Warren, a bounty hunter, to arrest him, and Donald Morrison shot Jack Warren.

After that Donald was seriously in trouble, but again the Lewis community closed ranks around him. For over a year he evaded capture, but eventually he was caught, tried and jailed. In jail he took ill with tuberculosis, and was released just in time to die. He, with the others of his family, is buried in the little cemetery in the woods at Giosla.

Donald's case became a cause célèbre, partly because no one liked MacAulay, the money-lender, and partly because the man Donald had shot was a known ruffian, and the story became the folk myth of the townships. One of the earliest versions was by Oscar Dhu,[201] who told the story in 118 eight-line stanzas. Here is a sample:

Vindictive stories, glibly told,
Regarding Don's career
Were caught by slander's poisoned tongue
And whispered far and near
In justice therefor to the lad
Whom vengeful darts assail
We now would fain, in simple strain
Relate his mournful tale.

I warn you, it gets worse!

Cnip, like the other townships in the area, was affected by the emigrations of 1851, not as a clearance area, but as a reception township. This was not according to the original plan of John Munro MacKenzie:[202]

> I think Kneep can be cleared and the whole pasture attached to it may be added to Reef, which will improve that farm very much. There are several in Kneep far behind in arrears of rent and some in Valtos, those should be sent to America, and those remaining in Kneep removed to Valtos in place of the emigrants from that place. The greater part of the arable of Kneep being adjoining to that of Valtos to continue in possession of the small tenants. By this arrangement Valtos would be the only township of small tenants left in the peninsula of Fourteen pence. Valtos is the best fishing port in Uig, and if small tenants can do in Uig, they should be able to support themselves here and pay their rents.
>
> Went to the Valtos Schoolhouse and with Mr Cameron and the Ground Officer's assistance went over the circumstances and condition of each family in Kneep and Valtos. Examining the State of their arrears, stock, etc. Explained to them the conditions offered them if they emigrated, their desperate prospects if they remained here, and the good prospects before them in America etc. etc. From Kneep the number of families which we fixed on to emigrate is six, only one consenting – the number of souls 43, the total of the 6 families arrears £74 and the probable value of their Stock £27.5/- All these are destitute except one family and have now little or no food. From Valtos we fixed on sending 8 families only one consenting, the number of souls 50. Total of arrears £111.15/- and value of their stock £39.15/- The greater number of these are also destitute. They are also very ill off for clothing and the value of the stock will not purchase enough for them.

However, MacKenzie's plans were not followed through: Cnip

was never cleared, though its boundary with Riof was altered to give more area to the farm. In 1851 Cnip had twenty-four households, and in 1861 it had twenty-five. This illustrates the danger of making up a history based wholly on the proposals in MacKenzie's *Diary 1851* – many of these were threats which were never carried out.

More recently Cnip had become known for its archaeological importance. Ian Armit introduces the area in his *The Archaeology of Skye and the Western Isles*:[203]

> Deep sands which formerly shrouded the east-facing slopes of the headland are gradually being peeled back by the wind, revealing year by year the remains of two old ground surfaces. The lower of these is occupied by Bronze Age cairns, and the upper by a Viking Age cemetery.

Between these eras is the ruined broch on Loch Bharabhat – a miniature broch compared with that on Loch na Berie, but nonetheless of the same pattern, though faulty foundations seem to have led to its collapse at an early date, perhaps even before completion.

Although Norse burial sites are scarce in the Hebrides, several have been excavated in Cnip and neighbouring Bhaltos. As Ian Armit points out,[204] one of the burials suggests a mixture of Celtic and Viking influences.

> The presence in this grave of two brooches and a belt buckle of Celtic design, including one penannular brooch, along with two Viking oval brooches, exemplifies the melding of cultural influences occurring in the Hebrides during the later part of the ninth century. Either this was a Scandinavian woman, a first- or second-generation settler, for whom Celtic fashions in personal ornaments were both available and apparently appropriate, or else she was a descendant of the indigenous peoples for whom Viking-style clothing and burial customs had become the norm.

There has been argument for a long time whether the Viking occupation of the Islands led to a thorough wipe-out of the previous population, or whether the new arrivals were quickly assimilated into the existing community. Armit makes the point that the dominance of Norse placenames does not mean than the native people were obliterated, or that earlier languages did not survive in daily parlance. We see the same today, when many Gaelic placenames are being

85. Brooch and comb from Viking grave at Cnip

officially dropped in favour of English equivalents. As Armit says, this may help to explain the otherwise rather puzzling reassertion of Gaelic as the Norse grip relaxed in the later Middle Ages.

The devastations of the Islands as told in the Viking sagas are well known:

> In Lewis Isle with fearful blaze
> The house-destroying fire plays;
> To hills and rocks the people fly
> Fearing all refuge but the sky
> In Uist the king deep crimson made
> The lighting of his glancing blade[205]

– but we tend to forget that this was King Magnus avenging a rebellion by his own Viking chiefs in the Hebrides, not their original arrival in the Islands. After the shock of the initial conquest, life in Viking times may have been relatively peaceable.

Bhaltos (Valtos)

As we saw at Pabaigh, the MacLeods were responsible for a massacre of the MacAulays, only one MacAulay, John Roy, being left alive and fostered at Mealasta. When he came to manhood, he avenged the massacre by killing all the sons of the MacLeods. One was killed, as we shall see, at Baile na Cille, but the others at Bhaltos, as told by the Sgoilear Ban:[206]

> Four sons of old Norman MacLeod were ashore, courting girls at Valtos. They were taken quite by surprise by the arrival of John Roy MacAulay. One of them was killed by John Roy on a plain piece of ground called ever since William's plain. The other sons were despatched by MacAulay on a stretch of sand at Valtos, called ever since Allan's strand.

Murdo MacAulay, son of Angus of Breanais, became tacksman of Bhaltos, and appears in a document of 1658, which Rev. William Matheson noted in the estate papers in Dunvegan:

> We Murdo McAngus vic Donald and Donald McAngus vic Donald, brethren-german and indwellers in the Lewis, bindis and obleiss us that nather we nor any of us shall either by gun or pistol shot, shot of bow, hunting of dogs or any other way kill any deire within the Forest of Harris.

We can guess how well they observed this agreement!

Zachary MacAulay, son of Murdo, became factor for Seaforth in the early 1700s, a difficult time for the estate, as Seaforth had been involved in the first Jacobite Rebellions and his estate forfeited. Zachary appears to have managed to gather most of the rents, and sent them to Seaforth in exile, whilst explaining to the government why the Lewis tenants could not pay the rents to them:

> As for resistance or disobedience there is no danger at all; there being no spot of ground in GB more effectively disposed into passive obedience than the poor Lewis island. But I can assure you shall find one rugged hag that will resist King and Government – viz. Poverty.

Iain Ruadh, son of Murdo, is remembered in tradition as a great hunter, on one occasion falling foul of Campbell of Scalpaigh, the forester of Harris. Iain Ruadh had shot a deer, but it ran off, badly wounded, and crossed the Harris border – at least so said Iain Ruadh! So much for his father's undertaking of 1658.

After this Iain Ruadh is said to have given up hunting, to concentrate on fishing, and, according to the Sgoilear Ban,[207] it was this which caused his death:

Zachary, the factor, along with his brothers John and Donald, prepared to go to Loch Langavat to fish trout, and began fishing opposite to an island on the loch. Suddenly they observed a stag grazing on the island. John MacAulay considered how he should be able to swim and carry his gun dry to the island – and he accomplished it. But the stag, on seeing him, disappeared in an instant. John searched for the stag throughout every foot of the island, but could find it nowhere. He swam ashore to where his brothers were fishing, and told them how he had missed the stag. Then all the party, looking toward the island, saw the same stag browsing in the same place. The brothers charged John with negligence in his search and Donald said to John 'I'll go along with you this time so that the deer shall not escape us both.' Both brothers swam to the island; the deer instantly went out of sight, and though they hunted for it everywhere, the deer could not be found. John MacAulay now began to feel very sick and to shiver all over. In a little while they both took to the water to swim ashore. Donald remarked to his brother that he was swimming too deep and slow, but John only answered 'Dear brother, mind yourself for I am gone!' He sank to rise no more.

The death of this young man caused many tears in the Lewis, and his mother on every Wednesday – the day he was drowned – for

86. Loch Langabhat

a whole year composed an elegiac song on the good qualities and sterling virtues of her lost son.

Bhaltos passed to Zachary's brother Donald, who appears as tacksman in 1726 – it may have been his daughter who, according to tradition, was kidnapped by the skipper of a Norwegian ship – but by 1740 the township was let to joint tenants, as it appears to have been until it was crofted in 1807.

Donald, last tacksman of Bhaltos, had a son Murdo, who, with his son Angus, appears later among the joint tenants of the township. Angus was the father of Captain Kenneth MacAulay of Fraserburgh, whose son, Robertson MacAulay was, after his father's death, brought up by his Robertson relatives in Steornabhagh, before emigrating to Canada, where his son Thomas Bassett MacAulay became chairman of the Sun Life Company of Canada.

Bhaltos was the largest township in Uig in its day, and was the centre of the fishing industry – as is told in the *Statistical Account*:[208]

> The length of the coast, following the shore in all its windings around Loch Roag, is 40 computed miles; the shore is rocky. Dogfish, cod, ling and colefish are abundant here. Great quantities of herrings, of

87. Bhaltos

uncommonly large size, have begun to be caught in this loch within
these few years. The herrings make their appearance about the 20th
of December, and remain to the middle of January; this last year
(1794) upwards of 90 sail came from different parts of the kingdom;
they both fished, and bought the herring fresh from the country-
people, at the great price of from 9s to 12s per crane (which is the
full of a barrel of green fish, as taken out of the net). The uncommon
gales of wind which prevailed this winter became fatal to some of
the fishers, and rendered their success upon the whole much less
than it was any year since the fishing last commenced.

Forty years back, and long before, there was an immense herring
fishery in Loch Roag. Sweden was then the only market for the fish,
and the abundance was such that the country-people sold them for
1s per foresaid crane. The cod is very plentiful in this loch during
the herring-fishing, and when the herrings emigrate, they soon
disappear. Such of the inhabitants as incline to take the trouble of
curing them, can be supplied with salt for the purpose from two
storehouses erected there by Mr Mackenzie of Seaforth, in which
salt is kept for the benefit of the people.

And in the *New Statistical Account*[209] of 1830:

The failure of the herring fishery in Loch Roag for thirty years back,
has contributed to impoverish the people of this parish. Ever since
the failure of the herring fishery in Loch Roag, the cod and ling
fishing is that to which the inhabitants have turned their attention.
In this, they engage with commendable industry, and are frequently
very successful. They cure the fish in shore-houses, and sell it at 4d
per cod and 7d per ling. About thirty tons of cod and ling are taken
annually; and about 100,000 lobsters are annually exported to the
London market. There are about 80 open boats in the parish, and
one decked vessel.

The happiness and comfort of the people would also be promoted
were men of capital to engage in the fishing trade. It is a well-known
fact, that, of late, there were abundance of herring on the whole
coast here, which remained for seven or eight weeks; but most of
the inhabitants had no nets that could fish so far out from shore. I
am confident that, had there been a number of boats and vessels
here upon the herring fishing, their success and profits would have
been considerable.

Even in these days it is clear that the fishing industry was not a
reliable one, subject to gluts and shortages as the herring, for no

explicable reason, would shun the coast where they had previously swarmed. It was suggested that the disturbance of the shore by the kelp industry at its peak could have had some effect, but the true reasons for the waywardness of the shoals is still not really known.

In 1839 when Dr MacAulay of Linsiadar obtained the tack of Bhaltos and the surrounding area, his plans for clearance were thwarted, in part due to pressure from the British Fisheries Society, and, as we saw at Miabhag, the fishing industry was sufficiently important in the 1850s to justify the establishment of a post office there.

It is strange, then, that Sir James Matheson's plans to improve the economy of Lewis did not include its fishery. John Munro MacKenzie[210] told the Napier Commission how he constantly called Sir James's attention to the need for piers and harbours:

> But that was one of the few points which he and I differed on. I constantly wished that some of the money expended on other things should be expended upon harbours, and he always said 'Well the fish-curer should do it – the people who are getting the benefit of this fish trade should do it.' I said 'You will get it in another way – you will get it in rents', but I could never get him to see the advantage to him. He always said that the fishermen and curers, and the people engaged in the trade, should do it for themselves.

Bhaltos was one of the largest townships in Uig, and had a population in 1901 of over 350. As in most Lewis townships, tuberculosis was a great killer in this period, possibly brought back to the Islands by girls working in the cities, and it is in my mind that I have heard a story that the Uig girls were warned not to make any attachments to Balaich na Leine Gheala – the boys in white shirts – since these could only be worn by those who were too frail to get involved in the usual labour of the men there.

Bhaltos had its emigrants too:

Hi horo tha mi duilich, tha m' aigne bho ghruam
Bho thainig mi Chanada fhrasach an fhuachd
Gun chaill mi an ribheadh a bha na mo ghruaidh
'S a 'n diugh tha mo shnuadh air caochladh

Tha cuimhn' agam fhathast 'n uair bha me gle og
Dol suas an Stuighe dhan an Eaglais Mhor
Measg oigridh bha snasail is banail nan doigh
'S an diugh tha gu leor bhon uir dhiubh

Ged thillinn-sa dhachaidh a Bhaltos an drasd
Chan fhaic mi na bodaich a bh' ann na mo la;
Aonghas Ruadh, Gille-Moire, an Leireach, 's Iain Ban
Iad sin is an Taillear Crubach.

Hioro, I am sad, my spirit is gloomy / since I came to Canada of the
cold showers / since I lost the glow that was in my cheeks / today my
appearance has changed. / I still remember when I was very young,
/ going up the Stiugha to the Church / among youngsters who were
smart and modest in their ways / today many of them are under the
ground. / If I were to come home to Bhaltos now / I wouldn't see the
old boys who were there in my day / Aonghas Ruadh, Gille-Moire,
an Leireach and Iain Ban / those and the lame tailor.

(I couldn't resist the temptation to work out who each of the old
boys was – but at least I restrained myself from putting the answers
into this book!)

This song was used in a radio programme my wife Chris made
of recordings she had made with Gaelic speakers in different parts
of Canada. We were told that the author was a Donald Morrison,
but I have no knowledge of him other than his name.

Aird Uig

The earliest record I can find of Aird Uig as a township is in
1827, and since most of the families there are young and newly
married, that is probably about the date of the establishment of
the township. There is a strange note in John Munro MacKenzie's
Diary 1851[211] – 'the remaining tenants of Aird Uig except one family
followed me to Barnera to volunteer to emigrate, so that farm will
be clear at Whitsunday' – strange, because although two families
from Aird Uig did go to Quebec, the remaining seven stayed on
in Aird Uig, and the two emigrants were replaced by other crofters
from Carnais.

In 1870 Malcolm Matheson of Aird Uig joined his former
neighbours in Quebec:

Malcolm Matheson came to Stornoway in 1870 and shortly after went
to Providence R.I. In 1877 he started a general store in Lennoxville,
but the following year removed to Lac Megantic, where he has since
resided. Here he has been lumbering and in trade on an extensive

88. Aird Uig

scale. Mr Matheson, in company with the late celebrated Donald Morrison, cut the first tree for improvement in Lake Megantic village, on May 26, 1878. That summer he built the first building – it being 25 x 35, two and a half stories high. The boards were rafted nine miles from Moose Bay, shingles and dry pine were brought from Stornoway, distance eighteen miles, while the doors, windows and nails were hauled by team fifty-three miles from Robinson, Bury. There was then no road within one and a half miles of the village, and he had to build a small boat to carry the provisions from Sandy Bay, distant two and a half miles. He has been successful in business and acquired considerable property throughout the county. He has held many public offices with great satisfaction to his fellow townsmen. He is a Mason, Orangeman, but first, last and always a Highland Scotchman.[212]

At Gallan Head, beyond Aird Uig, there was at one time an RAF base, and in the usual way of service bases, it was left after the war to rot and disfigure the landscape. Out beyond that again is a navigation mast for aircraft, where a year or two ago new powerful strobe lights were fitted – so powerful that on a clear night we could see them from the south of Harris! I am sure that there were plenty of local complaints too, and the lights were at last removed – or at least modified.

89. Malcolm Matheson in Quebec

Martin Martin[213] tells of another danger at Gallan Head:

> Cod and Ling are of a very large size, and very plentiful near Loch-
> Carlvay; but the Whales very much interrupt the Fishing in this
> place. There is one sort of Whale remarkable for its Greatness,
> which the Fishermen distinguish from all others by the name of
> the Gallan-Whale; because they never see it but at the promontory
> of that name. I was told by the Natives that about 15 years ago, this
> great Whale overturn'd a Fishers-Boat, and devour'd three of the
> crew; the fourth Man was sav'd by another Boat which happen'd
> to be near, and saw this Accident.

I would be willing to bet he was nicknamed Jonah ever after!
On the west shore of Gallan Head T.S. Muir[214] notes:

> Very sweetly and picturesquely situated in a small hollow, a mile or
> two short of its summit, is Tigh Beannachadh, Blessing House, a
> not greatly dilapidated chapel, internally 18 feet 2 inches in length,

with a broken east window, altar, and a doorway and a niche in each
of the side walls – the south doorway entire and flat-headed, the
masonry very rude and without lime.

The report of the Royal Commission on the Ancient and Historic
Monuments of Scotland (RCAHMS) in 1928[215] expands on this:

> Facing the full Atlantic blast, no wilder or more exposed site could
> be chosen for human habitation, and it is almost denuded of soil by
> the spray of winter storms. The Loch a' Bheannaich, which lies 200
> yards inland, becomes quite salt during the winter. The promontory
> is known as Am Beannachadh, and has always been considered a
> holy place.

Baile na Cille (Balnacille)

T.S. Muir barely mentions the old church site at Baile na Cille, but
his earlier book – *Characteristics of Old Church Architecture*[216] tells
us why not – he had been all day making notes on the various
buildings of the area, and sat down at night to write them up,
all with a night-cap – a 'thimble-ful', he says – and found in the
morning he had written nothing at all!

Happily, the reporter for RCAHMS was more conscientious – or
more sober!

> A short distance to the east of the manse at Uig, at Baile na Cille,
> there is an old kirkyard, beside the highest part of which stood the
> old church, built in 1724. The site was occupied by an earlier church,
> Capail Mor ('Big Chapel'), the foundations of which are said to be
> traceable in spring. To the south of it is the site of Capail Beg ('Little
> Chapel'), possibly a still older Church.[217]

Presumably it was the Capail Beag which was the site of the
revenge of John Roy MacAulay on one the MacLeods of Pabaigh,
who was then the tacksman of Baile na Cille.

> This MacLeod, dreading revenge at John Roy's hands, watched for
> three hours every day from a crevice in a rock that lies beyond the
> manse at Uig. The rock is known as Craig Orvell and the crevice
> is termed Sgorr-a-Chiomper. Next day, young MacLeod and two
> attendants were keeping a look-out at the rock, when suddenly
> MacLeod asked 'Who can this tall man be, coming over the sands?'
> The servants replied that it was one of the parish people coming to

Church, but MacLeod looked very serious and said 'If John Roy MacAulay is alive, he is the very person of such uncommon size among the crowd. I'll soon know. I mind that John Roy had a habit – that so soon as he wet his feet in the river, he used to put his hand to his hat.' By now John Roy was about to take the river, and as usual, he put his hand up to his hat. At once Norman MacLeod exclaimed 'It is he!' and away he went, to get within the walls of the sanctuary. John Roy needed no urging; he ran fast, and as Norman MacLeod was jumping over the wall of the sanctuary, John Roy thrust his sword through MacLeod's belly. He raised his sword to his nose and said 'That will do for Norman MacLeod.'[218]

The bounds of the sanctuary surrounding the old churches were usually marked by stones, often crosses, and I wonder whether any of these are still visible around the old churchyard at Baile na Cille.

According to Rev. Hugh Munro in the *Statistical Account* in 1797:[219]

The manse was built about fourteen years ago. Two kirks were built two years ago. The value of the minister's living, including the glebe, is £80. The present incumbent has been sixteen years settled; he is a widower, and has three daughters and one son; he is the third (minister) since the erection of the parish. (John) MacLeod and Norman Morison were his predecessors.

We know that there had been a parish of Uig much earlier, as an obligation by Roderick MacLeod of the Lews to the Bishop of the Isles in 1573[220] is witnessed as follows:

I Ronald Anguson persoun of Wig in Lewes, subscryvis this present obligatioun at the command of ane honourable man, Roderick McCloid of the Lewis, because he could not writt himself, his hand led on the pen.

Rev. John MacLeod, minister from 1726 to 1741, appears in the *Treatise on Second Sight*[221] by Theophilus Insulanus, now known to have been William MacLeod of Hamer, writing in 1763:

The deceased Mr John MacLeod, when minister in Lewis, dreamed that a neighbouring gentleman, who he intimately knew, came to his house, and told him a neighbour had been dead that morning, and he came to invite him to the interment; when he awoke, he told the dream to his spouse, with distinguishing circumstances of his informer's garb; and that same day in the afternoon, the same man came really to his house, exactly in the same manner as he had seen him in his dream, with tidings of the neighbour's decease. This I heard from the minister's own mouth, at different times, and also from his spouse, yet in life.

Another example is given of second sight in Lewis,[222] by 'a gentleman, one Donald MacLeod, lineally descended of the MacLeods of Lewes':

A young girl was contracted to a gentleman in Lewes, equal to her in birth and other circumstances; yet a Seer that lived about the family frequently told her, she should never be married to that man; and even upon the night when the Parson who came to the place to join their hands, the bride and bridegroom being completely dressed, and ready waiting to fulfil the ceremony, the Seer persisted in what he had so often asserted. In the meantime, the bride having stepped out of the room after night fell, she was met with by a gentleman, at the head of twelve persons, who carried her to a boat hard by, and conducting her to an island at some distance from the continent, waited there until they were married, and the Seer's prediction fulfilled.

That may have been an example of the second sight, but it strikes me as more like a pre-arrangement on the bride's part!

We met Rev. Hugh Munro's son previously: Ensign John Munro who was killed in the then Dutch East Indies in 1811. Ensign Munro was an uncle of John Munro MacKenzie, who tells the story to the Napier Commission:[223]

There were two battalions (of the 78th), and I had uncles in both battalions. The first battalion was raised mainly on the mainland, but I know that in the parish of Uig, when Seaforth came to the Parish to get recruits, the people all took to the hills. There was a ferry of twelve miles across Loch Roag, and they sent a boat for Seaforth, manned by six women. This set up Seaforth's rage, and he came very wroth to the Manse of Uig, where my grandfather was minister, and was very wroth at them. The minister told him to be quiet – that the people would find the tops of the hills rather cold, and just to let them alone. Next day, the minister went up and had a talk with them, and told them their conduct was very unbecoming and unpatriotic, and that they should come down and meet Seaforth. They said they would be very ready to do so, but they were afraid he would clear off the whole generation of young men. The minister said 'No, I will be responsible for that – wherever a man has one son, that son will not be taken, but where there is a large family perhaps two will be taken; but I will see that there is no hardship, and I will send my only son with you'.

But there is a problem here. The soldiers who were enlisted in 1793 were known as Saighdearan MhicChoinnich Bhodhair – Deaf MacKenzie's soldiers – and it was a later enlistment for a Second Battalion in 1804 that was known as Saighdearan mhic a' Mhinisteir – the minister's son's soldiers. Besides, John Munro was born in 1781, according to the Fasti of the Church of Scotland,[224] and could hardly have enlisted in 1793! I think that MacKenzie has got his enlistments confused, and the promise of the minister's son belongs to the second enlistment.

John Munro MacKenzie[225] adds:

> They were in Egypt in 1801 with Sir Ralph Abercromby. In Egypt they most all lost their sight by ophthalmia, and they came back to Lewis with hardly a single exception. When they came home the Government was very liberal to them. They gave them a large pension, and not only a pension to themselves but a pension for a guide for each man. I think, between themselves and their guides, they had a pension of £39 a year each. When I went to the Lewis I found upwards of twenty of these men still living. I asked them 'Have you got medals?' 'No, we never heard of medals.' I got their names and their regimental numbers and I wrote to the War Office for them and got medals for them. They were at Maidi and Alexandria. I got medals for them and they were highly delighted and pleased.

The Seaforths themselves were much involved in the army. The old earls of Seaforth had lost the title through their involvement in the Jacobite Rebellions of 1715 and 1719. The title was restored in 1771 for Kenneth MacKenzie, formerly Lord Fortrose, who, probably as a proof of his loyalty to the government, raised the 78th Regiment, or Seaforth Highlanders. They were sent to India, but conditions on the ships were so poor that Seaforth died before they reached St Helena, and it is claimed that 230 of his soldiers died also before reaching India. Seaforth was succeeded in charge of the 78th by his cousin Lt Col Thomas MacKenzie Humberston.

Col. David Stewart[226] tells us of how Humberston died:

Colonels MacLeod and Humberstone had gone to Bombay, and, on their return in the *Ranger* sloop, accompanied by Major Shaw, on the 7th of April 1783, they fell in with a Mahratta fleet off Geriale. In a vain attempt to resist so superior a force, the *Ranger* was taken and almost every man on board either killed or wounded, Major Shaw was killed, and Colonel Humberstone so severely wounded, that he died a few days afterwards in his twenty-eighth year, universally lamented as a young man of superior accomplishments and of great promise in his profession.

Lewis and the Seaforth title passed to Humberston's younger brother, Francis Humberston MacKenzie, who was deaf and dumb; he carried out the Uig enlistment, and hence the name Saighdearan MhicChoinnich Bhodhair.

Like most of the eighteenth-century ministers, Rev. Norman Morrison had been as much a farmer as a minister. In 1754 he held not only the glebe at Baile na Cille, but also Crabhlastadh, Cliof, Timsgearraidh, Eireastadh, Ceann Reusort and Aird Uig.

Rev. Hugh Munro was also interested in farming – according to his entry in the *Statistical Account*,[227] although his glebe seems to have been restricted to Baile na Cille itself, and perhaps Cliof:

The parish never supplies itself with sufficiency of provision. The people have lately acquired a superior knowledge and practice of the culture of potatoes to what they formerly had, and in proportion to the increase of this useful root, their buying of provision diminishes, and bears small proportion to their outlays in former years. About 15 years ago, the present minister was obliged to give over the cultivation of potatoes, except a little for his own private domestic use, because prejudices hindered the people from eating them; but his perseverance in using them in his own family at last convinced the people of their error, and of the vast utility of that article.

Here they sow small or black oats (the only kinds used) in the months of March and April; they reap in September and October; they sow a little earlier than in any other part of the country, in order to be employed in manufacturing kelp as soon as possible. Barley is sown in May, and reaped in the latter end of August, and some of it in September. The oats are all cut with the sickle, but the barley is plucked; the reason for their plucking the latter is that the root of it makes good thatch for their houses; and although they pluck it in rainy weather, when they cannot carry on any other harvest-work, it never heats, and is easily dried with the first fair weather. Kail or cabbage of any kind is not used here; since their prejudice against potatoes has been overcome, they chuse to bestow their manure on the latter rather than the former.

Here we can see the beginning of the reliance on the potato beyond any other crop which was to prove so disastrous in the 1840s, when the crop was destroyed year after year by blight.

William MacGillivray, the ornithologist, who lived for a time at Northtown in Harris was not very impressed by Munro when he visited him in 1817:[228]

> He is an old man of clear complexion, sub-sickly, sub-grave phiz, not very robust habit. He wears a white cotton nightcap – aye, even in the pulpit. The kirk is a thatched house, without regular seats, and having a most miserable pulpit composed of a few fir sticks. Mr Munro, honest man, is but a lame preacher.

– but then MacGillivray never was much impressed by anyone but himself!

Rev. Hugh Munro also includes what he terms a *lusus naturae* in the *Statistical Account*:[229]

> Very near the manse there lives a woman who has four distinct breasts or mammae. She has had several stout healthy children, and suckled each of them, and likewise one of the minister's children. She has nipples and milk in each of the four breasts; the upper two are situated immediately under the arm-pits and by being distended with milk, are very troublesome to her for the first two or three months after her delivery.

Rev. Hugh Munro was replaced in 1824 by Alexander MacLeod, a staunch evangelical and a great favourite of the then Lady Seaforth. It may have been a justified complaint of the evangelicals that the earlier 'moderate' ministers had been more interested in farming than religion, but Mr MacLeod himself was a considerable farmer also, according to the estate papers of the day:

> The Timsgarry tenants are not willing to move to make a glebe for Mr MacLeod, and have been told that they are not bound to do so without warning. Mr MacLeod expected much more for pasture than the factor could allow. Only allowed grass for the one horse and two cows they are entitled to after having an arable glebe set

apart, and just now MacLeod has twelve large milk cows and a bull
and seems to expect as much to continue.

The Timsgearraidh crofters, of course, lost the land at the next
term day!

A new church was built in MacLeod's time, as he tells in the *New
Statistical Account*:[230]

> The parish church is situated in the most convenient and centrical
> part of the parish; notwithstanding of which, those inhabiting
> the north and north-east coast of Loch Roag are thirteen miles
> from Church. The church was built in the year 1829 and affords
> accommodation for 1000 sitters. The manse was repaired with
> additions in 1824. The present incumbent has an arable glebe of no
> great value, and the amount of stipend is £150 Sterling per annum.

Baile na Cille is also the site of one of the great Uig stories – that
of Coinneach Odhar, the Brahan Seer. Coinneach's mother was
spinning and watching her flock by night near the old graveyard.
She saw the graves open and a great number of spirits rise into the
air and fly away. Before dawn they all returned to their graves except
one, and Coinneach's mother laid her distaff across the mouth of the
open grave. In time the spirit returned, but could not enter the grave
because of the distaff. She explained that she was Gradhag, nighean
Righ Lochlainn – daughter of the king of Norway – and the great
distance she had to travel home was the cause of her being late. As
a reward for removing the distaff, she told Coinneach's mother that
she had dropped a stone of vision in a pool, and that if Coinneach
found it, he would be able to see into the future. This happened,
and Coinneach became a famous seer and foreteller.

Many of Coinneach Odhar's prophecies are well known in the
Highlands of Scotland, but, of course, many 'prophecies' are actually
poetic re-tellings of past events. Rev. William Matheson has shown
conclusively that the real Coinneach Odhar in fact belonged to
Easter Ross, a century before the dates usually ascribed to him
in Lewis, and suggests that the stories about him may have been
brought to Lewis with the MacKenzie tacksmen, after the defeat of
the old MacLeod chiefs in the early 1600s. The story of Gradhag,
nighean Righ Lochlainn, may well be a Lewis one, but the story of
Coinneach Odhar has become grafted on to it.

Crabhlastadh (Crowlista)

The first tacksman to appear in Crabhlastadh in the forfeited estate rentals of 1718 and 1726 is a Malcolm Smith, but by 1740 it had been added to Rev. John MacLeod's tack of Baile na Cille. By 1766 it had been divided again among eleven joint tenants – Donald Macgillychalom, Donald his son, Malcom MacHorrimot, Murdo MacAulay, Kenth Breppiter, Malcom MacChristiny, Donald MacKay, John MacHorrimot, Malcom Maccoilvicinnes, John Maceonvichorrimot and Normand Beg.

By 1804 there were sixteen crofters in Crabhlastadh, though by 1841 there were thirty-six households there: a total of 196 persons – no wonder it was considered over-crowded!

John Munro MacKenzie has an unusual note in his *Diary 1851*:[231]

> Next met the people of Croulista and Aird Uig; several in both these townships are much in arrear while others pay up; a deputation from each place came to me to say that there were people on both farms who could take and pay the places if some of the most desparate were deprived of land & others put in their places who could pay; I replied that if the present arrears were paid up by Martinmas next except that due by a very few old & poor people I would recommend the proprietor to give them a short lease of say 7 years to make a trial of what they proposed, on which severals came forward and made payments.

There had already been an emigration from Crabhlastadh to Cape Breton in the 1820s, but another nine families left for Quebec in the 1850s. Among them was an Angus MacAulay, whose great-granddaughter Shirley MacAulay died recently in Saskatoon after a lifetime spent researching the later generations of the families who came from Lewis to Quebec, and their descendants all over the world. Her correspondents will remember her letters well – beautifully handwritten, and rarely amounting to less than forty pages! Angus's father, John MacAulay, was another of those who returned to Uig from the Java campaign, nicknamed 'Java', of course. He had a wound through his cheek which had never closed – and I remember being told that he was the only man in Crabhlastadh who could spit sideways!

Murdo MacLeod of Crabhlastadh wrote many songs – many of them extremely funny – but very hard to summarise and even harder to translate! He also wrote of the attractions of the moors above Morsgail:[232]

A' fagail Mhoirsgil nan craobh
Gu fallain faoin as t-samhradh,
A' cur ar n-aghaidh air an fhraoch
'S a' sreap ri maoil nam beanntan;

A Challtraiseal, na biodh ort turs
'S tu air ar cul a' sealltainn,
Na tarraing ceo a-nuas le gruaim
Gu ruig sinn suas na gleanntan.

Chan eil m'aighir anns an fhraoch
Ged 's mithich fhaoilt san am leam;
Cha neil mo run gu leir 's na flur
Tha bruchdadh tre na gleanntan;
Chan neil mo sholas no mo mhuirn
An tarraing chiuin nam beanntan,
Ach O! air maighdeannan na h-airigh –
'S gheibh mi failt nach gann uap'.

Leaving Morsgail of the trees, / happy and carefree in summer, / turning our face to the heather, / climbing the bare hill-tops; / Don't be sad, Calltraiseal, / watching at our back, / don't bring the dark fog down / before we reach the glens. / My gladness is not from the heather, / though it is pleasant in its time; / my pleasure is not wholly in the flowers / bursting out through the glen; / it's not my delight / or the peaceful draw of the mountains / but oh! the girls at the shieling / and the plentiful welcome they will give me.

Timsgearraidh and Eireastadh (Timsgarry and Erista)

In the earliest rentals these townships were held with the glebe of Uig, though each was split among five joint tenants in the rental of 1766. By 1780 Timsgearraidh was back with the glebe, but Eireastadh was still tenanted. In a rental of 1806 Eireastadh had six tenants, including John MacAskill, Schoolmaster, but by 1814 it had been cleared to make a farm for Kenneth Stewart, who later moved as tacksman to Tacleit in Bearnaraigh. Uig shooting lodge was made on part of the farm and still remains as a rather exotic landmark in the scenery.

RCAHMS mentions a dun:[233]

> On a tidal islet rising about 7 feet above high-water mark some 20 yards from a southerly projecting promontory at the east side of Uig Bay about ½ mile south by east of Uig Manse, is the much dilapidated Dun Borranish, or Dun Cuithach as it is sometimes called from a mythological giant, who, after oppressing the country, was slain by the Fians.

– and the same report mentions a grouping of stones at Geo Ruadh, near Taigh Bheannaich on Aird Uig moor, which are supposed to mark Cuithach's grave. You may remember that Darge, who had the dun at Carlabhagh, was a brother of Cuithach, and so was Tid, whose dun at Circeabost, Dun Tiddaborra, we should have mentioned there.

Eadar dha Fhadhail (Ardroil)

Eadar dha Fhadhail – between the two fords, one towards Eireastadh and the other toward Carnais – comprises three early villages: Capadail, Baileniceal (Balnicol) and Peighinn Dhomhnaill (Penny Donald). The forfeited estate rentals of 1726 show 'Adderaivill' as tenanted by a Donald MacAulay, who appears also in 1740 at 'Ederaisle', while by 1754 they were all a part of the tack of Breanais, being the 'five farthing land of Capidil, three farthing lands of Peindonil with pendicle of Ceanchusil, and seven farthing land of Balnickel, with pendicle of Ishlivik'.

In 1780 Edrachile passed to Kenneth Nicolson of the Carnais family, along with the liberty of change-keeping in the parish of Uig, but he appears in a list of 'Warnings-Away' in 1796 and the tack was thereafter split, Balnicol with Torray being leased to Donald MacAulay's widow and Malcolm MacAulay, while Capadail was shared among seventeen crofters.

A note of the State of Education in Uig in 1819 shows every household in these townships, not only those paying rent, but also shows shepherds living on the grazing lands. So Capadle has nine houses and three bothies, with two houses at 'Kenchusli', Peindonil has eleven houses, four bothies and a house at 'Penhelchen' and Balnicol has ten houses, one bothy and a house at Torray. Torraigh is on Loch Reusort-side and Ceann Chuisil between Mealasta and Thamnabhagh; Penhelchen is not known to me – I cannot even be sure that I have read the name correctly – but presumably it will lie between the other two, perhaps in the area of Loch Reusort-side known to me as Lamadail and Sgianuilt.

All three townships appear in a list of stock in Uig in 1824, when Balnicol has 46 cattle, 49 sheep and 3 horses, Penny Donald has 68 cattle, 97 sheep and 11 horses, and Capidol has 45 cattle, 106 sheep, and no horses – which incidentally shows the emphasis on different types of agriculture among the three townships.

> One day in 1831 Malcolm MacLeod of Penny Donald, known as Calum nan Sprot, was herding his cattle among the sand dunes when he saw one of the beasts rubbing itself against a sand-bank and acting in a queer manner, so he went along, and saw her pull out some whitish objects with her horn. He lifted some of them up and examined them and took them to be idols or graven images of some kind which he did not understand. A gentleman from Stornoway heard of their discovery and came over and dug out all the pieces, for Calum nan Sprot would meddle no more with them.[234]

These were, of course, the celebrated Uig chessmen, and though there is some disagreement about the detail of their finding, for it is also said that they were found within a stone chamber in the sand dune. There is no doubt that, whatever their provenance, they were sold through Roderick Ryrie, merchant in Steornabhagh, for £30. Eighty-two of the chess-pieces found their way to the British Museum and a further eleven to the National Museum of Scotland. Frederic Madden, Assistant Keeper of Manuscripts in the British Museum, made this report on their consignment:[235]

> There are 82 pieces of different descriptions, all made (apparently) of the teeth of the sea-horse, or morse, of which number 48 are the superior chess-men – forming parts of four or five sets, but none of them perfect per se, although two complete sets can be selected from them. Beside these there are the pawns, which are plain, and a set of draughts or table-men. An Ivory buckle also was discovered with them. These pieces are apparently of the 12th century and of fine workmanship.

90. Lewis Chessmen

The main source of morse, or walrus, ivory would have been the Greenland settlements, whose main trading commodity this was. Greenland was then subject to the see of Trondheim in Norway, as were the Hebrides in their period of Norse rule. Trondheim was also the centre of trading for the Atlantic coasts, and there is nothing inherently improbable in the suggestion that the chessmen may have been part of the sale-stock of a Trondheim merchant, trading in the Scottish islands.

In 1840 all three townships were cleared, and most of their tenants sent to Suaineabost in Nis, where a part of the former farm was broken up to make crofts for them. John Munro MacKenzie notes in 1851:[236]

> Those who wish to emigrate from Swanabost are people who removed from Uig nearly 20 years ago; they are now comparatively comfortable but are most anxious to emigrate – Not so the Ness men who are determined to a man not to leave the Country on any account.

The farm passed to the brothers James and John MacKenzie, who had followed a common pattern in having come from Lochalsh as shepherds to Losgaintir in Harris, and then moved up to a farm in

Lewis. The factor in Lewis in the late 1820s was Alexander Stewart, son of Donald Stewart, tacksman of Losgaintir, and it may not be coincidence that a few of the shepherds from Losgaintir later obtained farms in Lewis.

We noted earlier MacKenzie's comment that neither of the MacKenzie brothers could read or write, which had made them a bad choice to put in charge of the distribution of relief meal in the days of the potato blight. James later moved to Linsiadar, while John took a sheep farm in Gairloch.

One of the later shepherds at Eadar dha Fhadhail was an Alexander Finlayson from Lochalsh, whose son Alex Dan was widely recognised as an authority on the oral tradition of the Uig area – an ability inherited in no little degree by his daughter Mrs Anna MacKinnon, with whom I have often collaborated – and just as often disagreed! But that is of the essence of historical research – different views arising from different approaches, together helping to establish a more rounded view of the subject.

Rev. Peter MacLean was a native of Baile Niceal, though his family moved in the 1830s to Crabhlastadh. Here is a summary of a part of his life from the biography by Rev. Neil Dewar of Kingussie in *Disruption Worthies*:[237]

> In 1832 he undertook a mission among Highlanders, especially non-churchgoers, in Edinburgh and Leith. It was very reluctantly that in 1832, yielding to the solicitations of friends in Lewis, he quitted this field, and accepted the Parish School of Uig. In 1836 he was licensed. Soon thereafter a call was sent to him from Highland settlers in Cape Breton, some of whom had known him before they emigrated. Taking up his headquarters at Whycocomah, he extended his labours over the whole island, and preached almost daily. After labouring in the colony for five years, his strength completely gave way, and he was obliged to return to Scotland in 1842. After a short period of rest, he recovered his strength in good measure and accepted a call from the Free Church congregation of Tobermory and was inducted into that charge in August 1843.
>
> In 1853, Mr MacLean visited the Lower Canadian Provinces and one of his first services was to dispense the Lord's Supper at Whycocomah. Such a large gathering had never been witnessed in these quarters. Two hundred boats moored in the bay, and five hundred horses tied in the woods, may serve to give an idea of it. It

was estimated at about ten thousand. In the course of this mission he travelled 7289 miles and preached ninety-one times.

In 1866 he was again induced to undertake a mission to Nova Scotia and Cape Breton, with a view of endeavouring to heal divisions and strifes arising out of the union of the Presbyterian Churches.

On his return home, he resumed his duties, but that winter, while returning from the Communion at Uig, he got wet, and caught a severe cold accompanied with a cough, which baffled every remedy. He died on the 28th of March 1868.

Carnais (Carnish)

Carnais is in a lovely spot on the south side of Traigh Uige, but the entrance to the township is rather spoiled by open quarries on one side and the sprawl of a fish hatchery on the other. However, it is these which have maintained employment in the area and a balance has to be drawn between picturesqueness and the means of earning a living if a community is to be maintained – a message yet to be understood by some of the conservation bodies, to whom, one cannot help but feel, the human population of the Islands are at best an inconvenience and at worst an encumbrance. Where no employment is available, the young people who are the lifeblood of a community are forced to leave, and the community will sink, first into retirement homes, and then into holiday homes, as has already been seen in many parts of the Islands. Now, with fish-farming in decline in the Islands, there must be worries about the future of employment in the area.

In the rental of 1718 and 1726 Carnais is tenanted by a Malcolm MacAulay, but by 1754 it had passed to a John Nicolson, whose far-flung tack included Scalascro and Cirbhig at Carlabhagh, where his father may have been the tenant originally. By 1766 he has Carnais only, though by 1778 he had added Eadar dha Fhadail to his tack. From 1780 the tacks were divided again, with John Nicolson retaining Carnais and Kenneth Nicolson, probably his son, taking Eadar dha Fhadhail. John retained Carnais until 1796, when he was 'warned away' from his lease, and by 1807 the township was let to thirteen crofters.

Angus Nicolson, son of John, became a fishcurer in Stornoway,

91. Fish hatchery near Carnais

and was followed there by his son Roderick, whose son Angus, along with his brothers, was responsible for the founding of the Nicolson Institute – but more of that in the next volume!

John Munro MacKenzie noted in February 1851:[238]

> from Carnish we fixed on sending 12 families (five consenting) consisting of 61 souls. The total of their arrears £183.10.8 and the probable value of their stock £57.5. The greater part of the people fixed on today for America are even now destitute of food, several families have not even one meal of food. Carnish should be cleared altogether, the people left can be sent to Mangersta and Islivick in place of those removed. Carnish would make a good addition to Edereol adjoining.

And in September of that year:[239]

> Next called the tenants of Carnish few of whom appeared and the few who did paid little or nothing. 6 families from this farm emigrated this year and the remaining tenants despair of being continued in the farm as they are so much in arrear and on that account shewed no wish to pay. They are almost all desperate characters in this farm. Two or three heads of families have been confined to bed for years and there are some widows. This would

make a good addition to Arderoil Farm and the sooner it is cleared the better as the present tenants will never pay a tithe of the rents. Those who are able to emigrate should be sent, and those who cannot to get places elsewhere.

Carnais was indeed cleared: of the twenty-three families who appear there in the census of 1851, none were left in the following year. Most were scattered among the adjoining townships, but we can trace nine families who moved to the Eastern Townships of Quebec.

Mangurstadh (Mangersta)

Mangurstadh does not appear in the forfeited estate rentals of 1718 and 1726, and must have then been part of another tack, probably Breanais, but by 1755 it is in the hands of joint tenants. In 1766 there are six tenants, of whom the first-named is 'Donald mcJohndowie' – Domhnall mac Iain Duibh. Ian Dubh is said to have been the first of this family of MacLeans, and to have come to Lewis from Mull to teach better use of the commercial fishery there.

The MacLeans gradually spread all over west Uig and as far as Siabost and Liurbost. James Thomson refers to them in his article on Lewis in *Am Measg nam Bodach*[240] to which Rev. Malcolm MacLean of Conon Bridge, himself of Clann Iain Duibh, has added a handwritten note in my copy:

> Is e Iain Dubh seo a cheud fhear de na Leathanaich a thainig gu ruige Leodhas. B'iad mic Iain Duibh, Murchadh (Eirista) Domhnull is Aonghas (Mangursta) Gille-Padruig (Capadil) Iain Og (Siabost) is Tormod. Bha Gille-Padruig posda aig Anna nighean Iain Ruaidh Bhail' Ailein. B'e Calum MacGilleathain an Scarpa mac Iain Bhain mhic Gille-Phadraig mhic Iain Duibh.

> This Iain Dubh was the first of the MacLeans to come to the district of Lewis. These were the sons of Iain Dubh – Murdo in Eireastadh, Donald and Angus in Mangurstadh, Gille-Padruig in Capadil, Iain Og in Siabost, and Norman. Gille-Padruig was married to Anna, daughter of Iain Ruadh of Baile Ailein. Malcolm MacLean in Scarp [great-grandfather of Rev. Malcolm] was the son of Iain Ban son of Gille-Padruig son of Iain Dubh.

My friend Angus MacLeod – Angaidh Eubaidh – of Bru, a
good family historian and himself of teaghlach Iain Duibh on his
mother's side, has produced a chart of the main lines of the family,
which spreads to every corner of the island, and there are more
branches still to be added.

By 1787 Mangurstadh was in the hands of six joint tenants –
three of them of Clann Iain Duibh – and in 1807 there were nine
crofters – four of them MacLeans.

John Munro MacKenzie visited Mangurstadh early in 1851:[241]
'from Mangersta we fixed on sending six families composed of
thirty-five souls, two consenting, the total of their arrears £72.15.5
and the probable value of their stock £38.12/.' Later in that year
he was more hopeful: 'Went over their accounts with the tenants
of Mangersta who are also much in arrear, but who occupy much
better land for tillage and have larger stocks of Cattle and Sheep
than the other farms & on that account I have better hopes of their
reviving.'

Six families did indeed emigrate from Mangurstadh to Quebec,
their places being filled up by tenants evicted from Carnais.

Among the families who remained were those of Cain Morrison
and his brother Kenneth who had come to Uig from the Isle of
Tarasaigh in Harris, when that island was cleared in the 1830s. They
had settled first at Tamna, near Gobhaig in North Harris, where the
Tarasaigh people had been accustomed to cut their peats, the peats
on Tarasaigh having long been exhausted, but then moved across
to Uig. Kenneth was married in 1839, when his place of residence as
shown in the Old Parochial Register looks like 'Achileg' – wherever
that may have been – but by the next year he is living with his wife's
family in Mangurstadh.

MacKenzie's hopes for Mangurstadh were not fulfilled in the long
term, as the Napier Commission were told by Donald MacDonald
of Dun Charlabhaigh:[242]

> We, the people of Dun of Carloway, were in a township at the other
> end of the parish of Uig, called Mangersta. Now, a shepherd lives
> there. Our ancestors were there for 140 years. It was as good land as
> was in the whole country side, but the sea destroyed their crops now
> and again. No tacksman in the country would have cows and sheep
> better than ours, or that would secure higher prices at market. We

were thus enabled to keep ourselves going from year to year without falling into any debt whatever. In one year in particular, our crofts were destroyed by the sea, and we asked Rev. Mr Campbell, the Free Church minister of Uig, to speak to Sir James Matheson in order to get an exchange from Mangersta, where we were, to Dun of Carloway, where we are now.

The removal took place in 1872, but it has always seemed to me rather strange that the Mangurstadh people were so keen to move as far away as Dun Charlabhaigh because of one bad year. I wonder whether they had originally hoped to get Eadar dha Fhadhail or one of the other tacks in the area, but were only offered Dun, and having asked to be moved, could hardly refuse to go.

Mangurstadh then became a farm tenanted by Donald MacKay, son of a crofter from Bhaltos, until 1911 when it was settled again, mainly by cottars from Breanais, and though, like all of far Uig, it suffers now from depopulation, at least the sea does not seem to have been too much of a trouble since then.

Among the new settlers in Mangurstadh was a household of Buchanans from Breanais, including a son Donald – known as Stuircean – who died a few years ago. To him and to his wife Dolina I am indebted for much of my traditional information on genealogies in Uig. At the time, I was in charge of the project team for a development project in the island, and on one occasion I was holding a public meeting for crofters in Uig which was also being attended by top-brass civil servants from Edinburgh. I was rather worried that the meeting might follow the pattern of many meetings in the Islands, with nothing being said by the audience during the meeting, and two hours spent talking in the car park afterwards, so I asked Murdanie, Stuircean's son, to make a point of asking questions and keeping the meeting going. Well, he developed a cross-talk act with me which certainly prevented any danger of silence at the meeting – so much so that one of the Edinburgh contingent asked how often we had rehearsed beforehand!

Off the shore behind Mangurstadh is a sea rock known as Stac Dhomhnaill Chaim. Domhnall Cam is the folk hero of the MacAulays in Uig, as we saw earlier, but at this point in his life, having allied himself to the old MacLeod chiefs against the Scottish king and the MacKenzies, he was being pursued even more than usual. So he fortified the stac, where he was attended by his daughter Anna, who brought him provisions and water up the cliff-face. She is said to have been so sure-footed that she could climb the stac with a pail of milk in each hand! One wonders how long the occupant of a stac could have held out against an enemy, without supplies, but there are several such fortified stacs around the coasts of the Islands, and their use cannot be in doubt, if only as temporary hiding-places.

The red cliffs of Mangurstadh found themselves in the news again this year, when they were used for the 'cliff-dancing' episodes in *St Kilda, the Opera*. No doubt they were safer than St Kilda – and the National Trust would probably not have given permission in St Kilda anyway – but to anyone who knows the black cliffs of St Kilda, the red cliffs of Mangurstadh did seem rather odd! Having said that, the cliffs and the sands to the south of Mangurstadh are, to my mind, one of the most beautiful areas of Uig, especially with white breakers coming in from the Atlantic.

Islibhig (Islivig)

Islibhig can be thought of as MacAulay country – in 1851 nine of the eleven households there were MacAulays – and in our earliest rental of the township, in 1754, it is a part of Donald MacAulay's tack of Breanais. Before that its tacksman was William MacAulay, the youngest son of Domhnall Cam. It is said that he was so ambidextrous he could fight with swords in both hands. At the battle of Auldearn in 1645, he defended himself successfully with a sword in each hand and his back against a wall, until an enemy got into the loft above his head, and killed him from there.

A list of households in 1819 shows five households in Islivig, but it does not appear as a separate township until about 1841 – perhaps it was reckoned until then as part of Breanais.

One of the tenants of Islibhig in 1861 and 1871 was a John MacIver, who later moved as a schoolmaster to Sgiogarstaidh. His son Donald was actually born in his mother's family home in Crabhlastadh, but it was in Islibhig that he grew up. He also became a teacher, in Leumrabhagh, Breacleit and Pabail, but he is better remembered as a bard, especially for his poem 'An Ataireachd Ard':

An ataireachd bhuan,
Cluinn fuaim na h-ataireachd ard,
Tha toruinn a' chuain
Mar chualas leam-s' e 'n am phaisd
Gun mhuthadh gun truas,
A' sluaisreadh gainneamh na tragh'd
An ataireachd bhuan,
Cluinn fuaim na h-ataireachd ard.

'S na coilltean a siar
Cha'n iarrainn fuireach gu brath
Bha m'inntinn ' s mo mhiann
A riamh air lagan a' Bhaigh
Ach iadsan bha fial
An gniomh, an caidreamh, 's an agh
Air sgapadh gun dion
Mar thriallas ealtainn roimh namh

Seileach 'us luachair
Cluaran, muran, 'us starr,
Air tachdadh nam fuaran
'N d'fhuair mi iomadh deoch-phait'
Na tobhtaichean fuar
Le bualan, 's cuiseag gu'm barr,
'S an eanntagach ruadh
Fas suas 's a' chagailt ' bha blath

Ach siubhlaidh mi uat;
Cha ghluais mi tuilleadh 'n ad dhail;
Tha m' aois ' us mo shnuadh
'Toirt luaidh air giorrad mo la,
An am dhomh bhi suaint'
Am fuachd ' s an cadal a' bhais
Mo leabaidh dean suas
Ri fuaim na h-ataireachd ard.

The everlasting swell of the sea / listen to the sound of the great
swell / the thunder of the ocean / as I heard it when I was a child /
without change, without pity / sweeping the sand of the shore / the
everlasting swell; / listen to the sound of the swell. / In the forests
of the west / I would not want to remain forever / my mind and my
wish were always / in the hollow at the bay / but those who were
hospitable / in their deeds, their friendship, their happiness / are

scattered without shelter / like birds scattering before an enemy. / Willow and rushes / thistles, marram and reeds / have choked the springs / where I took many a drink / the cold ruins / with ragwort and docken over them / and red nettles growing / upon the hearth that was warm. But I will go away / and not delay longer / my face and my age / show the shortness of my days / but when it is my time to be laid / in the cold and sleep of death / make up my bed / by the sound of the great swell.

It is said that Donald MacIver wrote this poem after paying a visit to his uncle, another Donald MacIver, who had been cleared from Carnais to Quebec in 1851, and who had returned to Uig, only to find everything changed: 'Cha'n eil ni a seo mar a bha e, ach ataireachd na mara air an traigh.' – 'Nothing here is as it was, except the surge of the sea on the shore.'

The poem itself is deservedly popular, but I find it hard to think of except when being sung by Ishbel MacAskill, her voice full of pathos, and the last notes of each phrase held and floated, as on the breeze of the very sea itself.

On the moor above Islibhig shore is a blowhole known as Geodha Islaca – a tunnel bored in the rock by the sea, with the

92. Mealasbhal

inland end of the tunnel roof collapsed. In the right conditions
of tide and wind, the sea is forced into the end of the tunnel with
such force that a plume of spray is forced out many feet into the
air. If my description seems rather lacking in detail, it is because
I have never yet happened to be there at the right time to see the
blow in action!

Breanais (Brenish)

The first MacAulay tacksman here was Angus, son of Donald
Cam, who was killed with many of his compatriots at the battle of
Auldearn. He had four sons – Zachary, who was killed in the last
clan battle with the Morrisons at Druim nan Carnan; Dugald, who
succeeded at Breanais; Murdo, who was tacksman of Bhaltos; and
Donald; tacksman of Carnais.

By the time of the judicial rental of 1754[243] the tack of Breanais,
which included Capadail, Peighinn Dhomhnaill, Baile Niceal,
Ceann Chuisil and Islibhig, had passed to Donald MacAulay, son
of Dugald, and the evidence given shows a fascinating picture of
life in one of the oldest tacks:

> Compeared Ludovick McFinlay, tenant in Brenish, a married man,
> aged about fourty years, being solemnly sworn etc. & interrogated
> as to the rent payed by the said Donald McAulay his subtenants to
> him, depones that the whole town of Brenish consists of One pennie
> One farthing land; That he & two other of his neighbours payes for
> one farthing which they possess in said Brenish Two Pound thirteen
> shillings & four pence sterling; Depones the other four farthing
> lands in Brenish are possessed by the said Donald McAulay himself,
> but that they are not so good as that possest by the deponent and
> his neighbours, & that he and his neighbours are oblidged to work
> a day each week to the said Donald McAulay when required to do
> so; that he has been born in the neighbourhood and lived in Brenish
> since he took up land. The Deponent further adds that while he &
> his neighbours are at worke to the said Donald McAulay they get
> their victualls from and are entertained by him; And that they are
> bound to pay a cock and a hen to the said Donald McAulay yearly
> Together with a peck of meal yearly & a Coil of heather ropes for
> thatching his houses . . . Depones he cannot write and this is truth
> as he shall answer to God.

By 1766 the tack is in the name of Widow MacAulay and Zachary her son – and the widow signs the lease 'Bettey Macalay' – surely a most unusual accomplishment for a woman in these days. She was actually Donald's second wife and there was an unofficial wife as well, so there were three lots of half-brothers, all fighting for the inheritance!

John, a son of the first wife, became minister in Barra and then in South Uist – not a very time-consuming task in these wholly Roman Catholic islands! He then concentrated on encouraging emigration from Lewis to America, to where he himself emigrated in 1773 with several hundred of the Lewis tenantry. So worried was Seaforth by this loss of workforce that he actually proposed sending an army regiment to Lewis to forcibly prevent the people from leaving – rather a different reaction to what was being proposed by his successors only fifty years later!

Elizabeth MacAulay is the tenant until 1776, when Donald MacAulay is entered in the rental. By 1780 he is joined by Murdoch MacAulay. The two MacAulays were warned away from their lease in an action in the sheriff court in Steornabhagh, but this does not mean, as is often assumed, that they were forced to leave. A 'warning away' had been introduced in Scots Law as early as 1449 as a necessary part of altering the terms of a lease, such as changing the rent. They were warned away again in 1796, and this time the lease was ended, as in 1804 we find Breanais in the possession of sixteen tenants. By 1819 there were twenty-four households in Breanais, and two single people in bothies, a total population over the age of twelve of thirty-two men and forty-six women, of whom only one man, a Donald MacKay, was educated.

The township was badly affected by the potato blight in the 1840s and John Munro MacKenzie's note in *Diary 1851*[244] is:

> Met the people of Brenish a few of whom pay their rents & the greater portion are in arrear – some very desparate having already parted with almost all their stock to pay their rents, on account of the continuance of low prices they had reduced their stock much to meet the demands for rent & meal. Those who pay most are engaged in fishing lobsters etc. This township must be cleared at no distant day if the price of Cattle does not improve & the potatoe crop does not succeed.

Despite MacKenzie's worries, only four families emigrated to Quebec from Breanais, and two of these went in the 1840s, before there was any compulsion from the estate.

Norman Morrison gave evidence to the Napier Commission[245] in 1883:

> Our places were crowded first when the neighbouring township of Miolasta was cleared. Six families of that township were thrown in among us; the rest were hounded away to Australia and America, and I think that I hear the cry of the children till this day. The half of the island of Miolasta belonged in the time of my grandfather to our township and a neighbouring township. We were deprived of that. My father never earned a penny out of the island of Lewis, and he was not a penny in arrears when he died. Neither did my grandfather earn a penny out of the island. My great-grandfather marked thirty-six black lambs of his own in one year, in addition to the white ones in Miolasta. Then they had horses, cattle and sheep in addition; and we have no doubt whatever it was the crowding upon us of other people and the subdivision of the lots, and the land being taken from us that has reduced us to our present state. We have no hope of being improved in our condition except by getting enlarged holdings.

The cottars in Breanais did eventually get the farm of Mangurstadh broken down for crofts, but the population of Breanais has now plummeted, and only a few houses there are occupied except in the summertime.

It was off Breanais that Brian Wilson – no, not that Brian Wilson! – got the biggest fright of his kayaking trip round the whole of Scotland's coasts.[246]

> Suddenly, off the headland of Aird Brenish, I found myself at odds with a gigantic swell which was actually breaking from a height several feet above my head. I was over a mile out to sea, for inshore the waves had the driving power to dash me against the torn rocks and reefs which ringed the cliffs. So in every direction the sea was a heaving, seething mass, shaded grey where the gradients were sheer on massive walls of moving water, and white where the leaning crests collapsed into tumbling cauldrons of froth.
>
> For the three miles around Aird Brenish the thunder of the waves dashing on offshore skerries filled my ears like the rush of blood that is the roar of fear itself. The final stretch, around Aird

Brenish and nearing the sanctuary of Camas Islivig, was the worst of all; a confined area where the swell reflected and broke in several directions, stirred and torn by skerries and Dubhsgeirs. Then, as I lined up on the race which forged dangerously between two serrated skerries, a great heaving 'mother' of a wave picked the boat up and threw me, high and far, over the skerries and into the sheltered bay of Islivig.

I have read many descriptions of bad seas, but few from quite so close to the waves themselves.

Mealasta

Rev. Hugh Munro merely mentions 'the remains of a nunnery, called still in the language of the country Teagh na n cailichan dou, or the house of the old black women'.[247]

T.S. Muir gives only a little more – but at least his Gaelic spelling is better – I wonder whether it was Rev. Hugh Munro or Sir John Sinclair, who collated and published the *Statistical Account* who was responsible for the barbarous spelling:

> At Mealasta, on its south-west side, are traces of a small building called Tigh nan Cailleachan Dubha – House of the old black women – and in an open, grassy and flowery burial ground, the foundations of a chapel, internally about 19 feet in length, and a rudely formed font of elliptical shape.

One tradition claims that the nunnery was set up by nuns shipwrecked from the Spanish Armada, but I have always had suspicions about the Armada – I doubt whether anyone coming ashore from an Armada ship would have been left alive for very long. I imagine that in pre-Reformation times – and the Reformation took a long time to gain a hold in remote places like Lewis – there would have been local nunneries, even if the later evangelical ministers preferred to think of them as an alien importation!

The first tenant we know of in Mealasta was a Finlay Ciar MacRitchie – though MacRisnidh would probably be closer to the original Gaelic. We mentioned John Roy MacAulay, who escaped from the massacre of the MacAulays through being fostered away from home, and it was with Finlay Ciar MacRisnidh that he was living at Mealasta. If, as we suggested under Pabaigh, the massacre

93. The end of the road at Mealasta

was in, or shortly after 1506, then John Roy would have been born in the later 1490s. According to the Sgoilear Ban,[248] when the MacLeods recovered their power in Lewis, the Bearnaraigh family were forced to take John Roy into their care in recompense for the murder of his relatives. On one occasion, they had gone on a deer hunt to the Harris boundary, when they were forced by snow to take shelter in a shieling at Tobhta Choinnich. The chance was too good to miss, and the MacLeods left John Roy tied outside in the cold, wearing only a shirt, in the hope that he would be dead in the morning of what could be claimed were natural causes.

However, Finlay Ciar MacRisnidh saw John Roy's plight in a dream and came in time to rescue him. One story is that he walked the whole way from Ceann Loch Reusort to Tobhta Choinnich backwards, then returned in the same footprints with John Roy on his back, so that the MacLeods would think that John Roy had got away on his own, and would have perished in the snow. For better safety Finlay Ciar then hid John Roy in a cave called Uamh Tayvall, but the MacLeods found him there also, and he had to defend himself against them again, by his prowess as an archer. After that he headed to MacLean of Lochbuie on Mull for shelter. John

Roy became an accomplished swordsman, and decided to return to Lewis to avenge himself on the MacLeods, as we saw at Baile na Cille and Bhaltos.

It was a Ludovick macFinlay who gave evidence in Breanais in 1754, and Ludovick – Maoldomhnaich in its original Gaelic – is very much a Nicolson name. Could it be that there were Nicolsons in Breanais before the MacAulays came there? The Nicolsons have a very old history in Lewis, and it is said that it was through a Nicolson heiress that the MacLeods came first to Lewis. There is confusion in the old registers between MacRisnidh – MacRitchie – and MacCriceal – Nicolson. Could it be that Finlay Ciar MacRisnidh of Mealasta may have been the ancestor of the Uig Nicolsons?

Mealasta appears in the forfeited estate rentals as a part of Breanais, but by 1740 it was occupied by joint tenants. The rental of 1766 names eleven tenants there, but this had been reduced by 1776 to three, then increased again by 1787 to six. In 1807, when the trend was towards breaking tacks up into crofting townships, Mealasta went the other way, and was leased to just two men – Donald MacAulay and Donald MacLeod. However, when we look at the list of households in 1819, there are sixteen households and three bothies in Mealasta. It looks as though the changes in tenancies reflected more the relationship of those paying rent direct to Seaforth and their subtenants, and not necessarily changes in the actual population of the township. This is always the difficulty in constructing a history based solely on legal documents – the legal position and the actual position can have been very different.

It was a group of families evicted from Mealasta, along with some families who had earlier gone to Cape Breton from Lewis, who were the first settlers from Lewis in the Eastern Townships of Quebec.

There is a story about the murder of a boat crew from Mealasta, but it happened at Bagh Ciarach in the Pairc area of na Lochan, so we will leave it until we reach that area in the second volume.

Beunusbac

To me this is merely a placename on a map and, as Benisbac, in rentals, though some of our readers will know it better. Across the hills from Mealasta, on the shore of Loch Thamnabhagh, and at the mouth of Gleann Sgaladal, was a shepherd's bothy, occupied in 1819 by a Donald MacLeod – and that is all I know about it!

Ceann Chuisil

A mile beyond Beunusbac lies Ceann Chuisil, at the head of the loch of that name. The grazings there were on the boundary of the tacks of Breanais and Carnais, and there was always trouble about it. When Donald MacAulay of Breanais died suddenly in a boat in about 1762, the comment of Nicolson of Carnais was 'Seallaibh 'na phocaidean ach a bheil sgath a dh'fheur Cheann Chuisil ann' – 'check his pockets that there isn't any of the grass from Ceann Chuisil in them'. A lease of Carnais in 1780 includes 'the pendicle of Keanchuslich presently possesst by the tacksman of Brenish', so Nicolson won in the end.

There was a family living in Ceann Chuisil – some say they were MacDonalds, but this is not certain – who moved to the Gabhsann area. To their new neighbours they were Chuislich, and in the estate papers they ended up as Chisholm, which looked close enough to the original to satisfy the English-speaking clerk – and he could spell it!

In 1827 there is a note in the Seaforth Papers that 'Alexander MacRa, Husinis, offers £72 for part of Loch Resort Farm and Island of Mealista for five years' – the remainder of the farm at Loch Hamanavay could be let to Mitchell or another fishcurer. George Mitchell was originally from the Fochabers area of Banffshire and had come as a fishcurer to Steornabhagh. He took up the suggestion of a lease at Ceann Chuisil as a sheep-farmer, and apparently with success, as a few years later he was able to move into the farm of Timsgearraidh. He was the first of the family now in Siabost and Steornabhagh.

Thamnabhagh (Hamnavay)

Thamnabhagh is now at the end of a track cut through the hills from near Carnais, and is definitely Uig, whereas the country to the south and east of it is a land unto itself, with connections in many ways more to Scarp in Harris than to the rest of Uig. D.D. Pochin Mould describes a walk, or rather a trek, there from the Harris end, in her *West Over Sea*:[249]

I know how this country would look in the height of summer. There
would be greens of grass, patches of cotton grass, and everywhere
great beds of scented heather. The cloud shadows would dapple the
green shapes of the Harris hills to the south and the grey humps of
the Lewis mountains in the north. I know also how it looked that
evening in May, when we had December weather. It was brown
and colourless, the lochs steely, the wet peat sucking at my boots. A
wind came out of the west, so that I had to lean into it to make any
headway, and with the wind came a lashing storm of sleety rain. I
was blinded by it, floundered deeper in the bogs, found a trace of
a muddy path down a steep cliff slope and so came to the keeper's
house at Tamanavay.

She was a brave woman to attempt this trek alone, if not rather
foolhardy – to my mind these are not moors to be alone in, unless
you know the area really well.

An Aird Bheag

An Aird Bheag is the peninsula north of Loch Theallasbhaigh, and
a little township once lay on the north side, on the shore of Loch
Thamnabhaigh. At one time this was a grazing belonging to Baile
na Cille, and the Sgoilear Ban[250] tells a story about it then. A young
man was employed there as a cattle herd, and one stormy night a
ship was driven ashore. The herd saw a sailor swimming ashore,
with a small bag on his back, and killed him in the hope that the
bag contained treasure. When he examined the bag, all it contained
were carved relics, so he hid it in the sands near the manse. The herd
went from crime to crime and was eventually hanged on Gallows
Hill in Steornabhagh, when he confessed to his crimes, including
the murder of the sailor and the hiding of the carved relics.

If this story were true, it would cast doubt on the provenance of
the Lewis Chessmen.

In 1841 there were two households at the Aird Bheag – a Donald
MacLeod and a Murdo MacLennan. Donald MacLeod is thought to
have been the father of Aonghas nam Beann – Angus of the Hills –
the 'Holy Fool' of Rev. Alexander MacLeod's evangelical movement
in Uig. The MacLeods later moved to Mangurstadh, but Donald's
son Murdo was still known as Murchadh na h-Airde Bige.

94. An Aird Bheag

Murdo MacLennan was originally from Scarp, and was married
to Marion MacLean from Skye – Mor ni' Mhanuis – Marion
daughter of Magnus – a close relative of Professor Magnus MacLean
of Skye and Edinburgh. Prior to her marriage, Mor was in the habit
of taking summer work in the harvest fields of the Lothians, and on
one occasion she was on her way home with some money she had
saved from her wages – poor as they would have been. She stopped
for the night at the inn in Garve in Easter Ross, which was run by
an Alexander Stronach, son of the minister of Lochbroom. There
was little room at the inn, but Mor was happy enough to share a
bed with Stronach's daughter.

With a little of her wages, Mor had bought a string of beads,
which Stronach's daughter much admired, unfortunately within
the hearing of her brother who was already mentally unsound. The
brother's first name is not known, for he is remembered just as Mac
an t-Sronaich – Stronach's son. He decided he would get the beads
for his sister, and crept into their room at night, and strangled the
girl round whose neck he could see the beads glimmering in the
moonlight. What he did not know was that Mor had given his sister
the beads to wear for the night, and it was his own sister he had
strangled. After that his mind broke completely and he fled for the
Islands, living the life of a wanderer among the hills of Lewis and

Harris, to the danger of the local people, whom he would attack, and on occasion kill. His mother was of the Lewis gentry and he had important relatives there who no doubt fended off trouble for him as far as they could. Certainly the local fear of him would have been occasioned to some extent by his connection to the powerful tacksmen of the Island. Eventually he was caught, and no doubt hanged, but there are gaps in the court records of the time and there is no record of his hanging.

Because of this, some people have argued that he never existed at all, but oral traditions such as the story of Mor ni' Mhanuis exist all over the Islands, and are much too strong and too circumstantial for this to be the case. Admittedly, he has been blamed for murders outwith his period – it was always safer in a small community to blame a stranger – and the number of caves in which he slept is equalled only by the number of beds in which Queen Elizabeth of England is supposed to have slept. However, we can calculate fairly accurate dates for his period. Mor had her first child in 1826, so we can assume a marriage date of about 1824, so her brush with Mac an t-Sronaich has to be a little before that date. We will see at Ceann Reusort that he was there in the 1830s, so crimes within that period are probably justifiably blamed on him.

In due course Murdo was followed at the Aird Bheag by his son Donald, and by Donald's sons Kenneth and Magnus. In a place as remote as the Aird Bheag, it is always necessary to make use of whatever you can find for whatever purpose, and Manus na h-Airde Bige was an expert at this. My friend Tormod Alasdair at Beudarsaig in North Harris used to tell how Manus, having seen a barometer in one of the fishing lodges, set about constructing one from flotsam washed up on the beach – and it worked! Tormod Alasdair also told me that Manus made a set of false teeth from sheep's teeth and barbed wire – but I noticed that he only said that he made them – not that he used them!

Like most people of the area, the Aird Bheag brothers were lobster fishers in the season. Alasdair Alpin MacGregor in *The Haunted Isles*[251] tells:

> Manus and his brother sometimes walked over from Aird Bheag
> to Loch Resort. In the vicinity of Sgianait, a small boat awaited
> them to convey the lobsters up to Kinloch Resort at the head of

the loch. At Kinloch Resort they were carried across eight miles of moorland to Loch Meavaig, in Harris. There they were consigned to the postman, whose gig plied thrice weekly between Tarbert and Amhuinnsuidhe. This gives you some idea of the remoteness of the Back of Beyond.

The MacLennans were later joined in the Aird Bheag by John MacDonald from Teallasbhagh, and it is his son John who is the subject of Alasdair Alpin MacGregor's photograph of the Aird Bheag postman.

Teallasbhagh, Lamadail, Sgianuilt and Torraigh

Teallasbhagh was for a time a keeper's cottage at the back of the Aird Bheag, and the other names are of tiny villages along the northern shore of Loch Reusort. As the grazings there belonged to townships further north in Uig, each township would have had a shepherd living there, often a young family with no land in the main township.

Of Lamadail, which is on the wrist of the peninsula of the Aird Mhor, I know nothing except that it was always listed by my Scarpach friends as one of the villages of Loch Reusort-side – and there are indeed a few ruins there.

Sgianuilt appears in 1819 as a pendicle of Riof, and the tenant is Kenneth MacAskill, who from his name would have been a Harrisman. William MacGillivray, the ornithologist, visited there in 1818 on a trip from his aunt's house at Luachair to Uig[252] – 'I and Nelly went to Scianaid to see a goshti of hers' – goisdidh means strictly a foster parent, but probably here a nurse – infuriatingly, MacGillivray does not think to name the household!

Torraidh belonged to Baile Neacail, and was occupied in 1819 by a Duncan MacKinnon, whose family later settled in Bru, near Barabhas, but before that there had been MacLeans there, descendants of Iain Dubh whom we met in Mangurstadh. They left Torraidh to settle in Scarp when that island was first crofted in about 1810. MacKinnon cannot have been long in Torraidh, for when MacGillivray visited his aunt in Luachair,[253] he notes 'After breakfast the girls and I went to Toray, a small farm about two miles from Luchair on the Lewes side of the loch for the purpose

95. John MacDonald, the Aird Bheag postman

of seeing a child of Ewen's (his aunt's husband) kept there by
Tormod Ban.'

None of these little settlements on Loch Reusort-side lasted into
census times, and probably they all fell empty in the 1820s.

Crola

Less than a mile from the head of Loch Reusort was Crola, a single
shepherd's house. In the 1860s it was occupied by John MacDonald,
who had moved in from Teallasbhagh. He was followed by his son
Murdo, who had two children, Kate and Murdo. Murdo, though
all his schooling was in the little Sgoil na Leddies (school run by
the Ladies' Society in Edinburgh) in Luachair, across the loch

96. Crola

in Harris, was of near-genius ability and would have gone from Crola to university had he not died a young man. His sister Kate, who later moved to Scarp and then Gobhaig when Luachair was evacuated, was a great traditional historian, and used to tell me that her MacDonalds were originally of Glencoe, and had been given shelter after the massacre at Baile nam Bathach, near Beudarsaig in North Harris, before coming to Teallasbhagh.

James Shaw Grant, the then editor of the *Stornoway Gazette* wrote a very complimentary obituary for Kate – and she enjoyed reading it, for she was still alive at the time!

Ceann Loch Reusort (Kinlochresort)

A single house hardly deserves mention as a township, but Ceann Loch Reusort is important as the last house on the Lewis side of the boundary with Harris. It must have been a strange place to live in – at the head of Loch Reusort, yet a hook in the shape of the lochs bars it from any view out to sea. Across the stream which forms the boundary was the township of Luachair in Harris but this was cleared in the early 1800s. Until Luachair was resettled in 1885, the keeper's house at Ceann Loch Reusort was alone, and now that Luachair is deserted again, Ceann Loch Reusort is in utter solitude.

97. The Harris hills from Ceann Loch Reusort

To the south are the mountains of Harris, dominated from this angle by the sheer rock-face of Sron Ard, and to the north the wet peat-moors of Morsgail, at one time accessible by tracks, but the last time I was there, churned into porridge by the indiscriminate use of Sno-Cat tracked vehicles.

The shortest way from a road to Ceann Reusort is from Morsgail, keeping to a track on the side of the foothills of Sgalabhal and Beinn a' Bhoth until you reach a definite stream running to the head of Loch Reusort. Peter Clarke came this way on his walk through the Islands a few years ago:[254]

> The spurs marking the three glens to the south of Kinlochresort were now clear but the glens themselves were full of mist. A line of posts appeared, some broken down. Were they the remains of a line of telegraph poles? The bases looked like broken down tree trunks, but in one or two places the remains of the pole lay rotting alongside the stump.

Norman MacLeod, in an article in *Gairm*, vol. 17, tells of a conversation with Iain MacAskill, postman at Luachair, explaining the poles:

Cuireadh na polaichean suas ri linn Cogadh a' Chaisear, eadar
Morsgail agus Ceann Reusoirt; a sin, bha taod-fo-mhuir gu Loch
Thamnabhaigh far 'm bu tric a bhiodh loingeas chogaidh a' gabhail
tamh. 'Na latha fhein bha Morair Leverhulme an duil an acfhuinn
a chur an ordugh ceart ach dh-iarr Ughdarras a' Phuist a leithid de
mhal 's gun d'fhag Leverhulme aca e agus sin e nis a' breothadh.

They put poles up at the time of the Kaiser's War between Morsgail
and Ceann Reusort. At that time there was an undersea cable to
Loch Thamnabhadh where the warships often came in. In his day,
Lord Leverhulme wanted the apparatus put in order, but the post
office authorities wanted so much rent for it that Leverhulme gave
it up, and it is now rotting away.

Of course, there was no question of maintaining it for the benefit
of local people!

The track from Morsgail passes by Loch Sheilibridh, but it no
longer passes Loch nan Learga – because Loch nan Learga is no
longer there! One stormy night in 1958 Loch nan Learga burst
its banks, and poured all its contents into Loch Sheilibridh. It
could perhaps have been caused by extra-heavy rain, but local
people reckoned that the loch was hit by a meteorite, and that
was the story which hit the newspapers. Stewart Angus in his *The
Outer Hebrides – the Shaping of the Islands*[255] gives a more technical
explanation:

The two lochs were on peat overlying Lewisian gneiss, like most
of the smaller lochs in peaty areas in Lewis, but between the two
was a ridge of amphobolite. The key to the incident was not the
heavy rainfall, but the unusually dry early summer, which had
caused dessication cracks in the peat. As any peat cutter knows,
peat which has dried out never recovers its natural state, no matter
how much it is soaked, and the heavy rain of the winter soaked
through the cracks, creating a layer of sludge above the bedrock.
The peat between the ridge and Loch Sheilibridh was the first to
slide downhill using the lubricating effect of the sludge; without the
security of the weight of this peat, the shallower peat above the ridge
which had impounded Loch na Learga gave way suddenly under
the weight of water, easily breaching the sub-peat amphibolite ridge,
assisted by the underlying sludge.

Now I have known Stewart for many years, and I am sure that

his explanation is the correct one, but personally I still prefer the meteorite. There is no one so good at spoiling a perfectly good story as a scientist!

Near Loch Sheilibridh also are the well-known beehive houses – probably best described as igloos built of stone. Captain Thomas noted these as early as 1875:[256]

> The normal form of a beehive house is an irregular circle, six or seven feet in diameter, the walls rising perpendicularly for three feet; each successive course of stone then overlaps or projects beyond the one below it, and thus the roof gradually closes in and takes a beehive form. It is evident that in this style of architecture, the size of the rooms is limited by the nature of the stone; and although a tolerably safe roof may be made in this manner with rough moor stones to cover an area of six feet, it would have a most uncomfortable and suspicious appearance if extended over twice these dimensions. There are two doors and they are placed so that a line joining them cuts off on one side about two-thirds of the enclosed area. From door to door a row of flat stones, a few inches in height, forms the 'being', bench or seat, and behind this the area is filled up with hay or rushes for a bed. I had a native estimate of its capacity, and found it calculated to hold three people. In front of the bench, and midway between the two doors, is the fire – peat of course, and not much needed except for cooking. Above the fire, a longish stone draws in and out of the wall for the purpose of hanging a pot on, and in nearly every ruin did we find this primitive instrument in its place, shoved back into the wall.

The problem with dating beehive houses is that they are almost identical to the much later airidhean or shielings, except that the latter made more use of turf in the construction.

If you have made your way through the peat bogs from Morsgail to Ceann Loch Reusort – 'sploideaireachd' was the word coined by one of my Hearach friends – you might wonder why it was thought worthwhile maintaining a keeper's house in this wilderness, but you would soon cease to wonder if you were there when the salmon are running; I have never seen so many salmon, jostling their way up Abhainn Reusort, heading for the spawning beds in the little streams which drain the amphitheatre of the Harris hills. I remember being there on one occasion in bright moonlight when the salmon were packed so close as to look like the stones of a causewayed ford under

98. Dolaidh Dotair at beehive dwellings

the water, so close to the surface of the water that you might think that you could walk across on their backs – and I would prefer that you did not ask why I was there on that bright moonlit night!

In the days of the sheep farms, before they were converted to deer forests, there was a shepherd from Kintail living at Ceann Loch Reusort called William MacRae, with his wife Jessie Johnstone from Beattock in Dumfriesshire. One day William and his sons were out gathering sheep, when Mac an t-Sronaich the outlaw approached the house, where Jessie and her daughter Mor had stayed behind. Realising who the stranger was, Jessie got William's gun and started firing it, partly to scare Mac an t-Sronaich and partly to alert William and the boys. This was successful and Mac an t-Sronaich ran off. The MacRaes later moved to Harris, then emigrated to Australia, all except Mor, who married in Scalpaigh, and I remember her grandson there telling how she used to recall loading the gun for her mother to fire at Mac an t-Sronaich. Now Mor was born in 1827, and was just old enough to load the gun, which gives a date in the late 1830s for the skirmish, again helping to date Mac an t-Sronaich's period in the Islands.

From Ceann Loch Reusort the boundary with Harris runs generally eastward past Loch Langabhat to the shore of Loch Siophoirt. At one time, it is claimed, the boundary ran from Ceann

99. Loch Reusort from Crola

Loch Reusort in an almost straight line due east through Gleann Shanndaig to the narrows of Loch Langabhat – where the Uig people used to swim their cattle across on the way to their summer shielings in the Pairc – through the valley of Airigh Os Fid and down to Ceann Taragaigh at the head of Loch Siophoirt. This would certainly have been a more sensible boundary, following a natural geological fault, than the present boundary that wanders along hillsides and across valleys.

There was dispute about the boundary in 1805 and again in 1850, and the old boundary was stated then by several witnesses, though none of them could say why it had been changed. It is sometimes said that the intervening land was given from Harris to Lewis as part of the dowry of the daughter of a MacLeod of Harris chief when she married the son of a MacLeod of Lewis chief, but I can find no historical record of such a marriage – though they would tell you today that that was because neither side would want to acknowledge such an alliance!

Peter Clarke set out to follow the boundary:[257]

I took one last look at Kinlochresort. Cormorants were drying their wings on a rock in the bay. The retreating tide exposed banks of

stone at the river outflow. A heron ambled through the seaweed in
the estuary; one or two gulls circled, crying their whining call. The
overhanging cliff at Gleann Ulladale was crisp and the hill Sron Ard
in the next valley east was equally prominent. The sun shone over
the hills of North Harris. Some rain came in over the hills ahead,
shrouding them in grey. I could still see blue sky to the west, but
unfortunately, a rather cold rain began falling.

Peter Clarke was following the line of the old boundary from
Ceann Loch Reusort up the Abhainn Mhor as far as Tobhta
Choinnich, where John MacLeod of Ceann Loch Reusort, the
Lewis forester, used to have an airidh, but beyond that was in
dispute. The Hearaich claimed that the boundary went from there
to the top of a hill above Loch Langabhat named in the boundary
dispute as Eeun Tom, though the Ordnance Survey map now shows
it as Eun Toman. The witnesses to the boundary dispute agreed that
there was a special stone on Eeun Tom.

Norman MacLean of Einaclait told that 'he saw a stone there
about 2½ feet long, four-sided, with sharp corners, as if it had
been made by a plane; that there was writing on the stone; that he
does not read and cannot say what the writing was.' John MacKay
of Baile Ailein added 'that there was some writing on it, but not
proper writing; that it was done with a nail', and Donald MacKay of
Srannda told that he had heard from Kenneth Campbell of Scalpay,
the forester of Harris 'that there were the letters T.O.H. on one side
and T.A.L. on the other' – which would suggest that whatever the
other letters stood for, the H on one side was for Harris and the L
on the other was for Lewis.

Peter Smith from Iarsiadar told:[258]

> that his father said that he understood that the stone had been
> put up by a Mr John Campbell at Scalpa, who had also made the
> scratchings on it with the nail; that his father farther said that
> he understood that the stone had been so put up by Scalpa, in
> consequence of a quarrel he had with one McLeod, a Lewis tenant
> at Ken-Resort and Forrester. That the quarrel was in consequence of
> Campbell having taken a gun from McLeod, who was an old man,
> and McLeod's son having taken it back by force from Campbell and
> that the next time Campbell went to the hill, he placed the stone at
> Eeuntom, and Campbell's object in placing the stone was to reclaim
> the ground as far as Eeuntom.

According to several witnesses, the stone was taken away to Steornabhagh to show to the chamberlain there, and sent back, but the man carrying it back got tired of it, and dumped it in a loch! When Kenneth Campbell of Scalpaigh was told that, his remark was 'I don't care though they have taken the stone, they have not taken the hill' – but in fact they did, for the boundary finally agreed was well to the south of where the stone had been.

The line claimed by the Lewismen was along the river Abhainn a' Chlair Bhig up to Loch Chleistir, then through the pass between Stuabhal and Rapaire, and into the valley of Gleann Langadail at the head of Loch Langabhat. At the summit of the pass were the ruins of an airidh called 'Braidhanfhiachlachan' in the court case, which they claimed was directly on the line of the boundary.

Malcolm Roy Matheson of Peighinn Dhomhnaill had told the earlier hearing of the same case in 1810 that his father had good reason to remember where the boundary was at this point:

> . . . that his father, who died about twenty years ago, at the age of eighty, told him that when he was a boy herding John MacAulay of Brenish's cattle, Donald Campbell, the present Scalpa's father, and the said John MacAulay, met at Braidhanfhiachlachan on purpose to fix and renew the march, and they whipped his father soundly

100. Stalking

in order that he might remember the circumstance, and recite it to posterity; that his father told him, that when he was whipped, the gentlemen gave him five shillings a-piece for allowing himself to be flogged.

And there on the hill of Braidhanfhiachlachan we will leave Donald Matheson, Malcolm's father, alternately nursing his sore back and counting his shillings, until we reach this area again in the second volume of *Lewis in History and Legend*.

EPILOGUE

It is sometimes said that the more eyes you can look through, the more likely you are to see truly. In this book, I have tried to look at the west coast of Lewis from Nis to Uig through as many eyes as I can find – some sharp, some dulled, some almost blind, some determined to see only what they want, some searching to the far horizon, and others steadfastly gazing no further than their own feet.

From this mixture of quotations and comments of my own I hope that readers will be able to construct their own picture of the area and its history.

I have, of course, used only a selection of the tales told in the area, and if I have not used your own favourite then you will have to wait to see whether it appears in the second volume, which will deal with the east coast of Lewis from Tolastadh to Airidh a' Bhruthaich and the Pairc.

REFERENCES

1 James Fraser of Wardlaw, *Polychronicon, 1699*
2 John MacCulloch, *Description of the Western Islands of Scotland,* London, 1819, vol 1, p. 179
3 Quoted by William Matheson, 'Families of Lewis' *Stornoway Gazette,* 1977
4 *Acts of the Lords of the Isles,* Scottish History Society Edinburgh, 1986, p. 188
5 MacFarlane's Geographical Collections, vol. 2, Scottish History Society, 1907 p. 214
6 Capt F.W.L. Thomas, *Traditions of the Morrisons* in PSAS, 1870, p. 508
7 Gillanders of Highfield Papers, SRO GD427
8 Alasdair Alpin MacGregor, *Haunted Isles*, London, 1933, p. 215
9 J. Wilson Dougal, *Island Memories*, Edinburgh, 1937, p. 125–6
10 J. Wilson Dougal, *Island Memories*, Edinburgh, 1937, p. 135–6
11 Published in *Na Nisich* by Comunn Eachdraidh Nis, p. 13
12 Martin Martin, *A Description of the Western Islands of Scotland*, London, 1703, p. 19
13 Martin Martin, *A Description of the Western Islands of Scotland*, London, 1703, p. 22
14 Martin Martin, *A Description of the Western Islands of Scotland*, London, 1703, p. 22
15 Martin Martin, *A Description of the Western Islands of Scotland*, London, 1703, pp. 24–5
16 John MacCulloch, *Description of the Western Islands of Scotland*, London, 1819, vol. 1, p. 207
17 Michael Robson, *Rona – the Distant Island*, Steornabhagh, 1991
18 F. Fraser Darling, *A Naturalist on Rona*, Oxford, 1939, pp. 48–9
19 Translated in *The Blaeu Atlas of Scotland*, Birlinn, Edinburgh, 2006
20 John Beatty, *Sula, the Seabird Hunters of Lewis*, London, 1992
21 Angus Campbell, Ness *Orain Ghaidhlig*, Glasgow, 1943, p. 30
22 Ian Armit, *The Archaeology of Skye and the Western Isles*, Edinburgh, 1996, p. 101
23 J. Anderson, *Proceedings of the Society of Antiquaries*, vol. 45, p. 35 in PSAS, 1910–11, vol 45
24 John MacCulloch, *Description of the Western Islands of Scotland*, London, 1819, vol. 1, p. 179
25 J. Wilson, *Voyage round the Coasts of Scotland*, Edinburgh, 1842, vol. 2, p. 119

26 W. Anderson Smith, *Lewsiana or Life in the Outer Hebrides*, London, 1875,
     pp. 124–6
27 Donald MacDonald, *Lewis – A History of the Island*, Edinburgh, 1978, p.
     99
28 Napier Commission, 1884, pp. 1013–14
29 Napier Commission, 1884, p. 1004–5
30 Napier Commission, 1884, p. 1021
31 *Bardachd a Leodhas*, Glasgow, 1969, p. 69
32 *Eilean Fraoich*, Acair, Steornabhagh, 1982, pp. 153–4
33 William Matheson in *Transactions of the Gaelic Society of Inverness*, in
     TGSI, 1972–4, vol. 48, pp. 395–6
34 Martin Martin, *A Description of the Western Islands of Scotland*, London,
     1703, pp. 28–9
35 William Daniell, *Scotland*, Edinburgh, 2006, vol. 1, p. 207
36 John MacCulloch, *Description of the Western Islands of Scotland*, London,
     1819, vol. 1, p. 173
37 R.W. Munro, *Munro's Western Isles of Scotland*, Edinburgh, 1961, pp. 82–3
38 W.C. MacKenzie in *Proceedings of the Society of Antiquaries of Scotland*, in
     PSAS, 1905, vol. 39, p. 255
39 W.C. MacKenzie in *Proceedings of the Society of Antiquaries of Scotland*, in
     PSAS, 1905, vol. 39, p. 255
40 *Eilean Fraoich*, Steornabhagh, 1982, pp. 172–3
41 John Munro MacKenzie, *Diary 1851*, Acair, Steornabhagh, 1994, pp. 38–9
42 Bill Lawson. *Harris in History and Legend*, Edinburgh, 2002, p. 13–14
43 William Matheson. 'Families of Lewis', *Stornoway Gazette*, 1977
44 *Eilean Fraoich*, Acair, Steornabhagh, 1982, pp. 185–6
45 *Eilean Fraoich*, Acair, Steornabhagh, 1982, pp. 196–7
46 L.S. Channell. *History of Compton County*, Quebec, 1896, p. 264
47 Gillanders of Highfield Papers, SRO GD 427/2/1
48 Statistical Account of Scotland, Parish of Barvas, 1795, p. 6
49 New Statistical Account of Scotland, Parish of Barvas, 1836, p. 141
50 Roderick Campbell, *The Father of St Kilda* London, 1901, p. 8
51 Published in *Na Nisich* by Comunn Eachdraidh Nis, p. 7
52 Published in *Na Nisich* by Comunn Eachdraidh Nis, p. 8
53 Bill Lawson, *Croft History of Lewis*, vol. 13, Northton, 2007, p. 73
54 Napier Commission, 1884, Appendix A, p.162
55 Napier Commission, 1884, p. 1012
56 Roderick Campbell, *The Father of St Kilda*, London, 1901, p. xiv
57 Ian Armit, *The Archaeology of Skye and the Western Isles*, Edinburgh, 1996,
     p. 182
58 T.S. Muir, *Ecclesiological Notes*, Edinburgh, 1885, p. 42
59 William Daniell, *Scotland*, Edinburgh, 2006, vol. 1, p. 205
60 Statistical Account of Scotland, Parish of Barvas, 1795, p. 8
61 Donald Morrison, *Traditions of the Western Isles*, Steornabhagh, 1975, p. 19
62 Gillanders of Highfield Papers, SRO GD427/15/5

256   LEWIS IN HISTORY AND LEGEND

63 Col. David Stewart, *Sketches of the Highlanders*, Edinburgh, 1822, vol. 2,
    p. 129
64 Col. David Stewart, *Sketches of the Highlanders*, Edinburgh, 1822, vol. 2, p.
    130
65 Gillanders of Highfield Papers, SRO GD427/49/1
66 John Munro MacKenzie, *Diary 1851*, Acair, Steornabhagh, 1994, p. 131
67 Gillanders of Highfield Papers, SRO GD427
68 Seaforth Papers SRO GD/46/17/63
69 John Munro MacKenzie, *Diary 1851*, Acair, Steornabhagh, 1994, p. 131
70 J.S. Grant, *The Hub of my Universe*, Edinburgh 1982
71 Finlay MacLeod, *The Chapels in the Western Isles*, Steornabhagh, 1997,
    p. 17
72 Martin Martin, *A Description of the Western Islands of Scotland*, London,
    1703, pp. 7–8
73 Duncan MacLeod, *History of Milan*, Quebec, p. 69
74 Seaforth Papers, SRO GD 46/17/53
75 Bill Lawson, *The Clearances in Lewis*, Steornabhagh, 2006, pp. 8–9
76 John Munro MacKenzie, *Diary 1851*, Steornabhagh, 1994, p. 130
77 Norman Robertson, *History of the County of Bruce*, Toronto, 1906,
    p. 418–19
78 *Ripley – Huron's Hub*, Ontario, 1994, p. 268
79 *Families and Farms of Huron*, Ontario, 1985, p. 208
80 *Ripley – Huron's Hub*, Ontario, 1994, p. 287
81 Jane Yemen, *Scrapbook*, Ontario, 1983, p. 45
82 Jane Yemen, *Scrapbook*, Ontario, 1983, p. 207
83 *Eilean Fraoich*, Acair, Steornabhagh, 1982, pp. 165–6
84 Statistical Account of Scotland, Parish of Barvas, 1795, p. 9
85 Charles Macleod, *Devil in the Wind*, Edinburgh, 1979
86 William Daniell, *Scotland*, Edinburgh, 2006, vol. 1, p. 205–20
87 Ian Stephen (ed.) *Siud an t-Eilean*, Steornabhagh, 1993, pp. 16–17
88 Donald Morrison, *Traditions of the Western Isles*, Steornabhagh, 1975, p. 22
89 Statistical Account of Scotland, Parish of Barvas, 1795, p. 6
90 New Statistical Account of Scotland, Parish of Barvas, 1836, p. 149
91 Ian Stephen (ed.), *Siud an t-Eilean*, Acair, Steornabhagh, 1993, p85
92 James Hogg, *Highland Tours*, Hawick, 1981, p. 113
93 New Statistical Account of Scotland, Parish of Barvas, 1836, p. 142
94 George C. Atkinson, *Expeditions to the Hebrides*, Skye, 2001, p. 134
95 George C. Atkinson, *Expeditions to the Hebrides*, Skye, 2001, p. 134
96 Bill Lawson, *Croft History of Lewis*, vol. 9, Northton, 2003, p. 28
97 Martin Martin, *A Description of the Western Islands of Scotland*, London,
    1703, p. 7
98 Arthur Mitchell, *The Past in the Present*, Edinburgh, 1880, pp. 25–7
99 Donald MacDonald, *Bard Bharabhais*, Glasgow, 1920, pp. 5–7
100 Donald MacDonald, *Bard Bharabhais*, Glasgow, 1920, pp. 28–9
101 Arthur Mitchell, *The Past in the Present*, Edinburgh, 1880, pp. 50–2

102 Statistical Account of Scotland, Parish of Barvas, 1795, pp. 2–3
103 New Statistical Account of Scotland, Parish of Barvas, 1836, p. 142
104 New Statistical Account of Scotland, Parish of Barvas, 1836, p. 143
105 T.S. Muir, *Ecclesiological Notes*, Edinburgh, 1885, p. 42
106 Statistical Account of Scotland, Parish of Barvas, 1795, p. 3
107 *Eilean Fraoich*, Acair, Steornabhagh, 1982, pp. 170–1
108 *Eilean Fraoich*, Acair, Steornabhagh, 1982, pp. 44–5
109 W. Matheson, *The Blind Harper*, Glasgow, 1970, pp. 210 & 216
110 Martin Martin, *A Description of the Western Islands of Scotland*, London, 1703, p. 13
111 W. Matheson, *The Blind Harper*, Glasgow, 1970, p. 217
112 *Eilean Fraoich*, Acair, Steornabhagh, 1982, pp. 8–9
113 Helene Scott, *Old Timers' Tales*, Canada, 1989, p. 120
114 Helene Scott, *Old Timers' Tales*, Canada, 1989, p. 124
115 New Statistical Account of Scotland, Parish of Lochs, 1833, p. 167
116 Napier Commission, 1884, p. 960
117 John Munro MacKenzie, *Diary 1851*, Steornabhagh, 1994, p. 121
118 Napier Commission, 1884, p. 967
119 Napier Commission, 1884, p. 970–2
120 *Eilean Fraoich*, Acair, Steornabhagh, 1982, p160
121 Bill Lawson, *Harris in History and Legend*, Edinburgh, 2002
122 John Munro MacKenzie, *Diary 1851*, Acair, Steornabhagh, 1994, p. 35
123 Napier Commission, 1884, p. 953
124 Col. David Stewart, *Sketches of the Highlanders*, Edinburgh, 1822, vol. 2, p. 189
125 Napier Commission, 1884, p. 953
126 Napier Commission, 1884, p. 955
127 John Munro MacKenzie, *Diary 1851*, Acair, Steornabhagh, 1994, p. 85–6
128 John Munro MacKenzie, *Diary 1851*, Acair, Steornabhagh, 1994, p. 73–4
129 Duncan MacLeod, *History of Milan*, Quebec, pp. 87–8
130 Alasdair Alpin MacGregor, *The Haunted Isles*, London, 1933, pp. 3–5
131 J.P. Day, *Public Administration in the Highlands and Islands of Scotland*, London, 1918
132 Arthur Geddes, *The Isle of Lewis and Harris*, Edinburgh, 1955, pp. 249–250
133 *Eilean Fraoich*, Acair, Steornabhagh, 1982, p. 193
134 Bill Lawson, *Croft History of Lewis*, vol. 5, Northton, 1995, p. 29–30
135 Bill Lawson, *Croft History of Lewis*, vol. 5, Northton 1995, p. 19
136 Historic Scotland, *The Ancient Monuments of the Western Isles*, 2003, p. 19
137 Ian Armit, *Towers in the North*, Stroud, 2003, pp. 70–3
138 Ian Armit and Noel Fojut, *Dun Charlabhagh and the Hebridean Iron Age*, Steornabhagh, 1998
139 Donald Morrison, *Traditions of the Western Isles*, Steornabhagh, 1975, pp. 21–2
140 Bill Lawson, *Croft History of Lewis*, vol. 5, Northton, 1995, p. 21

141 J.S. Grant *The Gaelic Vikings*, Edinburgh, 1984, pp. 89–91
142 John Munro MacKenzie, *Diary 1851*, Acair, Steornabhagh, 1994, p. 113
143 Napier Commission, 1884, p. 932
144 Francis Thomson, *St Kilda and other Hebridean Outliers*, Newton Abbott, 1970, pp. 169–70
145 R.W. Munro, *Munro's Western Isles of Scotland*, Edinburgh, 1961, p. 81
146 Martin Martin, *A Description of the Western Islands of Scotland*, London, 1703, pp. 15–19
147 MacFarlane's Geographical Collections, vol. 2, Scottish History Society, 1907, p. 211
148 John MacCulloch, *Description of the Western Islands of Scotland*, London, 1819, vol. 1, p. 199
149 Alasdair Alpin MacGregor, *The Haunted Isles*, London, 1933, pp. 265–71
150 *Reminiscences of the Lews by 'Sixty-One'*, London, 1875, pp. 14–15
151 Historic Scotland, *The Ancient Monuments of the Western Isles*, 2003, p. 13
152 Lesley Riddoch, *Riddoch on the Outer Hebrides*, Edinburgh, 2007, pp. 135–9
153 Elizabeth Ogilvie, *The Silent Ones*, 1981, p. 1
154 *Bardachd a Leodhas*, Glasgow, 1969, p. 61
155 *Ripley – Huron's Hub*, Ontario, 1994, p. 202
156 *Reminiscences of the Lews by 'Sixty-One'*, London, 1875, p. 81–2
157 W.C. MacKenzie, *The War Diary of a London Scot*, Paisley, 1916
158 Gillanders of Highfield Papers SRO GD 427/2/1
159 *Reminiscences of the Lews by 'Sixty-One'*, London, 1875, p. 17–18
160 Dr Donald MacDonald, *Tales and Traditions of the Lews*, Steornabhagh, 1967, pp. 57–8
161 Donald Morrison, *Traditions of the Western Isles*, Steornabhagh, 1975, p. 22
162 William Matheson, 'Families of Lewis', *Stornoway Gazette*, 1977
163 William Black, *A Princess in Thule*, London, 1886, pp. 4–5
164 T.S. Muir *Ecclesiological Notes*, Edinburgh, 1885, p. 57
165 Iona Club, *Collectanea de Rebus Albanicis*, Edinburgh, 1839, p. 48
166 Donald Morrison, *Traditions of the Western Isles*, Steornabhagh, 1975, p. 32
167 John N. MacLeod, *Bardachd Leodhais*, Glasgow, 1916, p188–190
168 Anne Lorne Gillies, *Songs of Gaelic Scotland*, Edinburgh, 2005, pp. 70
169 Cairstiona Sheadha, *Orain*, Steornabhagh, 1980, p. 3
170 I.M.M. MacPhail, *The Crofters' War*, Steornabhagh, 1989, p. 14
171 L.S. Chanell, *History of Compton County*, Quebec, 1896, p. 34
172 Napier Commission, Appendix A, p. 167
173 Napier Commission, Appendix A, p. 166
174 Capt J.T. Newall, *Scottish Moors and Indian Jungles*, London, 1889, p. 178
175 Donald Morrison, *Traditions of the Western Isles*, Steornabhagh, 1975, p. 13
176 Daniel MacKinlay, *The Isle of Lewis and its Crofter-Fishermen*, 1878
177 Capt J.T. Newall, *Scottish Moors and Indian Jungles*, London, 1889, pp. 85–6
178 Capt J.T. Newall, *Scottish Moors and Indian Jungles*, London, 1889, pp. 3–5

179 Lewis-Harris Boundary Dispute, SRO GD/274/37/19, pp. 52–3
180 Duncan MacLeod, *History of Milan*, Quebec, p. 68
181 Hudson's Bay Company newsletter, December 1929
182 Statistical Account of Scotland, Parish of Uig, 1792, p. 42
183 John Munro MacKenzie, *Diary 1851*, Acair, Steornabhagh, 1994, p. 116
184 Capt J.T. Newall, *Scottish Moors and Indian Jungles*, London, 1889, pp. 93–5
185 Bonnie Thornhill, *The Road to Tarbot*, Englishtown, Nova Scotia, 2004
186 Dan Alex MacDonald, *Songs from Framboise*, Cape Breton, 1986
187 James A MacKay *Islands Postal History Series* no. 3 – Lewis, Dumfries, 1978, pp. 38–9
188 M.S. Campbell, *The Flora of Uig*, Arbroath, 1945, pp. 22 & 63
189 Martin Martin, *A Description of the Western Islands of Scotland*, London, 1703, pp. 14–15
190 Donald Morrison, *Traditions of the Western Isles*, Steornabhagh, 1975, pp. 3–4
191 Matheson, 'Families of Lewis', *Stornoway Gazette*, 1977
192 Dr Donald MacDonald, *Tales and Traditions of the Lews*, Steornabhagh, 1967, pp. 173–4
193 Anne Lorne Gillies, *Songs of Gaelic Scotland*, Edinburgh, 2005, pp. 278
194 Napier Commission, Appendix A, p. 207
195 Ian Armit, *The Archaeology of Skye and the Western Isles*, Edinburgh, 1996, p. 120
196 Napier Commission, 1884, p. 886
197 Napier Commission, 1884, p897 & Appendix A, p. 161
198 Napier Commission, 1884, Appendix A, p. 207
199 Napier Commission, 1884, p. 927
200 Napier Commission, 1884, Appendix A, pp. 207–8
201 Oscar Dhu (Angus MacKay), *Donald Morrison, the Canadian Outlaw*, Quebec, 1892
202 Napier Commission, 1884, p. 3310–11
203 Ian Armit, *The Archaeology of Skye and the Western Isles*, Edinburgh, 1996, p. 96
204 Ian Armit, *The Archaeology of Skye and the Western Isles*, Edinburgh, 1996, p. 201
205 Heimskringla Saga as quoted in Donald MacDonald, *Lewis – a History of the Island*, p. 19
206 Donald Morrison, *Traditions of the Western Isles*, Steornabhagh, 1975, p. 7
207 Donald Morrison, *Traditions of the Western Isles*, Steornabhagh, 1975, p. 92–3
208 Statistical Account of Scotland, Parish of Uig, 1792, p. 41–2
209 New Statistical Account of Scotland, Parish of Uig, 1833, p. 156
210 Napier Commission, 1884, p. 3314
211 John Munro MacKenzie, *Diary 1851*, Acair, Steornabhagh, 1994 p. 34
212 L.S. Channell, *History of Compton County*, Quebec, 1896, p. 277

213   Martin Martin, *A Description of the Western Islands of Scotland*, London, 1703, p. 5

214   T.S. Muir, *Ecclesiological Notes on some of the Islands of Scotland*, Edinburgh, 1885, p. 41

215   RCAHMS, Edinburgh, 1928, p. 17

216   T.S. Muir, *Characteristics of Old Church Architecture*, Edinburgh, 1861, pp. 174–6

217   RCAHMS, Edinburgh, 1928, p. 18

218   Donald Morrison, *Traditions of the Western Isles*, Steornabhagh, 1975, pp. 6–7

219   Statistical Account of Scotland, Parish of Uig, 1792, p. 46

220   Iona Club, *Collectanea de Rebus Albanicis*, Edinburgh, 1839, p. 8

221   Miscellanea Scotica, vol. III, Glasgow, 1820, pp. 34–5

222   Miscellanea Scotica, vol. III, Glasgow, 1820, pp. 62–3

223   Napier Commission, 1884, p. 3309

224   Fasti Ecclesiae Scoticanae, vol. 7, p. 208

225   Napier Commission, p. 3310–11

226   Col. David Stewart, *Sketches of the Highlanders of Scotland*, Edinburgh, 1822, vol. 2, p. 133

227   Statistical Account of Scotland, Parish of Uig, 1792, p. 45–6

228   William McGillivray, *A Hebridean Naturalist's Journal*, Acair, Steornabhagh, 1996, p. 57

229   Statistical Account of Scotland, Parish of Uig, 1792, p. 48

230   New Statistical Account of Scotland, Parish of Uig, 1833, p. 155

231   John Munro MacKenzie, *Diary 1851*, Acair, Steornabhagh, 1994 p. 115

232   *Bardachd a Leodhas*, Glasgow, 1969, p. 39

233   RCAHMS, Edinburgh, 1928, p.21

234   Dr Donald MacDonald, *Tales and Traditions of the Lews*, Steornabhagh, 1967, p. 122

235   National Museum of Scotland, The Lewis Chessmen

236   John Munro MacKenzie, *Diary 1851*, Acair, Steornabhagh, 1994, p. 38

237   *Disruption Worthies of the Highlands*, Edinburgh, 1877, p. 214–19

238   John Munro MacKenzie, *Diary 1851*, Acair, Steornabhagh, 1994, p. 32

239   John Munro MacKenzie, *Diary 1851*, Acair, Steornabhagh, 1994, pp. 114–15

240   An Comunn Gaidhealach, *Am Measg nam Bodach*, Glasgow, 1938, p. 99

241   John Munro MacKenzie, *Diary 1851*, Acair, Steornabhagh, 1994, p. 32

242   Napier Commission, 1884, p. 941

243   Gillanders of Highfield Papers, SRO GD427

244   John Munro MacKenzie, *Diary 1851*, Acair, Steornabhagh, 1994, p. 114

245   Napier Commission, 1884, pp. 887–9

246   Brian Wilson, *Blazing Paddles*, Oxford, 1988, pp. 110–11

247   Statistical Account of Scotland, Parish of Uig, 1792, p. 48

248   Donald Morrison, *Traditions of the Western Isles*, Steornabhagh, 1975, p. 3

249   D.D. Pochin Mould *West over Sea*, 1953, p. 239

250 Donald Morrison, *Traditions of the Western Isles*, Steornabhagh, 1975, p. 86

251 Alasdair Alpin MacGregor, *The Haunted Isles*, London, 1933, pp. 307–8

252 William McGillivray, *A Hebridean Naturalist's Journal*, Acair, Steornabhagh, 1996 p. 90

253 William McGillivray, *A Hebridean Naturalist's Journal*, Acair, Steornabhagh, 1996 p. 90

254 Peter Clarke, *The Outer Hebrides, The Timeless Way*, Steornabhagh, 2006, p. 77–8

255 Stewart Angus, *The Outer Hebrides – the Shaping of the Islands*, Harris, 1997, p. 195

256 Capt F.W.L. Thomas *Beehive House in Lewis*, in PSAS, vol. 7, p. 153

257 Peter Clarke, *The Outer Hebrides, The Timeless Way*, Steornabhagh, 2006, pp. 80–1

258 Lewis-Harris Boundary Dispute, SRO GD/274/37/19

PICTURE CREDITS

The illustrations in this book are sourced partly from photographs taken by the author and partly from the collection of old photographs gathered by the late Bob Charnley. Use has also been made of several of the excellent photographs taken by Alasdair Alpin MacGregor. Details of these and the other illustrations are shown below.

1. Dun Charlabhaigh
   Bill Lawson

2. Diagram of possible interior layout of Dun Charlabhaigh
   Ian Armit in *The Archaeology of Skye and the Western Isles*

3. Dun Charlabhaigh
   Western Isles Tourist Association Guide, *c.* 1950

4. Dun Charlabhaigh township
   Bob Charnley in *The Western Isles – a Postcard Tour*

5. Tabost, Nis
   Bob Charnley in *The Western Isles – a Postcard Tour*

6. Ruins of Dun Fhiliscleitir
   Bill Lawson

7. Church at Filiscleitir
   Bill Lawson

8. Taigh Iain Fhiosaich, Filiscleitir
   Bill Lawson

9. Taigh Effer, Cuisiadar
   Bill Lawson

10. Fianuis on Ronaidh
    Bill Lawson

11. Teampall Ronaidh
    Bill Lawson

12. Tobha Ronaidh
    Bill Lawson

13. Heading for Ronaidh
    Bill Lawson

14. Sulaisgeir
    Bill Lawson

92. Mealasbhal
    M.S. Campbell in *The Flora of Uig*

93. The end of the road at Mealasta
    Alasdair Alpin MacGregor in *The Western Isles*

94. An Aird Bheag
    Alasdair Alpin MacGraegor in *Haunted Isles*

95. John MacDonald, the Aird Bheag postman
    Alasdair Alpin MacGregor in *The Western Isles*

96. Crola
    Alasdair Alpin MacGregor in *Behold the Hebrides*

97. The Harris hills from Ceann Loch Reusort
    Alasdair Alpin MacGraegor in *Haunted Isles*

98. Dolaidh Dotair at beehive dwellings
    Emily MacDonald in *Twenty Years of Hebridean Memories*

99. Loch Reusort from Crola
    Bill Lawson

100. Stalking
     Bill Lawson

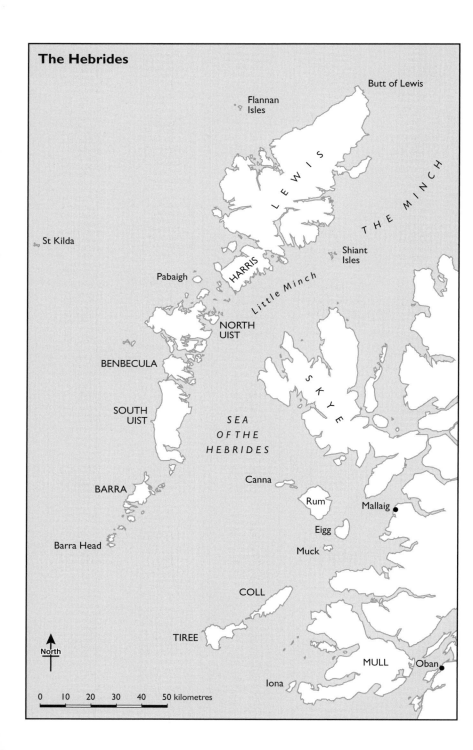

The Hebrides

Butt of Lewis

Flannan
Isles

L E W I S

T H E   M I N C H

St Kilda

HARRIS

Shiant
Isles

Pabaigh

Little Minch

NORTH
UIST

BENBECULA

S K Y E

SOUTH
UIST

S E A
O F T H E
H E B R I D E S

BARRA

Canna

Rum

Mallaig

Eigg

Muck

Barra Head

COLL

TIREE

MULL

Oban

North

Iona

0   10   20   30   40   50 kilometres

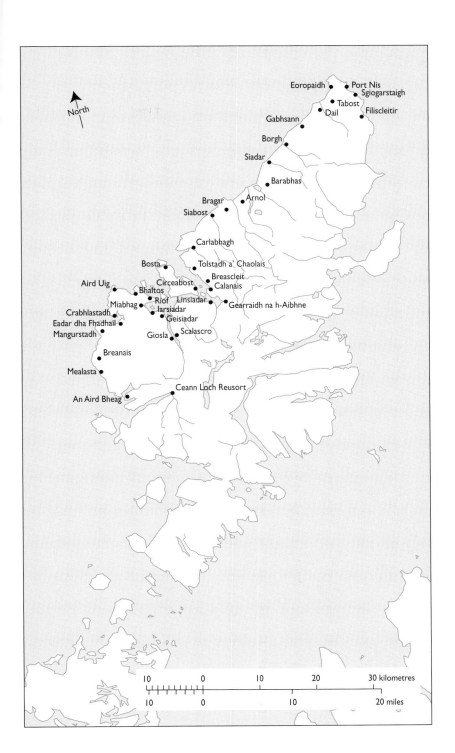

North

Eoropaidh
Port Nis
Sgiogarstaigh
Tabost
Filiscleitir
Gabhsann
Dail
Borgh
Siadar
Barabhas
Bragar
Arnol
Siabost
Carlabhagh
Tolstadh a' Chaolais
Bosta
Circeabost
Breascleit
Aird Uig
Bhaltos
Calanais
Miabhag
Riof
Linsiadar
Iarsiadar
Gearraidh na h-Aibhne
Crabhlastadh
Geisiadar
Eadar dha Fhadhail
Scalascro
Mangurstadh
Giosla
Breanais
Mealasta
Ceann Loch Reusort
An Aird Bheag

| 10 | 0 | 10 | 20 | 30 kilometres |
| 10 | 0 | | 10 | 20 miles |

INDEX OF PLACES

INDEX OF PERSONS

INDEX OF MAIN TOPICS